DATE DUE

.

Child Composers and Their Works

A Historical Survey

Barry Cooper

THE SCARECROW PRESS, INC.
Lanham, Maryland • Toronto • Plymouth, UK
2009

SCARECROW PRESS, INC.

Published in the United States of America
by Scarecrow Press, Inc.
A wholly owned subsidary of
The Rowman & Littlefield Publishing Group, Inc.
4501 Forbes Boulevard, Suite 200, Lanham, Maryland 20706
www.scarecrowpress.com

Estover Road
Plymouth PL6 7PY
United Kingdom

British Library Cataloguing in Publication Information Available

Library of Congress Cataloging-in-Publication Data

Cooper, Barry, 1949–
   Child composers and their works : a historical survey / Barry Cooper.
     p. cm.
   Includes bibliographical references and index.
   ISBN 978-0-8108-6911-0 (cloth : alk. paper) — ISBN 978-0-8108-6912-7 (ebook)
   1. Child musicians. 2. Music by child composers. 3. Gifted children. I. Title.
ML81.C66 2009
780.92'2—dc22   2009000236

∞ ™   The paper used in this publication meets the minimum requirements of
American National Standard for Information Sciences—Permanence of Paper
for Printed Library Materials, ANSI/NISO Z39.48-1992.
Manufactured in the United States of America.

Contents

Illustrations

MUSIC EXAMPLES

TABLES

Preface

This book came about as a result of a gradually increasing awareness during the 1990s that children's compositions had not been given a fair assessment in most historical studies of music. To redress the imbalance properly would require a much more forceful advocacy of these works than has been attempted here, but one of the main aims has been to raise awareness of this previous imbalance and work toward a more equitable assessment without prejudice one way or the other. The difficulties of surveying in detail such a wide range of composers and compositions across several centuries need no exaggeration, and apologies are offered for any omissions, misrepresentations, or other defects. My hope is that the present study will form a starting point for many further investigations of this neglected music, and also provide a firmer basis in this field for interdisciplinary childhood studies than has previously been available.

I would like to express my sincere thanks to all who have helped in the preparation of this book with useful advice or pieces of information, in particular David Fallows, David Fanning, Louise Lansdown, Hugh Macdonald, Bruce Phillips, Jim Samson, Irene Schallhorn, Jan Smaczny, John Turner, and Dario van Gammeren. Finally, I am especially grateful to my wife, Susan, for all her support throughout the time I have been engaged on this project.

Part 1

OVERVIEW

• 1 •

Introduction

A Virgin Field

*I*n recent years historical musicology has significantly expanded its horizons, both by encompassing repertoires previously excluded (such as non-Western music) and by introducing new approaches to the discipline. One particularly conspicuous development has been the appearance of numerous studies of women's music, culminating in *The New Grove Dictionary of Women Composers.*[1] This trend has come about through developments in society at large, with the rise of feminist movements that actively promote women's interests. Other groups such as homosexuals and certain other minorities have also developed similar pressure groups that have occasionally impinged on the world of musicology.[2] One important group that has been neglected in this process, however, is children. Their very considerable contributions to music in past centuries—notably in the field of composition—have commanded extraordinarily little attention, and the number of books and anthologies devoted exclusively to music composed by children is very small. Although there are a few exceptions by Denis Dille, Géza Révész, and others,[3] these studies are generally devoted to a single child composer. Various studies of Mozart's childhood provide further examples. Ever since he began appearing in public, Mozart has generally been regarded as the child composer par excellence, if not the only child composer of note, but his achievements are rarely placed alongside those of other child composers. Mozart is, moreover, usually the only musical reference point in historical–psychological studies of child geniuses or "prodigies," since authors of such studies are generally non-musicians who are unlikely to be acquainted with the work of other child composers. What is more, studies of child musicians have normally focused mainly on the children themselves and their environment, rather than on the actual music they wrote,[4] and there has been a widespread reluctance to engage seriously with the musical substance of the most outstanding compositions by children of the past. In some cases almost the only literature on the early works of a composer is found in the early chapters of general biographies of that composer. Here these works are often regarded as a mere prelude to the main matter, a kind of scene-setting that need not be investigated in any detail.

The contrast with women composers is quite striking. There is certainly nothing on child composers in general that is comparable with the plethora of books on women composers that have appeared in recent years, and the subject of significant compositions by children is almost a virgin field.[5] Yet there are some striking similarities between recent treatment of child composers and former neglect of women composers, as will be shown, and one cannot let the obvious differences between the two groups cloud this fact. Although there are more women than children in the world—very roughly, women form about 40 percent of the population as a whole whereas children form little more than 20 percent (and some of these are too young to compose)—so that one might expect more literature on women composers than on child composers, children still form a very large minority of the population, a much larger portion than some minorities that have attracted rather more attention in the literature on music.

The issue to be addressed is not the childhood works of major composers, but the major works of all child composers, which are not necessarily the same. What concerns us here is music composed by children of the past (chiefly those born before 1900), regardless of how they developed in later life. One cannot assume that the most successful child composers became the most successful adult composers, or even continued composing at all. The extent to which they did so is one of many questions to be investigated in this study, since it has not previously been considered.

Literature on "children's music" is actually quite plentiful, but it is almost always one of two types, as can readily be ascertained by standard bibliographical searches. One type is concerned with music written by adults for children—a "children's opera," for example. There are plenty of these, such as Aaron Copland's *The Second Hurricane* (1937) or Seymour Barab's *Little Red Riding Hood: A Children's Opera in One Act*.[6] Works such as Schumann's *Album für die Jugend* and Debussy's *Children's Corner* are particularly noteworthy early examples of music written by adults with children in mind. Study of such repertoires within the aesthetic framework of childhood is only a recent development,[7] and it concerns music written *for* children rather than music written *by* them. The second common type of literature on "children's music" is concerned with pedagogy and teaching children to compose in the context of the classroom. This sometimes includes assessments of what has been composed by whole groups of schoolchildren, and there is some useful research in this field.[8] It is worth observing, however, that this type of approach has never been adopted for assessing the compositions of adults. The idea of assembling a random group of adults of mixed and generally very limited musical ability and asking them to compose something, which is then assessed, is so far from the normal approach to adult compositions that it is almost laughable. In serious scholarly studies of adult composers, only the works of those who are able and well-trained are generally given any attention, with the most outstanding composers being given much greater attention than the merely able, though these are at least mentioned in music dictionaries. This therefore suggests an alternative way forward for examining the works of child composers. Those who are able need to be identified, while the most outstanding child composers, of whom Mozart is widely accepted as the prime example, can be placed in the context of the others.

The aim of the present investigation, therefore, is to make a preliminary exploration of works written by children in the past, and to provide an overview of the subject as a springboard for further investigation. Music by children from non-Western cultures lies outside the scope of this study, partly because the distinctions between performance, improvisation, and composition are much less distinct, and the issues involved are very different. It is worth noting, however, that music by non-Western children does not appear to have been so extensively disregarded in the literature, and there are some notable case studies.[9] At present there is a curious inconsistency in that, while musical outputs from all parts of the globe are now deemed worthy of examination whether or not they show great skill or sophistication and whether or not they involve children, music by Western children has been left largely unstudied. This applies whatever age boundary is chosen, but preliminary surveys of the literature suggest that scholarly neglect of young people's compositions appears to become progressively more common for composers younger than the age of twenty-one down to about the age of fifteen; music composed by those aged fifteen and younger is sometimes even dismissed under the heading "juvenilia" in catalogues and work lists. The present study therefore focuses on works by children younger than sixteen, although the boundary is inevitably somewhat arbitrary and could have been drawn earlier or later, or varied depending on the period, the place, and even the individual concerned. Sixteen has often been used as an official boundary between childhood and adulthood (or at least "youth") in legal and other circles, which suggests that it should work well as a convenient cutoff date. Of course there are obvious drawbacks to using a rigid boundary at all: for example, some compositions may have been written sometime around the sixteenth birthday, or begun before it but finished after it; hence, some flexibility is necessary in such situations. There is also a gray area between childhood and adulthood, and different aspects of childhood disappear at different times even within a single individual. In this respect childhood differs from qualities such as race or sex, in which bound-aries are sharper. (Even with race and sex, however, there are some blurred boundaries, including people of mixed race, people living within a community of a different race from themselves, and transsexuals.) Such gray areas must not be allowed to obscure the issues, and these issues come into sharper focus if the age boundary is drawn at sixteen rather than, say, eighteen or twenty, or left completely vague.

The most basic issue is that many fundamental questions relating to child composers in general have simply never been asked. Posing the right questions is the first step toward many discoveries, and among those that have not been considered (except occasionally at the most superficial level) are the following: Who are the most important child composers of the past, and did they gener-ally become leading adult composers? Is Mozart particularly exceptional in this respect? Have there been particular periods when child composers were more prominent than normal, and, if so, what are the reasons for this? What level of technical competence can be produced by a child younger than sixteen, and what is the youngest age at which a child might compose something that can be recognized as a complete and competently written piece of music? Are there any significant levels of originality in children's works, or are they entirely derivative in style? Which works might be regarded as particularly outstanding, and is it legitimate to use the term *masterpiece* to describe them? How far back in childhood can distinguishing hallmarks of a composer's adult style be found? How often is the neglect of children's works due to prejudice rather than in-herently poor musical quality or some other reason (such as unavailability of sources)? If there is demonstrable lack of quality, to what extent is this sufficient justification for ignoring this music? Is children's music in general different in nature from music written by adults, with distinctive childlike qualities and dif-ferent sets of values that require some alternative critical approach? If so, what are these differences, how consistently can they be found in child composers in general, and what evaluative criteria should be adopted for such works? Which works, if any, are stylistically indistinguishable from those of adults, and, on the other hand, which are most obviously written by children? Not all of these questions may be answerable, but they clearly need to be asked.

The first step toward investigating the history of children's compositions in general must be the compilation of some kind of list, however provisional, of the principal child composers. Astonishingly, no such list appears to have existed hitherto, and a first attempt has therefore been made in the present book (see the Checklist in Part 2). There are problems, however, with identifying child composers born before about 1750 or after about 1900. In the former case, loss of source material becomes a major drawback, and is compounded by the fact that, even though childhood compositions may have survived, they cannot usually be definitively dated. Moreover, before about 1600, uncertainty about many composers' dates of birth compounds the problem. Thus, although there are a few known cases of child composers from before 1750 whose works survive—for example, Monteverdi, Humfrey, and Bononcini—the total is relatively meager. For the twentieth and twenty-first centuries, the problems are different and more diverse. First, there are so many children's compositions surviving, even from the first half of the twentieth century, that selection would have to be made on a somewhat arbitrary basis. The extent of the problem is illustrated by the fact that, of the composers listed in *A Dictionary of Twentieth-Century Composers 1911–1971,*[10] most of whom were born around the end of the nineteenth century, about half reported to have composed something before the age of sixteen. Thus childhood composition seems to have been a widespread phenomenon in the twentieth century. Second, since today whole classes of schoolchildren in several countries are producing "compositions" (if one can dignify their efforts with such an imposing term) as part of their general education, any realistic selection on the basis of quality becomes impossible, while attempts at a more comprehensive overview are impracticable and would be largely meaningless. Study of such compositions would have to be confined to individual classes or groups, as has occurred in the pedagogical studies cited earlier. Some kind of rudimentary selection could be made on the basis of choosing adult composers and examining their childhood works; but such works have generally been rejected by the composers themselves on reaching adulthood.[11] Another problem in assessing children's compositions of recent years is the difficulty of establishing reliable criteria. For music of earlier centuries, one criterion was always how well the composer had grasped and exploited the conventions of the day with regard to such elements as form, harmony, rhythm, and tonality. In a period when such conventions scarcely exist, and works are being written concurrently in a huge variety of styles, it becomes almost impossible to assess children's output on this basis, and one must rely on much more elusive concepts such as organization and manipulation of material, and coherence of thought. An even greater problem is that nearly all children's compositions from more recent years are still unpublished and in private hands, and access to a representative selection is nearly impossible. It is also perhaps significant that an important book on Korngold (born 1897) describes him in the title as "the last prodigy,"[12] with the implication that the main period for composer "prodigies" lasted to Korngold and no further. Although this is not entirely true, Korngold does provide a useful landmark in the history of childhood composition, and his childhood music is the last major corpus that does not raise any of the problems outlined to a significant extent.

    Accordingly, the Checklist of child composers compiled for the present study is confined to those born before 1900 and therefore reaching adulthood by 1915 to 1920 at the latest. The list, which has been compiled mainly from standard dictionaries, biographies, and thematic catalogues, is based on an extensive search. It must, however, be seen as extremely provisional, since there is no search mechanism that can reliably assemble all relevant names, and it is therefore only a tentative first step toward a more comprehensive dictionary of child composers that might be produced some time in the future. It appears that most major composers wrote something before the age of sixteen; but when this music is entirely lost or of indeterminate date, their names have not been included in this study. Despite the previously mentioned limitations, the Checklist includes well over one hundred child composers, who together wrote nearly 2,000 extant works (plus many now lost), the longest of which lasts more than two hours in performance. These figures provide for the first time some idea of the scale of the corpus in need of appraisal.

The Checklist also enables many general questions about significant child composers to be answered or at least examined for the first time. First, it makes possible at last a chronological résumé of the development of composition by children (see chapter 2) in a narrative that expands on the only previous such résumé,[13] on which the present study is partly based. Although the Checklist itself covers only children born before 1900, this historical narrative offers a provisional outline up to the present day, and might provide a starting point for further research in the later period. This overview is followed by a discussion of other issues associated with the works and composers in question, and their reception in the scholarly literature (see chapters 3–5). Frequently there is just a passing mention of a particular composer or work, perhaps as illustrative of a general characteristic. Although no reference to the literature or sources is given in such cases, further details on the composers and works in question can normally be found in the Checklist, or in the literature cited there.

NOTES

1. Julie Anne Sadie and Rhian Samuel, eds., *The New Grove Dictionary of Women Composers* (London: Macmillan, 1994). See also Jane Bowers and Judith Tick, eds., *Women Making Music: The Western Art Tradition, 1150–1950* (Urbana: University of Illinois Press, 1986); James R. Briscoe, ed., *Historical Anthology of Music by Women* (Bloomington: Indiana University Press, 1987); Barbara Garvey Jackson, *"Say Can You Deny Me": A Guide to Surviving Music by Women from the 16th through the 18th Centuries* (Fayetteville: University of Arkansas Press, 1994); Kimberly Marshall, ed., *Rediscovering the Muses: Women's Musical Traditions* (Boston: Northeastern University Press, 1993).

The phrase "woman composers" seems preferable to the commonly used "women composers," by analogy with "boy sopranos," "child prodigies," "girl guides," and so on, but linguists have noted that irregular plurals such as "women" can be used adjectivally whereas regular ones cannot (e.g., see Stephen Pinker, *The Language Instinct* [New York: W. Morrow, 1994], 146–47). On that basis one ought to say "children composers." The present study, however, adopts the more usual phrase "child composers," while retaining the widely used but arguably incorrect "women composers."

2. See, for example, Philip Brett, Elizabeth Wood, and Gary C. Thomas, eds., *Queering the Pitch: The New Gay and Lesbian Musicology* (New York: Routledge, 1994); Leo Treitler, "Gender and Other Dualities of Music History," in *Musicology and Difference: Gender and Sexuality in Music Scholarship,* ed. Ruth A. Solie (Berkeley: University of California Press, 1993), 23–45.

3. Denis Dille, *Thematisches Verzeichnis der Jugendwerke Béla Bartóks,* 2nd ed. (Kassel, Germany: Bärenreiter, 1974); Géza Révész, *The Psychology of a Musical Prodigy (Erwin Nyiregyházy)* (London: Kegan Paul, 1925). Originally published as *Erwin Nyiregyházy: psychologische Analyse eines musikalisch hervorragenden Kindes* (Leipzig, Germany, 1916).

4. See, for example, Claude Kenneson, *Musical Prodigies: Perilous Journeys, Remarkable Lives* (Portland, Ore.: Amadeus Press, 1998).

5. This was even more the case in 1996 when an article appeared that made this point, and which has formed a starting point for the present study: Barry Cooper, "Major Minors," *The Musical Times* 137 (August 1996): 5–10.

6. Vocal score published New York: Boosey & Hawkes, 1965. Reviewed by Dena J. Epstein in *Notes* 23, no. 2 (1966): 337.

7. Susan Boynton and Roe-Min Kok, eds., *Musical Childhoods and the Cultures of Youth* (Middletown, Conn.: Wesleyan University Press, 2006), ix, xvi, and the literature cited there.

8. See, for example, Sarah J. Wilson and Roger J. Wales, "An Exploration of Children's Musical Compositions," *Journal of Research in Music Education* 43 (1995): 94–111; Joanna Glover, *Children Composing: 4–14* (London: Falmer, 2000).

9. See, for example, John Blacking, *Venda Children's Songs: A Study in Ethnomusicological Analysis* (Johannesburg, South Africa: Witwatersrand University Press, 1967).

10. Kenneth Thompson, *A Dictionary of Twentieth-Century Composers 1911–1971* (London: Faber, 1973).

11. Cooper, "Major Minors," 8–9.

12. Brendan G. Carroll, *The Last Prodigy: A Biography of Erich Wolfgang Korngold* (Portland, Ore.: Amadeus Press, 1997).

13. Cooper, "Major Minors," 6–8.

· 2 ·

Chronological Résumé from the Middle Ages to the Present Day

$\mathcal{N}$o child composers can be identified from medieval times or before, but, based on what children have achieved in more recent centuries, there must certainly have been some. Medieval children were in any case required to take on the roles of adults at a much younger age, which might include composing music. This requirement was partly necessitated by a high mortality rate and much lower life expectancy; marriage generally occurred far earlier as well. Whether childhood was even much recognized as a concept in medieval times has been hotly debated,[1] but child composers would not have attracted particular comment about their age. It is easy to imagine that a few of the many thousands of chants composed for monastic purposes in the Middle Ages were written by child oblates or novices, who often played a full part in the singing of such chants.[2] Similarly, some of the thousands of troubadour and trouvère songs from the twelfth and thirteenth centuries could well have been composed by very young members of the nobility. Nothing has yet been positively identified from this period, however, or from the next two or three centuries as having been certainly composed by a child. Most of the secular music and much of the sacred music from this period has been lost. Much of what survives is anonymous or of uncertain attribution. Dates of composition are rarely known to within ten years, and the dates of birth of individual composers are often equally uncertain. Thus any identification of a composition written by a child before the sixteenth century would have to depend on a very exceptional combination of circumstances. The case of Philippe Basiron (c. 1449–91) illustrates the difficulty of reaching firm conclusions on child composers of this period. Basiron evidently wrote four known chansons before the age of twenty—perhaps long before—and may have written other even earlier works now lost. Meanwhile Prince Henry of England

(1491–1547), later King Henry VIII, offers a different kind of evidence. His earliest known works show so little competence, surviving only because of who he was, that a very young age has been inferred. His skill then developed so rapidly in later works, culminating in two polyphonic masses written at the age of nineteen, as to suggest that he may have been as young as ten when he began composing. Again, however, we are left with speculation and inference rather than solid data.

The rise of music printing in the sixteenth century has enabled works to be dated far more reliably than those of earlier times, since most printed music can be dated to within a narrow time frame, giving us at least the latest possible date of composition. Also, works surviving from this period usually bear the names of their composers. Thus two of the main barriers to identifying child composers of earlier centuries are no longer present. Even so, only two have yet been discovered from the sixteenth century—Barthélemy Beaulaigue (c. 1543–59 or later) and Claudio Monteverdi (1567–1643). It was stated that Beaulaigue was fifteen years old when he published a collection of polyphonic chansons followed by a collection of motets in 1558–59, and his date of birth has been deduced from this, but nothing more is heard from him in later years. Monteverdi, however, embarked on a long and highly successful career as a composer with his first collection of twenty-three motets, published with a dedication dated 1 August 1582. Since they must have taken at least several months to compose, the earliest must have been composed at the age of fourteen or younger.

During the Baroque era, child composers rarely attained any prominence, a notable exception being some Chapel Royal choirboys trained by Captain Henry Cooke immediately after the Restoration in 1660. The evidence indicates that at least fifteen anthems were composed by choirboys within four years (six by Smith, five by Humfrey, three by Blow, and at least one by another choirboy—probably Turner or Wise), although most of these anthems are now lost. There is no reason to suppose this tradition did not continue, at least until Cooke's death in 1672, but precise information is lacking.

Not many years afterward, Giovanni Bononcini (1670–1747) at the age of fifteen published three instrumental collections totaling thirty-six works, but few other child composers are known from this period. No music by Bach is known to have been composed as a child, despite intensive investigation. Nearly all the earliest works of Händel (1685–1759) are lost, though there were a considerable number; Händel composed a cantata-like work almost every week for three years, but these are lost. Those that do survive cannot be securely dated.

It was Mozart (1756–91) who changed the image of the child composer irrevocably when he burst on the scene in the early 1760s with a series of remarkable compositions. Had there been other young child composers shortly before him, even if a little older and less skillful than he was when he first made his mark, he would not have created such a stir; but there were no immediate predecessors remotely comparable. His father, Leopold, a composer and violin teacher, gave him every opportunity and encouragement to develop his obvious talent, and allowed him to perform first in his native Salzburg, then in Munich, Vienna, Paris, and London, where he performed at the age of eight. Inevitable suspicions arose that there must be some trickery or a hoax involved, but these were easily rebuffed by various tests. While in London he attracted the attention of Daines Barrington, a polymath who wrote about a variety of curious phenomena, at a time when scientific enquiry of such phenomena was becoming popular. Barrington's account of Mozart, written in 1770 and republished in 1781, relates how Mozart was tested in various ways and demonstrated outstanding ability in keyboard playing, extemporization, score reading at sight, and composition.[3] Barrington then suspected that Leopold Mozart had misrepresented the boy's age, but he managed to obtain confirmation that it was correct. It was from Barrington's account that the phenomenon of the child composer first passed into general public consciousness, at least in English-speaking countries.

Within a few years of Mozart's first lengthy tour of 1763–66, several more child composers appeared on the scene. It seems probable that these two circumstances are related, and that Mozart himself gave rise to the concept of the "child composer" per se. Thomas Linley (1756–78), Joseph Martin Kraus (1756–92), François-Joseph Darcis (c. 1760–c. 1783), Johann Heinrich Schroeter (c. 1762–after 1784), Elizabeth Weichsell (1765–1818), Samuel Wesley (1766–1837), Ludwig van Beethoven (1770–1827), and William Crotch (1775–1847) were all born within twenty years of Mozart, and were all able to benefit from the tide of interest that he engendered. Wesley and Crotch became the subject of further articles by Barrington, as did Wesley's elder brother Charles, who excelled as a keyboard player at an early age, although not as a composer.[4] The contrast with composers born in the twenty years before Mozart is striking. The few who did compose at an early age were not given any special attention beyond what might be given to a composer of any age, and no publications by them have yet been traced.

If there was a Mozart "bandwagon," however, very few children attempted to jump onto it. After Mozart's birth, the remainder of the eighteenth century produced fewer than one child composer per year in the whole of Europe, as far as can be judged at present. This suggests that children's desire to compose is not much influenced by trends and fashions, but is more likely to be conditioned by innate responses in a few rare individuals, who may flourish in more favorable periods or go unrecognized or unsupported in less favorable ones. Many of those who flourished in the late eighteenth century were so outstanding that they did not need any Mozart bandwagon, and could well have created their own, even if they did benefit to some extent from Mozart's example. Wesley wrote at least two full-scale oratorios, the first completed at the age of eight, plus numerous lesser works. Crotch wrote an even larger oratorio, completed at the age of thirteen, which preliminary assessment suggests is also more imaginative and skillfully written than Wesley's. Darcis and Beethoven were of a similar age when Darcis wrote the opera *La fausse peur* and Beethoven wrote his early Piano Concerto in E flat. They are both very substantial works, composed after several shorter ones. Although the outputs of these composers do not match that of Mozart, this was probably due mainly to the outstanding support Mozart received from his father, not merely as a teacher but also through Leopold's willingness to take him to the main music capitals of Europe and introduce him to the various composers and styles that were prevalent. Such a high quality of parental assistance and guidance was not experienced by any of the other child composers mentioned, even though they all had supportive parents and did travel to some extent.

Conditions for the development of child composers continued to be relatively favorable into the nineteenth century. Increasing population and more widespread education facilitated the development of a larger number of child composers, and some were quite prolific: Felix Mendelssohn (1809–47) leads the way here with about 150 works, including thirteen string symphonies completed by the age of fourteen. Schubert (1797–1828) wrote about fifty works that survive, while Arriaga (1806–26) and Liszt (1811–86) wrote at least twenty each, including an opera (*Los esclavos felices* and *Don Sanche* respectively). Although none of these four composers is known to have started composing before the age of ten, there were a few who started younger, such as Chopin (1810–49), whose Polonaise in G minor was actually published when he was only seven. The youngest beginners, however, were born slightly later: Ouseley (1825–89) is the youngest known, composing his first work, a perfectly presentable little piano piece, at the age of three years, three months (ex. 2.1),[5] while Saint-Saëns (1835–1921) was close behind with his first work at three years, four months. Some of these composers lived to a ripe old age: Liszt to 74 and Saint-Saëns to 86. Others from this period died tragically young: Schubert at 31, Arriaga and Aspull (1813–32) at 19, and Filtsch (1830–45) at only 14.

During the latter part of the nineteenth century there seems to have been something of a decline in notable children's compositions, though not a very marked or obvious one. The number of composers from 1851 through 1900 included in the Checklist in Part 2 is only slightly greater than the number from 1801 through 1850, even though there were far more composers and

Example 2.1. Ouseley's first composition.

music publications (and a larger population) in general in the second half of the century. Moreover, most of the child composers known from the second half of the century composed relatively little: only Strauss (1864–1949) and Busoni (1866–1924) produced works in numbers that rival those of Mozart and Mendelssohn, with Bartók (1881–1945), Enescu (1881–1955), Prokofiev (1891–1953), Langgaard (1893–1952), and Korngold (1897–1957) some way behind. The reasons for this slight decline are difficult to fathom, but there are several possibilities. It may be that composers became increasingly critical of their early works and tended more often to destroy them deliberately, as Verdi, Brahms, and Dvořák apparently did. This reaction had occasionally occurred in earlier times (for example with C. P. E. Bach), but it seems to have become more prevalent in the late nineteenth century, continuing into the twentieth. Another possibility is that children's education tended to become wider and more varied, and opportunities for the type of intensive musical study that Mozart underwent became less common. A further factor may have been an increasing reluctance to put young children in the spotlight. This changing attitude is illustrated, for example, in Joseph Bennett's comments in *The Musical Times* in 1897:

> With much pleasure I quote from the *Musical Standard* the subjoined remarks upon the appearance of little Bruno Steindel [a young piano virtuoso] at the Crystal Palace: "The Society for the Protection of Children might surely stand, like Moses, 'in the gap' and try to stop such exhibitions. All contemporary journalists write to the same effect." Not all, unfortunately, but I, for one, will have nor part nor lot in the showing of a poor baby of seven, and I cry "Shame!" upon those who abet it.[6]

A similar attitude appeared in the same journal a month later, after Steindel's appearance in Manchester, in which the anonymous writer condemns the fact that young pianists such as Steindel have been "allowed to appear on concert platforms instead of being restricted to the drawing room for the entertaining of their cousins and their aunts."[7] With such attitudes becoming prevalent, child composers no longer had a concert platform on which to exhibit their latest works, and therefore had far less incentive to put effort into producing new works of high quality merely "for the entertaining of their cousins and their aunts." Hence fewer child composers were likely to come to public attention. Certainly the type of concert tour that had been undertaken by child composers such as Mozart, Crotch, and Liszt seems to have more or less died out by 1900.

In the twentieth century, child composers continued to appear from time to time, sometimes producing very fine work. Korngold was arguably the last composer to be presented before the public as a prodigy in the way that earlier child composers had been, but he was certainly not "the last prodigy" in the sense of being the last notable child composer. The works of the others, however, often remained hidden from view and in many cases still do. One who attracted much attention for a short time was Ervin Nyiregyházy (1903–87), who became the subject of a detailed study in 1916 after starting to compose at the age of four;[8] but he failed to live up to early promise, despite gaining some fame as a pianist and continuing to compose in later life. Other composers born in the early part of the twentieth century who began writing music as children attracted less attention at the time but include some notable examples. Olivier Messiaen (1908–92) wrote his first piece (*La dame de Shalott*) at the age of nine, and it is still apparently unpublished although it has been recorded; Dmitry Shostakovich (1906–75), who began composing in 1915, first came to prominence with a scherzo for orchestra, Op. 1, as early as 1919. The two most prolific, however, may have been Samuel Barber (1910–81), who was composing from the age of seven or younger; and Benjamin Britten (1913–76), who began at a similar age—his earliest known work, a partsong entitled "Do you no that my Daddy," dates from circa 1919, when Britten was five or six. Both composers wrote perhaps as many as one hundred works, and certainly not far short of this figure, while still younger than sixteen.[9]

Other young child composers worth mentioning from the early twentieth century include Morton Gould (1913–96), whose first composition was published at the age of six (as its name, *Just Six,* implies). Ruth Gipps (1921–99) is notable for being possibly the youngest girl ever to have a composition published, which she did at the age of eight, although Weichsell (1765–1818) was about the same age when her first pieces were published. Gipps's work is a sixty-four-bar piano piece in A minor entitled *The Fairy Shoemaker* (London: Forsyth, 1929). Slightly later, Glenn Gould (1932–82), who became famous as a pianist, performed his own composition in public on 9 December 1938 at the age of six.

With more recent composers, there has been a fairly consistent pattern of complete neglect of their early works. Even if they began composing at an early age, the earliest work they "recognize" or "acknowledge" in later life is generally one written around the age of twenty or later. This pattern is already evident, for example, with Giacinto Scelsi (1905–88), whose first "acknowledged" work is *Rotative,* written in 1929 and premiered in 1930.[10] John Adams (b. 1947) had an orchestral work performed at the age of fourteen, yet the earliest work currently listed dates from 1970.[11] Harrison Birtwistle (b. 1934) began composing at the age of about seven, initially in a "sub Vaughan Williams" style, but his first work now acknowledged, *Refrains and Choruses,* was not written until 1957.[12] I asked him once what had become of the works he had written before that time. He indicated that they were in some box somewhere, but was reluctant to give any further details. This has been the attitude of numerous composers in the past fifty years or more, and it is almost impossible to investigate what is being suppressed, or to estimate the size of the losses.

One small window and rare means of access into the field of compositions written by children of the middle to later twentieth century can, however, be provided by my own early works (b. 1949). Although not generally known as a composer, I wrote my first notated composition (after several had been improvised and forgotten) at the age of seven. By the age of twelve I had completed several works, though not all had actually been written down—partly because of a limited supply of manuscript paper. Some that were written down have since been mislaid, but one that survives is a rondo in G for piano, written at the age of eleven (ex. 2.2).

The main problems are obvious. Like many children of the time, I had scarcely encountered anything as chromatic as Debussy, and so it is hardly surprising that ex. 2.2 is closer to Mozart than the techniques of the mid-twentieth century, even though it exhibits some irregularities, such as the unusual trill in bar 8 and the curious modulatory chords (later deleted) in bars 9 and 10, with a change of key that scarcely belongs in Mozart's period. There was no chance of such works finding favor with the guardians of modern musical taste of the 1960s, no matter how well composed.

By the age of fifteen, however, I had been exposed to many major composers of the first half of the century, and was able to write an organ fugue in a much more "acceptable" style (ex. 2.3).[13] The rhythms may be almost entirely Bachian, and the reinvention of what is now known as the octatonic scale is scarcely worthy of note; but the way this scale is used is

Example 2.2.   Cooper, Rondo in G.

distinctive and original, as is its combination with a chorale melody ("Wir Christenleut") hidden in the alto part in bars 7–9. The work has been performed several times, even though it was far from the forefront of stylistic development of the 1960s.

Although these two examples are from an individual case, there is no reason to suppose that it is in any way exceptional. A huge stylistic gulf is evident between what I composed as an eleven-year-old, in a style deemed "unacceptable," and what I subsequently wrote in this second example, especially in terms of harmony and tonality. Such a gulf between very early and later works was in fact already apparent with some composers born in the late nineteenth century, such as Bartók. This gulf was surely one of the main reasons why so many composers from the twentieth century quickly discounted all their works written before a certain age, and why such works attracted very little adult attention.

In recent years, however, there has been a gradually increasing recognition that children might be capable of producing works worthy of notice. Whereas, in the mid-twentieth century, composition was generally regarded as an esoteric art (unlike, say, painting), to be practiced only by those who had studied an instrument and mastered the art of harmony and counterpoint over several years, pedagogues have since come to realize that composing is an activity that can actually be attempted by nearly all children, even if the outcomes cannot always be dignified by the term "composition" in the conventional sense. As Joanna Glover has said, composers were formerly regarded as "a rare species set apart, exceptional geniuses, with gifts and inspiration beyond those to which any ordinary person can aspire. This is a very specific

Example 2.3.　Cooper, "Fugue" from Chorale Sonata.

historical legacy of western nineteenth-century romanticism. . . ."[14] There have been many recent attempts to break free from this historical legacy, by encouraging children of varied abilities to attempt composition. One forward-looking example comes from as long ago as 1962 and was described at the time by "a comparative newcomer to teaching," Peter Maxwell Davies. As in his own compositions, Maxwell Davies adopted a strikingly individual approach to the teaching of composition, and elicited from his school pupils several interesting works, some of which were recorded. He concludes that "children are capable of producing vital and arresting original music, if all creative drive is not hounded out of them."[15] Nevertheless, it was some time before such ideas were widely accepted, and in the pages of the *Journal of Research in Music Education* there are no articles dating from before the 1980s on the teaching of composition or the assessment of children's compositions,[16] although there have been several since.

　　Thus children's compositions are now at times receiving considerable scholarly attention, if only in the context of educational studies. Meanwhile the rise of postmodernism has gradually loosened the rigid bounds of musical taste, and a much broader range of styles is now acceptable, sometimes even within a single work. The result is that children's works are less likely than before to be dismissed on stylistic grounds. At the same time, children have become exposed to a far wider range of music through a proliferation of available recordings of music in many styles, and are consequently less likely to compose a work in an entirely pre-1900 style. These three factors have helped create a much more positive attitude toward children's compositions—an attitude reflected in the creation of competitions specifically for child composers. A notable example in the United Kingdom is the annual Guardian/BBC Proms Young Composers Competition, begun in 1998–99 and open to composers up to the age of eighteen, with prizes having been awarded to children as young as thirteen.[17]

A few other children have sprung to prominence since the dawn of the twenty-first century. Two notable examples are Jay Greenberg (b. 1991), who composed numerous works, including five symphonies, as a child;[18] and Alexander Prior (b. 1992), who began composing at the age of eight and wrote a two-act ballet, *The Jungle Book,* which premiered at the Moscow Classical State Ballet in June 2007.[19] Despite this increased interest in compositions by today's children, however, literature on compositions by children of the past has remained sparse, and much has still to be done before children achieve parity in this field with comparable works by adults.

One thing that is very clear from this chronological résumé and the Checklist is that there has rarely been any concentration of child composers together, either geographically or chronologically. Almost all the major European countries and the United States are represented, and every decade from the 1750s is also represented by several composers. There seems to have been a slight surge in the late eighteenth century, which could have been partly due to Mozart's influence and prestige; on the other hand there was no substantial increase toward the end of the nineteenth century, despite an increase in numbers of composers and of the population in general—in other words, there was effectively a proportional decrease. The only cluster of notable child composers so far observed is the Chapel Royal choirboys of the English Restoration period. This anomaly requires some explanation. First, these boys were rounded up from across the country on the basis of exceptional talent (Blow, for example, had been brought from Newark), and so more composers than usual were likely to emerge. Second, Captain Cooke must clearly have given them positive and active encouragement of a kind scarcely seen again until the latter part of the twentieth century. The rare combination of these two features was evidently sufficient to produce several able child composers at the same time; but, apart from this group, the general pattern is of somewhat random appearances, in both place and time, of individual child composers whose remarkable abilities could not have been predicted.

There have been some claims that certain periods were not conducive to the development of child composers. Brendan Carroll's description of Korngold as "the last prodigy" implies that child composers did not flourish in the twentieth century. Paul Griffiths, in discussing Bartók's early works, alleged that "the time was not right for the flourishing of boyhood geniuses like Mendelssohn or Britten, let alone Mozart."[20] These claims need to be reassessed. Griffiths supports his opinion by naming six other composers of Bartók's generation who produced nothing distinctive as child composers: Schoenberg, Stravinsky, Sibelius, Debussy, Ives, and Ravel. But selecting a mere six composers is scarcely a strong argument, quite apart from the fact that Ives did actually produce some significant compositions as a child. So, too, did several other child composers of this period, including Strauss, Busoni, Scriabin, Enescu, and Prokofiev, even if one discounts Korngold as too late. Enescu was even born the same year as Bartók, and while still a child composed three symphonies and numerous other works that impressed his contemporaries, thus undermining Griffiths's claim.

The issue is more complicated than this, however. Child composers born around this time inevitably wrote in the prevailing tonal idiom with functional harmony, but this style quickly became outmoded in the early twentieth century, just as they reached adulthood. Most composers then took on this new style of increased dissonance—especially unresolved dissonance—and a loosening of tonal bounds, and were sometimes themselves path-breakers in this direction. Schoenberg, Bartók, and Prokofiev are examples. It thus becomes particularly difficult to appraise their early works, which use conventional tonal harmony, since it is hard to set aside expectations based on the dissonant style of their later works. With such rapid and dramatic changes in prevailing idiom, the gulf between their early and later works appears much larger than usual, as mentioned previously, so that their childhood works cannot easily be incorporated into a general summary of their complete oeuvre. These "immature" works are therefore more readily dismissed pejoratively as "juvenilia" than are those of a Mozart or Mendelssohn, and listeners who have been attracted by the later style of one of these composers are likely to find their early works unappealing. It is particularly important with these composers, therefore, to judge their childhood compositions by the standards applicable when they were written, rather than by anachronistic, twentieth-century criteria; when correct standards are applied, these works suddenly become far more interesting.

Not all child composers of the late nineteenth century made this stylistic leap, however. Some, notably Strauss, Langgaard, and Korngold, remained conservative, retaining the tonal idioms of the late nineteenth century. But this creates a different problem, for their later works have tended to be dismissed as outdated. Langgaard and Korngold were marginalized to a very great extent in their later years, and even Strauss has acquired a reputation built largely on works composed before 1915. Thus, although there is a smooth continuum rather than a stylistic gulf between their earlier and later works, the later works have tended to be sidelined by music historians on the grounds that they were not at the leading edge of stylistic innovation and are not typical of the period in which they were composed.

Meanwhile the problem of stylistic disjunction evident in the work of the more progressive composers born near the end of the nineteenth century continued almost throughout the twentieth century, creating even greater difficulties for child composers. These composers were rarely introduced to the most up-to-date and progressive musical styles until their student years (or shortly before), and by about 1960 the gulf between what children were playing and hearing and what was being written by the most advanced composers of the day was enormous, as noted earlier. Child composers of that period therefore tended to compose in somewhat outdated styles before making the kind of stylistic leap made earlier by Bartók and others, resulting in a disjunction between their childhood and mature styles. This factor, combined with the then-current aesthetic preference for compositional complexity of a kind that a child is unlikely to produce, and a prevailing cultural hostility toward childhood creations, inevitably resulted in adult composers refusing to acknowledge their childhood works, and they currently still do so almost without exception. With such attitudes from the composers themselves, musicologists have rarely thought fit to try to unearth these early works of recent composers in the hope that something might be learned from them. Thus, although the present study can begin to fill a gap in the investigation of child composers of earlier times, study of the childhood works of most composers from the later twentieth century has not yet begun.

NOTES

1. Susan Boynton and Roe-Min Kok, eds., *Musical Childhoods and the Cultures of Youth* (Middletown, Conn.: Wesleyan University Press, 2006), xi, and literature cited there.

2. Susan Boynton and Isabelle Cochelin, "The Sociomusical Role of Child Oblates at the Abbey of Cluny in the Eleventh Century," in *Musical Childhoods and the Cultures of Youth,* ed. Susan Boynton and Roe-Min Kok (Middletown, Conn.: Wesleyan University Press, 2006), 14–16.

3. Daines Barrington, *Miscellanies by the Honourable Daines Barrington* (London: J. Nichols, 1781), 279–88.

4. Barrington, *Miscellanies*, 289–317.

5. F. W. Joyce, *The Life of Rev. Sir F. A. G. Ouseley, Bart.* (London: Methuen, 1896), 242.

6. Joseph Bennett, "Facts, Rumours, and Remarks," *The Musical Times* 38 (1897): 742–43.

7. "Music in Manchester," *The Musical Times* 38 (1897), 835.

8. See Géza Révész, *The Psychology of a Musical Prodigy (Erwin Nyireghházy)* (London: Kegan Paul, 1925); originally published as *Erwin Nyiregyházy: psychologische Analyse eines musikalisch hervorragenden Kindes* (Leipzig, Germany, 1916).

9. Don A. Hennessee, *Samuel Barber: A Bio-Bibliography* (Westport, Conn.: Greenwood, 1985); John Evans, Philip Reed, and Paul Wilson, *A Britten Source Book,* 2nd ed. (Aldeburgh, U.K.: Britten Estate, 1987). The most up-to-date catalogue of Britten's early works is currently (April 2008) available online via the website of the Britten-Pears Foundation at http://www.brittenpears.org.

10. Julian Anderson, "La Note Juste," *The Musical Times* 136 (1995): 22–27.

11. Sarah Cahill, "Adams, John," *GMO,* http://www.grovemusic.com (accessed 3 June 2008).

12. Michael Hall, *Harrison Birtwistle* (London: Robson, 1984), 5, 154.

13. The fugue forms the first movement of a chorale sonata; a copy of the complete work, which was composed in Scotland, is held in the Scottish Music Centre, Glasgow.

14. Joanna Glover, *Children Composing: 4–14* (London: Falmer, 2000), 10.

15. Peter Maxwell Davies, "Music Composition by Children," in *Music in Education,* ed. Willis Grant (London: Butterworth, 1963), 108, 115. The paper was originally presented in April 1962.

16. The one exception—Israel Silberman, "Teaching Composition via Schenker's Theory," *Journal of Research in Music Education* 12 (1964): 295–303—merely reinforces the attitude that composition is an esoteric art, for it states on the first page that the article will be understood only by those with "thorough training in harmony and composition" and preferably "considerable experience with Schenker" too.

17. Details of these competitions can be found on numerous websites, including the the BBC's website at http://www.bbc.co.uk.

18. Information on Greenberg is available on many websites, notably *The Juilliard Journal Online* 18, no. 8 (May 2003); 22, no. 2 (Oct. 2006), http://www.juilliard.edu.

19. See Prior's website at www.alexprior.co.uk.

20. Paul Griffiths, *Bartók,* 2nd ed. (London: Dent, 1988), 4.

• 3 •

The Marginalization of Children's Compositions of the Past

$\mathcal{D}$espite the substantial amount of music written by children of the past, as indicated in the Checklist in Part 2, very little has received even a brief mention in recent music histories. Many reasons for this neglect can be identified, and they are worth exploring in some detail.[1] The most basic reason is simply that disproportionately large numbers of sources of children's compositions have been lost. Almost all of the anthems written by the choirboys of the Chapel Royal after the Restoration have disappeared, even though the words of many are known. Both Handel and Telemann composed much as children, but almost all is lost, including Telemann's first opera and all of Handel's weekly compositions for the church in Halle, for which we have only a single reference to their existence. All three of Cardonne's early motets are lost, and only the words of Clementi's oratorio have survived. All but one of Linley's seven violin sonatas are lost. Major works by later children that have suffered the same fate include two concertos by Fétis; one concerto by Spohr; Weber's first opera and most of his second; a symphony by Moscheles; two string quartets by Schubert; two quintets by Berlioz; the greater part of Arriaga's opera *Los esclavos felices*; two or perhaps three piano concertos by Liszt; all of Verdi's numerous childhood works; nearly all the childhood works by Eckert, including an opera and an oratorio; nearly all the childhood works by Smetana; a concerto by Franck; two operas by Paladilhe; almost all Bruch's early works, including two piano trios and a symphony; two symphonies and an opera by Fibich; two string quartets by Bartók; two piano trios and a string quartet by Hindemith (destroyed during World War II); and a cantata by Korngold. This impressive list represents only the major works; hundreds of minor ones have also disappeared. Moreover, these are just the works that are known to be lost; many more may have existed for which there is now no evidence at all. A few lost works may yet be discovered in private hands, but this is unlikely to be true for many. The efforts of children are often treasured only by their parents, and when the family is dead, the compositions may all too easily be casually discarded.

Sometimes, too, the destruction of childhood compositions has not been casual, and the composers themselves are often to blame, as was the case for C. P. E. Bach, Verdi, Brahms, and Dvořák. Saint-Saëns is another composer who is reported to have destroyed many of his childhood works, although, if he did so, he does not seem to have been very systematic; more than fifty still survive. Early works by Grieg and Schoenberg are among those that have had a lucky escape after their composers lost interest in them. Composers, however, are arguably not always the best judges of their early works. As their tastes and ambitions alter, they may come to regard these works as outdated or insufficiently sophisticated; or they may simply wish to turn their backs on the means by which they reached their current position, perhaps afraid that such works might lessen their image and reputation in the eyes of the public. What concerns us now about these works, however, is what the child composer thought of them at the time of composition, not what the composer thought of the works retrospectively, after reaching adulthood. Any composer who takes the trouble to write down a composition at all, fetching pen, ink, and manuscript paper, and laboriously writing out every single note, must have considerable regard for it. Although one can understand the reasons for later destruction of childhood compositions, such action is nevertheless regrettable. It can also rob us of one means of increasing our understanding of that composer's later works.

A third reason for the current neglect of children's compositions is their infrequent publication, making access and assessment of them difficult. Whether or not these works have been published in modern editions has often depended on whether a complete edition has been devoted to the composer in question; this in turn has depended largely on how successful that composer was in later life, rather than as a child. Thus there are complete editions for composers such as Mozart, Beethoven, Schubert, and Chopin, and these duly include the childhood compositions. There are also partially complete editions of the works of Hummel, Mendelssohn, Liszt, and Strauss, for example, and these contain at least some of the works of the composers in question. For composers regarded as of lesser significance on the basis of their later works, however, the situation is not so good, regardless of how successful they were as child composers. Many childhood works by composers such as Wesley, Crotch, Franck, Ouseley, Saint-Saëns, Rheinberger, Paladilhe, Busoni, Bloch, Furtwängler, and Tcherepnin have so far never appeared in print or in recordings, and are likely to be unfamiliar to anyone except perhaps one or two specialists. The same applies to works that were published shortly after they were written but not since then, as these will be equally unfamiliar today except to the occasional specialist. Works by composers such as Darcis, Welsh, Weichsell, Berwald, Blahetka, Moscheles, Fibich, and Castelnuovo-Tedesco come into this category, as do works by many of the composers in the previous list. With so much material not readily available for study, it is hardly surprising that there has been almost total neglect of these works in general histories of music, and even, in most cases, in specialist studies of the individual composers.

Surviving manuscripts of works left unpublished have generally found their way into public collections eventually, but it has often taken many decades. Thus unpublished works by earlier composers are generally accessible in libraries, and there may even be a catalogue of them, but those from more recent years are often in private hands, and access is sometimes impossible. A particular problem arises where a composer has decided to discard or withdraw a work, or simply refuses to acknowledge it. This has been a very common occurrence in the twentieth century, as indicated earlier; composers often refuse to recognize anything they wrote before the age of about twenty-one. These works are consigned to a kind of limbo. They may eventually reemerge, as happened with a group by Grieg that he instructed to be destroyed at his death and certainly never intended to be published, but their absence in the meantime gives the impression that childhood composition is a far less common activity than it actually is. Childhood composition consequently receives even less attention than would otherwise be the case. Works dismissed by their own authors within about ten years of their composition stand almost no chance of being reappraised by others.

In a few cases, an adult composer has recognized that an early composition contains some merit, but has simply extracted some material—a theme or two—and reworked it in a new way. This conscious appropriation of earlier material often passes unacknowledged, and is probably much more widespread than is generally realized. Beethoven, for example, borrowed two themes from his early piano quartets, written at the age of thirteen or fourteen, when composing his Piano Sonata Op. 2, and there could easily be many other unrecognized borrowings by various composers from works now lost. Sometimes the borrowings are even acknowledged openly, as in Elgar's *Wand of Youth* and Britten's *Simple Symphony*. Almost always, however, the earlier work is suppressed and treated as a quarry for useful ideas rather than as an artistic creation in its own right.

The implication of such practices is that a composer's output forms a kind of unified whole, almost like a journey of exploration, in which early works are regarded as preparatory. Such works can then automatically be assigned lesser significance—mere steps on the road to an accrued mastery of composition. These works are then liable to be judged anachronistically by the aesthetic norms of later works, and their failure to live up to later sophistication can be regarded as a defect. There can be an automatic assumption that a composer's skills gradually improve toward a final goal; from here it is a short step to assuming that the works furthest from that goal, namely the early works, have no intrinsic value, and that their only possible interest might be in how far they anticipate what came later.

Such attitudes can be exacerbated by the modern preference for complexity as aesthetically desirable. If a modern work is not complex, it tends to be considered weak and artistically deficient; twentieth-century critics have placed undue value on complexity, which is often regarded as an aesthetic goal (though this may be less so in the twenty-first century). Yet complexity is not a universal aesthetic axiom: In the later eighteenth century, simplicity was highly valued, and writers such as Charles Burney could condemn Bach's music for lacking this desirable attribute. It is hardly surprising, therefore, that child composers such as Mozart, Darcis, and Wesley flourished particularly easily at that time. Once complexity becomes prized, however, children's compositions are liable to be excluded, since this quality tends to be avoided by child composers, as it used to be by women composers. Marcia Citron has observed, "The cases of music and art both suggest that the greater value placed on complex art forms, which require education, may have been a way of keeping out women."[2] If an overvaluation of complexity keeps out women, it is clearly an equally effective way of keeping children's compositions from their place in the musical canon, though Citron does not seem to have noticed this.

Alongside the tendency to view a composer's career as one of growth and improvement, with the implication that early works have little or no interest, much of the terminology used for children's compositions has pejorative overtones, which tend surreptitiously to diminish the perceived value of such works. For example, a composer's childhood works are often dismissed as "juvenilia," a word that possesses strong negative overtones suggesting incompetence. Lewis Foreman actually catalogues Bax's early works under the heading "juvenilia," separate from the main body of Bax's works.[3] A similar approach is adopted for Enescu (1881–1955) by Noel Malcolm, who arbitrarily deems "juvenalia" to be between all of Enescu's works written before 1895, plus all those written between 1895 and 1900 that are still unpublished.[4] Enrique Alberto Arias does not actually use the term "juvenilia" for Tcherepnin's early works, but he too catalogues them separately from the rest of the composer's output, as "childhood works," with only the briefest of indications of what this category contains.[5] Several scholarly editions also marginalize composers' childhood compositions by relegating them to an appendix, as in the complete edition of Strauss's songs, in which all his childhood songs, or "Jugendlieder," are placed in an appendix.[6] The complete edition of Hindemith's songs also relegates his childhood works to an appendix. In this way childhood compositions are all too easily neglected, although this approach does confirm that childhood compositions can form a separate corpus for investigation in the same way that women's compositions can. The failure occurs when this corpus receives little or no attention, as with Arias's catalogue. Meanwhile, the pejorative term "juvenilia" cannot be accepted; it is no more appropriate than the descriptor "senilia" for works written after the age of about sixty. References to a composer's childhood compositions should use more neutral terms, such as "early works" or "youthful works."

Several other terms are best avoided as conveying possibly negative implications. Suggestions that a composer's later works show greater "maturity" and that children's compositions are "immature" can easily give a wrong impression that the later works are better and the early ones poor, rather than just different. Another term to avoid is "prodigy" as applied to child composers (and performers), since it implies something freakish and unnatural, and could be regarded as little short of an insult. One never hears of adult "prodigies," though outstanding figures such as Shakespeare and Michelangelo would just as easily qualify as any child "prodigy" if one were trying to indicate that the person in question had prodigious ability. For outstanding child composers, the German term *Wunderkind* is a little better, since it suggests wonderment on the part of adult observers, though even here comparable terms for adults, such as *Wundermann,* are rarely encountered. But it seems preferable simply to call child composers precisely this, without any a priori judgment on their level of ability. The current widespread use of such words as "juvenilia" and "prodigy" provides strong evidence that the principles of political correctness have so far been insufficiently applied to children as compared with other groups. These words must be rejected, just as the word "primitive" is no longer acceptable for describing the music (or the people) of the non-Western world.

Another term that is surreptitiously misleading is "women composers." Writers who vehemently insist that the sexes should be distinguished in written text (e.g., by using "he or she" rather than just "he" for someone unspecified) are often much less rigorous when age rather than sex is involved, and unthinkingly use "women composers" when they really mean "women and girl composers." Thus a sonata written by an eleven-year-old girl called Elizabeth Weichsell (1765–1818) has been included in a series with the inaccurate title *Women Composers: Music through the Ages.*[7] Anyone reading the title of this series might easily conclude that there have never been any girl composers, which would be unfortunate. It would be more accurate, if less elegant, to use the phrase "female composers" here and in all such contexts, including dictionaries of women composers, unless music written by girls is being explicitly excluded.[8] Clearly, inaccurate and pejorative terminology can be a powerful factor in marginalizing or diminishing the achievements of boy or girl composers.

Still more powerful are cases in which a composer's works are treated as simply nonexistent. This apparently improbable situation occurs surprisingly often. Beethoven, for example, composed and published thirty-five piano sonatas, but most editions include only thirty-two, and some books actually state that he wrote only thirty-two because the first three were issued when the composer was only twelve.[9] His first piano concerto, in E flat major, is similarly disregarded, and he is generally credited with only five piano concertos, rather than six (or more). In the case of Franck's substantial collection of early works, Laurence Davies deemed it not "necessary" to say much about them, and his list of Franck's works omits them entirely.[10] The common attribution to Bartók of only six quartets tacitly disregards two early ones. Although these are now lost, this cannot negate the fact that he did write them. An article on "Strauss Before Liszt and Wagner" discusses the music Strauss wrote in the 1880s, when he was sixteen or older, rather than his numerous childhood works.[11] Mendelssohn is often credited with only five symphonies, yet he wrote thirteen other symphonies (for strings) before the age of fifteen. A book devoted to his "early works" addresses mainly those he wrote after he was sixteen, with his childhood efforts deemed "pre-early" and discussed only briefly.[12] Ouseley wrote two early operas, of which the second, *L'isola disabitata,* was completed at the age of eight, using a text by Metastasio that had already been set by Haydn among others. The experienced critic William Ayrton, having heard the first aria and recitative of Ouseley's work, asserted that Ouseley's setting was superior to Haydn's.[13] Whether it was or not, the fact remains that if even one critic (whose view, incidentally, was endorsed by the great singer Maria Malibran)[14] had such a high opinion of the work, this is strong evidence that it deserves serious attention. Yet Ouseley's *L'isola disabitata* remains unpublished and, like his first opera, is not even mentioned in *The New Grove Dictionary of Opera*.[15] The total neglect of these operas in such a major reference tool is hard to account for, except as a symptom of how extensively the very existence of some children's compositions has been suppressed in recent times.

In all such cases it is tacitly assumed that, because the works were composed at an early age, they cannot be worthy of attention and can be treated as nonexistent. In this way they are quickly eliminated from historical surveys, as compositions by women often were in earlier times. Susan McClary has stated:

> When I began graduate training in musicology . . . no women appeared in the curriculum. It never even occurred to some of us to wonder why there

were no women in the histories of music we studied; if we asked, we were told that there had not been any—at least none worth remembering.[16]

A similar response would no doubt have resulted if she had asked why no works by children were in the curriculum, but feminist musicologists are unlikely to ask this question. Moreover, the absence of children's compositions is less obvious and therefore more insidious. When searching for women composers, one can simply look up a name in an index and not find it. Thus it is easy to notice that Hildegard of Bingen (1098–1179), one of the finest composers of chant in the Middle Ages, is completely absent from Gustave Reese's pioneering *Music in the Middle Ages*.[17] The names of most notable child composers, however, are present in music histories, since these composers continued to compose as adults. It is merely the childhood compositions themselves that are completely absent, as with Beethoven's first three piano sonatas. This absence is easily overlooked.

A suggested explanation of why women are not found in histories of music applies in large part equally well to children:

> The absence of women in the standard music histories is not due to their absence in the musical past. Rather, the questions so far asked by historians have tended to exclude them. . . . Musicologists have emphasized the development of musical style through the most progressive works and genres of a period, whereas most women composers were not leaders in style change.[18]

Not only have certain questions not been asked, as indicated earlier, but the emphasis on progressive works has tended to prioritize certain composers and genres at the expense of others—Schoenberg rather than Puccini, Stravinsky rather than Rachmaninoff, the string quartet rather than the glee or partsong, and men rather than women or children, who tended not to write conspicuously progressive works. However, one might challenge the assumption that children were not "leaders in style change." Although it is almost universally accepted that they were not—any suggestion that, say, the style of Mendelssohn's string symphonies was quickly taken up by his contemporaries would be wide of the mark—the situation is not as straightforward as might appear. Children did play a more significant role in style change than might be assumed, as will be seen in chapter 4.

The general assumption that compositions by children of the past are not worthy of attention is seen at its most conspicuous in some of the misguided criticism that has been given to individual works during the last half-century. Let us begin with Monteverdi, the earliest well-known child composer yet identified. His *Sacrae Cantiunculae,* a collection of twenty-three

motets published shortly after his fifteenth birthday, receive some rather negative criticism from Denis Arnold in *The New Grove Dictionary* (see "Monteverdi" in the Checklist), and these comments are amplified in Arnold's own
Monteverdi biography:

> Monteverdi at this stage in his career was rather inconsistent in the way
> that he decorated unimportant words with melismas while often ignoring
> expressive ones; but this is something we might expect of a boy, for the
> manipulation of words is often no little embarrassment to a beginner whose
> main concern is making the counterpoint fit together.[19]

This description gives an extremely misleading impression of Monteverdi's
approach to word setting at this date. Most of the words in the *Sacrae Cantiunculae* are set syllabically, with the careful attention to verbal rhythm that also
characterizes his later music. Melismas are mostly on important words, and a
word such as "surge" (rise up) may be set in a dramatic manner that anticipates
his *Vespers* of 1610 (ex. 3.1); but it would have been tedious to place a melisma
on almost every expressive word, as Arnold seems to demand. When a relatively unimportant word is given a long melisma, as in "patientia" (ex. 3.2),
this was clearly deliberate since it could easily have been avoided, and was not
because Monteverdi was a "beginner." Nor was "making the counterpoint fit
together" Monteverdi's main concern, for he shows himself extraordinarily
sensitive to the meaning of the words as well as to their rhythm. Indeed, "patientia" may have been given a melisma for poetic reasons, to suggest patience.
To imply that an older, more experienced composer would have set the words

Example 3.1.   Monteverdi, "Surge" from *Sacrae Cantiunculae*.

Example 3.2.   Monteverdi, "In tua patientia" from *Sacrae Cantiunculae*.

more sensitively at that date seems highly speculative; the hypothesis seems to be born out of (probably unintentional) prejudice against children's creations. It would in fact be difficult to imagine a more apposite and skilled setting of these texts within the scale on which Monteverdi was working.

Beethoven is another composer whose childhood works have been too often maligned—when they have not been ignored altogether. Among his finest early works are three piano quartets (WoO 36). Most recent discussions of these are very brief, saying merely that they were modeled on three Mozart violin sonatas, with the implication that they display no originality of their own.[20] A comparison of these quartets with their alleged models, however, reveals far more differences than similarities, as in the exposition of the first movement of No. 3 in C major, for example. Here the model is Mozart's sonata K. 296, also in C major, composed in 1778, some seven years before the quartets, and the two expositions, both marked "Allegro vivace," are almost identical in length. Beethoven's work, however, uses far more dynamic markings, over a wider dynamic range, and much more virtuosic piano figuration. He also introduces his second subject much earlier (in bar 23 instead of bar 43), creating entirely different proportions within the exposition—proportions that result in much greater forward thrust and enable him to explore a much wider range of keys. Whereas Mozart's exposition simply modulates to the dominant and remains there, Beethoven includes within the secondary key area a series of dramatic modulations through G minor, D minor, and C minor, using material that was so striking that he revived it in his piano sonata Op. 2, No. 3. While Beethoven, as usual, does not match Mozart's elegance, he easily overshadows him in terms of dramatic power, and any suggestion that he was merely modeling his quartet on Mozart is very wide of the mark. Here, then, the implication of the criticisms is not that Beethoven's work was poorly constructed but that it was entirely derivative, which is patently inaccurate.[21]

Liszt's opera *Don Sanche, ou Le château d'amour,* written at the age of thirteen and premiered in Paris on 17 October 1825, five days before his fourteenth birthday, has been even more heavily denigrated. A complete recording has been issued,[22] which reveals the opera to possess considerable tonal and harmonic imagination, soundly based forms, and sensitivity to the meaning of the words, but most of all great melodic charm and inventiveness. The air "Aimer, aimer," for example, is cast in C major to suit the idea of "gloire," with an appropriately contrasting middle section in the minor. The opening two phrases are carefully balanced to match melodically while displaying sufficient variety and contrast between them to dispel predictability (ex. 3.3). How easy, and how unsatisfactory and banal, it would have been to make the second "aimer, aimer" match the first exactly.

Example 3.3.   Liszt, "Aimer, aimer" from *Don Sanche*.

The opera includes some highly dramatic moments (see "Liszt" in the Checklist), and, although it is not a profound or elevated masterpiece, it fully reaches the standards one might expect from an average (or well-above-average) opera of its date. No critic has yet been able to demonstrate any obvious weaknesses or lack of technical competence, and one critic at the time of its first performance wrote in the *Gazette de France,* "Reasonable people, i.e. those who do not demand the impossible, were highly gratified by the remarkable skills of *notre petit Mozart en herbe.*"[23] Twentieth-century criticism of the opera, however, has been largely negative. Sacheverell Sitwell wrote that it was "completely unremarkable in every way,"[24] while Eleanor Perényi stated, "The whole thing went up like a Montgolfier balloon . . . , only to descend as rapidly. There was no disguising the thinness and immaturity of a work whose title alone would give it away."[25] Yet it seems clear that neither Sitwell nor Perényi actually consulted a score or heard the work, which lasts about ninety minutes, since they make no specific observations on the music. Perhaps they were misled by an unduly hostile criticism of the first performance in the *Journal des débats:* "The audience listened in chilly silence to this cold, humourless, lifeless and quite unoriginal composition, in which a mere handful of charming motifs can be found. . . . There was not a single number that aroused genuine applause."[26] Or perhaps they were simply basing their comments on unsound preconceptions that a child's composition cannot merit attention, rather than on proper acquaintance with what Liszt had written. Whatever the reason for their disdain, the extraordinary suggestion that the work's title on its own could betray thinness and immaturity in the actual music illustrates the extent to which rational judgment has been clouded; the music in fact displays no sign of these features.

Some of Strauss's early works have suffered in a similar way. His first major orchestral work, written for a large orchestra in 1876 at the age of twelve, is described most unhelpfully by Norman Del Mar: "*Festmarsch* is little more than a childhood attempt, the remarkable thing being, perhaps, that the boy had the tenacity, let alone the skill, to complete the full orchestral score."[27] Thus Del Mar implies that the work shows childish features, but does not identify any; he praises only the fact that Strauss had the skill to complete an orchestral score, rather than the skill shown in the actual orchestration, which is strikingly rich and well handled. Del Mar also comments that "we need not take seriously" such early works, even though Strauss himself did at the time.[28] These attitudes seem appalling. Such a work should clearly be considered with the utmost seriousness, both for its intrinsic merits and for its contribution to the development of Strauss's later music. Strauss's next major orchestral work, his Serenade, is described even more disparagingly by Walter Werbeck, who uses inappropriately pejorative terms to describe what are in fact perfectly normal musical devices such as four-bar phrase structures (see "Strauss" in the Checklist).

Bartók's largely unpublished early works offer another example of inappropriate criticism. He wrote thirty-two piano works, numbered by him from Op. 1 to Op. 32, between 1890 and 1894, though some are lost.[29] Paul Griffiths comments, "Of course it would be absurd to look for very much in these efforts of a boy of thirteen or fourteen. Most other composers would have taken care to destroy or lose such juvenilia."[30] As should be evident from the Checklist, the statement is itself misguided. It is by no means "absurd" to look for musical interest in the works of a thirteen-year-old, for plenty of other composers have produced excellent music at this age and younger, which we would not want destroyed. Equally unacceptable is Griffiths's earlier comment about one of these works, *A Duna folyása* (1890–94), which he says "is of interest only as a clue to the eleven-year-old's patriotic feelings"[31]—a dismissive attitude that has been all too prevalent in the literature. At the very least, the work, a multi-movement piece of 573 measures charting the course of the Danube, is of interest in that it reveals some of Bartók's early concerns and capabilities, as well as his ambition to work on a much larger canvas than he had done hitherto. Thus, where childhood works are discussed in the literature, they are often condemned with unjustified remarks, rather than offered a fair assessment; even where they are praised, authors often seem obliged to add or imply that the works are admirable only if the age of the composer is taken into account.

When the quality of a child's composition has been recognized and is unmistakable, there have been attempts to cast doubt on whether such works really were written by such young children. The assumption has too often been that, if a work is known to be by a child, it cannot be that good; if it is recognized as outstandingly good, then it cannot have been written by a child. This attitude was already evident in Barrington's doubts about Mozart's age (see page 13), when he guessed that Mozart might be quite a bit older than claimed until proof of his age was produced. Other doubters have gone further, suggesting the child must have received help to produce such a fine work. This occurred, for example, with Czerny's Variations Op. 1, which were so well written that, according to Czerny, nobody believed that he had had no assistance. Similarly, when Martinů presented himself at the Prague Conservatoire with a string quartet written at the age of about twelve, the director doubted whether it was his work, asking who had helped him (see "Martinů" in the Checklist). In actual fact, Martinů could not have received any help, since no one in his village had sufficient skill to do so.

In the case of Liszt's *Don Sanche,* some scholars found the music so good that they doubted that it could have been composed by a child of only thirteen; Emil Haraszti claimed the whole work must have been written by Liszt's teacher, Paër[32]—a claim that has been dismissed by recent Liszt scholars, who all accept *Don Sanche* as authentic. Paër does appear to have assisted with the orchestration. Yet Arriaga's excellent overture to his opera *Los esclavos felices* (1820), written in Bilbao at a similar age, shows equally imaginative orchestration without any help from Paër (though some have alleged, without firm evidence, that Arriaga was helped by his brother). Moreover, the supposition that children could not possibly know about orchestration is undermined by Mendelssohn's first orchestrated work, *Die Soldatenliebschaft,* which was orchestrated entirely without help. His mother reports, "It seemed to me impossible that a child could be so confident writing for each section of the orchestra . . . when one considers that no expert had seen even one line of it, let alone retouched it. The old musicians were most surprised to find everything fluent, correct and appropriate to the character of each instrument."[33] Korngold's first orchestral work was orchestrated by his teacher, Zemlinsky; yet when Korngold composed his own first orchestral score a few months later, the orchestration was equally skillful. This suggests that Paër helped with Liszt's *Don Sanche* to expedite the completion of the work, rather than because of any lack of skill on Liszt's part. The same may also be true of Arriaga's brother's help (if any) with *Los esclavos felices* and Schumann's contribution to the orchestration of Wieck's piano concerto. These people probably acted not so much as mentors but as assistants, like the assistants who helped with Lully's five-part scoring in the seventeenth century, or those who scored the music of Hollywood film composers in the twentieth. There is no reason to suppose that Liszt, Arriaga, and Wieck were necessarily any less capable at orchestration than either their assistants or Mendelssohn.

In other cases, not just the orchestration but the actual authorship of composers' early works has been questioned on grounds of their age. The earliest work ascribed to Henry Purcell, "Sweet Tyranness" (Z. S69), was published in 1667 when he was eight. Franklin Zimmerman's thematic catalogue, however, places it among the "spurious" works, claiming that the song must have been composed by Henry's father, also called Henry.[34] Two reasons are given: first, Zimmerman notes that the work is ascribed to "Mr." Henry Purcell, a title that today implies an adult; and second, Zimmerman found it hard to believe that Purcell could have written anything at such an early age. Both arguments are specious. In Purcell's day the term "Mr." was an abbreviation for "Master"; it bore no implications about a person's age until nearly a century later. Even then, its use was by no means confined exclusively to adults: Mozart's "God Is Our Refuge" was headed "by Mr: Wolfgang Mozart/1765," when he was only nine; and Vaughan Williams's "The Robin's Nest," written at the age of six in 1878, is headed "by mr R. Williams." Moreover, Purcell's age in 1667 cannot be used as evidence that he did not compose the thirteen-bar song since there is nothing in it that precludes composition by an eight-year-old—especially one with such natural ability as Purcell. Some eight-year-olds have composed far more ambitious works, as is evident from the Checklist. As for Purcell's father, although he was a musician, he died in 1664 and wrote no known compositions. Since there is no autograph score, the issue is unlikely to be resolved conclusively. But there are further reasons for believing the work to be by the younger Purcell. The song reappeared in print in 1673 in a version for solo voice and bass, and again in 1678 in a collection entitled *New Ayres and Dialogues* alongside five other songs ascribed to Henry Purcell. One could argue that all six must therefore be by Purcell Senior, but it is unlikely that so many songs would have been published so long after the composer's death in a collection of this kind, and the only likely explanation is that all six are by Purcell Junior. Thus only a blinkered view that a child could not compose songs at an early age has caused "Sweet Tyranness" to be marginalized as supposedly spurious.

A similar situation arises with six oboe sonatas said to have been written by Handel at the age of eleven. As with many works by children, the sonatas display occasional touches of extraordinary originality: for example, No. 4 begins out of key with the oboe and violin unaccompanied, answered by the continuo alone. There is a fairly reliable story that, when a copy of the sonatas was shown to Handel in England many years later, he made a comment about his partiality to the oboe in his early days, and did not deny the authenticity of the sonatas.[35] Since the sonatas do not differ greatly in style from Handel's later music, there seem no very reliable grounds, external or internal, for dismissing the attribution to Handel, as has been done by several recent scholars. It is certainly no longer possible to argue that they are too good to have been composed by someone as young as eleven—especially as Handel is reported to have composed a cantata-type work for the church every week for three years at around this period.[36] Although the source of the sonatas is late and unreliable, the only other grounds for serious doubt are whether anyone could have composed in such an advanced style as early as 1696, for the sonatas seem stylistically far more characteristic of the eighteenth century. But it could be that they were first drafted in 1696 before being substantially revised to produce the version we have today.

Domenico Scarlatti is another composer whose childhood output has been doubted. There is strong evidence that he was writing chamber cantatas by the age of thirteen, for two of them are dated 1699 (20 September in one case, and he did not reach his fourteenth birthday until late October that year). A slightly earlier cantata, *Belle pupille care,* is dated 1697. Since this is ascribed to Scarlatti's uncle Francesco in one source, and simply to "Scarlatti" in the other two, this one was probably not composed by Domenico, but there is no reason to discount him on grounds of age, as is done by Malcolm Boyd: "It is, at all events, unlikely that Domenico was composing cantatas at the age of eleven or twelve!"[37] Boyd's exclamation mark is very revealing, for it implies an automatic assumption that the notion of an eleven-year-old composing a cantata is slightly ridiculous. Such an unwarranted assumption would be a direct result of the suppression of children's compositions from standard music histories, and it demonstrates how easily prejudice can be unthinkingly reinforced. Since Scarlatti was almost certainly composing cantatas at the age of thirteen and was appointed as composer to the royal chapel in Naples at fifteen, it is actually rather likely that he was "composing cantatas at the age of eleven or twelve," even if none survive now and *Belle pupille care* was written by his uncle.

Beyond skeptics' doubts about a child composer's age, accusations of surreptitious help, or claims of misattribution, there have even been occasional accusations of deliberate deception, as occurred with Korngold. When his early works first came to public attention in Vienna in 1909 and 1910 and were recognized as being of outstanding quality, anti–child-composer attitudes were allied with anti-Jewish ones: the view was put about that these works were really written by Korngold's father, Julius, a music critic, and that the whole episode had been perpetrated by him as an elaborate hoax (see "Korngold" in Checklist). This view was clearly erroneous; in fact, in all the current investigations of children's compositions no hoaxes have been identified. They would anyway have been very difficult to sustain for any extended period. The worst that may have happened is that a child composer's age may have been deliberately understated by one or possibly two years; but it is just as likely that any such understatements were unintentional, given that, until relatively recently, not much attention was paid to the year of someone's birth (as in the case of Beethoven, in which there is no evidence of any grand conspiracy to misrepresent his true age).

In some cases, any suggestion of deception could be ruled out anyway because of the mediocre quality of the compositions in question, though surprisingly few compositions have survived that are badly written. Even where quality is lacking, however, this does not necessarily justify ignoring the music. Again a parallel with women's compositions can be seen, as is evident in the following editorial statement in *The New Grove Dictionary of Women Composers*:

> The issue of "quality" in music can provide a convenient means of dismissing women's music, both heard and unheard, particularly when the critic overlooks such vital issues as the fact that aesthetic judgments are never absolute and that criteria for musical quality are inextricably linked to the established repertoire in a spiral that constantly bypasses women composers.[38]

Just as quality has been used in the past as an excuse for dismissing or bypassing women's compositions, it has also been used against children's compositions, especially when criticisms denigrate the quality of children's compositions in ways that are patently unjustified. Yet children's compositions of the past, no matter how poor aesthetically, are as worthy of attention and investigation as those of women (or men) composers from the point of view of what they might reveal about their composers and their context. This needs to be more widely recognized, now that it is generally accepted that the history of music should embrace far more than just the major masterpieces, and should also examine a composition's historical context.

An analogy with the music of medieval times may be useful here. Any piece of medieval polyphony, no matter how mediocre, is considered worthy of attention by scholars. The thirteenth-century hymn "Nobilis, humilis," for example, which consists of barely sixteen bars in two-part harmony moving largely in parallel thirds, shows no more sophistication than the efforts of several composers aged eight or younger; yet because of its antiquity and rarity (as almost the earliest surviving piece of British polyphony of this type) it has been much cited and subjected to scrutiny.[39] There is no logical reason why this principle should not be applied equally to music written *at*, rather than *in*, a very early age: the music becomes particularly interesting precisely because it was composed by such a young child, and should attract greater rather than less attention. Where such music shows features such as a limited range of modulations, short-winded phrases, or lack of textural complexity, these features should be accepted as inherent aspects of its style, rather than as deficiencies to be condemned—just as it would be wrong to condemn "Nobilis, humilis" for failing to modulate or use more than two voices.

Perhaps the most potent and insidious way in which prejudice has operated to marginalize children's works is through writers being unaware that there is a problem. Judging by their unjustified criticisms, it seems that several writers cited previously have not noticed their own inbuilt prejudice against children's compositions. In fact the problem has sometimes been overlooked even when the marginalization of minorities is being specifically addressed. In one study Leo Treitler discusses dualities in music, and repeatedly returns to the fashionable dualities of race, ethnicity, and gender without once mentioning the child/adult duality. This is so despite the fact that he quotes several passages that refer implicitly or explicitly to this duality—for example, a description of Old Roman Chant as differing from Gregorian Chant in being "naive, youthfully fresh, blossom-like."[40] Similar neglect of children is evident in the following passage by Marcia Citron:

> Anthologies have stressed Western art music and generally ignored other idioms, such as folk music, popular music, and world music. Music by women and other "minorities" in Western culture has also been overlooked, and this shows the biases in gender, class, and race that are inherent in the seemingly comprehensive label "Western art music."[41]

Citron refers here to women and implicitly to lower classes and non-European races. Yet she conspicuously avoids any hint that age has been used as a barrier to recognition. She may have done so because to draw attention to children's compositions would somewhat undermine her case for promoting music written by women, since it would highlight a much stronger case of discrimination. More likely, however, she simply failed to notice that children's compositions were being neglected—both by herself and by the writers she was criticizing. This seems a classic case of unthinking prejudice in which the writer seems unaware that preconceptions are impeding a balanced assessment of children's music in general or of individual works. Equally revealing is a comment by Greg Vitercik: "It simply goes against the critical grain to devote serious effort to the explication of the works of a sixteen-year-old composer, no matter how fine those works might be."[42] In the prejudiced world described here, one does not even need to draw attention to alleged failings in children's compositions: any assessment of them is pointless because it is simply "against the critical grain." Mozart and Mendelssohn are curiously and somewhat arbitrarily exempted by Vitercik in this strange, anti-child world, but otherwise, we are told, "The juvenilia of no other composer . . . shows [sic] more than very occasional evidence" of youthful spontaneity.[43] What musical features would qualify as evidence of youthful spontaneity, and how far Vitercik has looked through the works of the one hundred or more composers named in the Checklist to support his view, remain unclear; but his claim clearly does not withstand scrutiny. Girls, too, are seemingly exempted from discrimination in some recent studies, where, as mentioned earlier, they are included unthinkingly in books and anthologies purportedly devoted to "women" composers.

Altogether, there are numerous ways in which past children's compositions have been marginalized in literature on the history of music, and they can be summarized as follows:

- disproportionate loss of sources compared with composers' later works
- some composers' deliberate destruction of their early works; other composers' withdrawal of early works, or refusal to acknowledge them
- rarity of publication, so that critical comment on privately owned works is almost impossible
- composers' reworking of their earlier ideas, which are then regarded as having been superseded
- a general assumption that a composer's output always advances, and therefore presumably is improving, implying that the earliest works can be disregarded
- a modern taste for complexity (rarely found in children's works) as a measure of aesthetic quality
- unthinking use of pejorative terminology; separation of early works from the main body in lists of composers' works and collected editions
- total disregard of childhood works in commentaries on or lists of a composer's output
- omission of such works from the canon of those worthy of study, especially when progressive works are being prioritized
- misguided criticism that does not stand up to scrutiny
- skepticism about the authenticity of the best child compositions
- a disregard of works of lesser quality, no matter what they might reveal
- a widespread blindness to the fact that this kind of marginalization is taking place

Thus the ways in which children's compositions have been discriminated against are extremely diverse, and operate in all sorts of different manners, but their cumulative effect is massive. Some of these types of discrimination also operated against women's compositions until relatively recently, for in both cases there have been witting or unwitting attempts to marginalize their output—notably through their exclusion from the canon of works deemed worthy of study, misguided criticism of fine compositions, disregard of works of lesser quality that might nonetheless be revealing in some way, and perhaps blindness in some quarters to the fact that any such discrimination was taking place. The range of factors that have operated against child composers, however, is clearly wider than the range that operated against women composers. Another important difference is that the discrimination against children's works has been both more profound and also less obvious (since child composers often gradually change into prominent adult composers and are therefore less easily seen as a distinct group). Furthermore, discrimination against child composers is still a powerful force today, whereas discrimination against women's works has largely disappeared in recent years, and there is even considerable evidence of attempts at reverse discrimination, such as the previously mentioned books devoted to music composed by women. There are therefore both significant similarities and significant differences between the two groups of composers in the recent reception of their music by the community.

Searching for reasons for this neglect of and discrimination against the music of child composers, however, is problematical. There may well prove to be a kind of cultural prejudice against children's productions and ideas in other arts too: children's paintings are rarely displayed in an art gallery, for example, or children's poetry anthologized alongside poetry by adults. Such prejudice is perhaps even evident in society in general: children are not allowed to vote, for example, even though some might use their vote more wisely than some adults. In pointing to the widespread neglect of women's compositions, Citron has observed that "the critical establishment has been overwhelmingly male";[44] but it is also overwhelmingly adult, and it must be suspected that this is one reason why some critics have subconsciously denigrated children's compositions without justification. Thus the question seems not to be a musical one and will need to be addressed by social historians in general. One element that has affected discrimination against children's works appears to be the increasing and welcome desire during the nineteenth and twentieth centuries to protect children from slavery, exploitation, and other evils, which resulted in an increasing reluctance to exhibit exceptional children for entertainment, as noted earlier. This then led to a concomitant increasing disrespect for their artistic output, since the quality of the most outstanding child composers was no longer visible, as it had been with Mozart, Crotch, Liszt, and others. It was but a short step from treating children's artistic output as not suitable for display to regarding it as not worthy of display, leading inevitably to a tacit assumption that children cannot produce true works of art. Once this stage was reached, however good a child's compositions might be, they would be likely to suffer the kinds of unjust criticism or neglect demonstrated in this chapter. Reversing such prejudices will be a long, slow process.

NOTES

1. Some of these reasons have already been explored briefly in Barry Cooper, "Major Minors," *The Musical Times* 137 (August 1996): 9–10.
2. Marcia J. Citron, *Gender and the Musical Canon* (Cambridge: Cambridge University Press, 1993), 131.

3. Lewis Foreman, *Bax: A Composer and His Times* (London: Scolar, 1983), 7, 449.

4. Noel Malcolm, *George Enescu: His Life and Music* (London: Toccata Press, 1990).

5. Enrique Alberto Arias, *Alexander Tcherepnin: A Bio-Bibliography* (Westport, Conn.: Greenwood, 1989), 117.

6. Richard Strauss, *Lieder Gesamtausgabe,* vol. 3, ed. Franz Trenner (London: Fürstner; Boosey & Hawkes, 1964).

7. Martha F. Scheifer and Sylvia Glickman, eds., *Women Composers: Music through the Ages* (New York: G. K. Hall, 1998).

8. Even the term "female composers" might be queried by some, since it would strictly have to include female birds and other nonhuman creatures that might be regarded as composers.

9. Even whole books on Beethoven's piano sonatas, by Donald Tovey, Charles Rosen, and others, fail to make the slightest mention of these three early sonatas.

10. Laurence Davies, *Franck* (London: Dent, 1973).

11. R. Larry Todd, "Strauss before Liszt and Wagner," in *Richard Strauss: New Perspectives on the Composer and His Work,* ed. Brian Gilliam (Durham, N.C.: Duke University, 1992).

12. Greg Vitercik, *The Early Works of Felix Mendelssohn: A Study in the Romantic Sonata Style* (Philadelphia: Gordon & Breach, 1992).

13. F. W. Joyce, *The Life of Rev. Sir F. A. G. Ouseley, Bart.* (London: Methuen, 1896), 9.

14. Joyce, *Life of Ouseley,* 12–13.

15. Stanley Sadie, ed., *The New Grove Dictionary of Opera,* 4 vols. (London: Macmillan, 1992). The score of the opera survives in Oxford, Bodleian Library, Tenbury MS 1087; see E. H. Fellowes, *The Catalogue of Manuscripts in the Library at St. Michael's College, Tenbury* (Paris: Oiseau-Lyre, 1934). It surely deserves to be resurrected and investigated more fully.

16. Susan McClary, "Of Patriarchs . . . and Matriarchs, Too," *The Musical Times* 135 (1994): 365.

17. Gustave Reese, *Music in the Middle Ages* (London: Dent, 1942).

18. Jane Bowers and Judith Tick, eds., *Women Making Music: The Western Art Tradition, 1150–1950* (Urbana: University of Illinois Press, 1986), 3.

19. Denis Arnold, *The Master Musicians: Monteverdi,* 3rd ed. (London: Dent, 1990), 124.

20. See, for example, Nicholas Marston's account in *The Beethoven Compendium,* 2nd ed., ed. Barry Cooper (London: Thames & Hudson, 1996), 228.

21. Further evidence of the high quality of these piano quartets is presented in Barry Cooper, "Beethoven's Childhood Compositions: A Reappraisal," *The Beethoven Journal* 12 (1997): 2–6.

22. Franz Liszt, *Don Sanche* (Hungaroton, LP: SLPD 12744-5; or CD: HCD 12744-5, 1986), with notes by András Batta.

23. Ronald Taylor, *Franz Liszt: The Man and the Musician* (London: Granada, 1986), 15.

24. Sacheverell Sitwell, *Liszt* (London: Faber & Faber, 1934), 15.

25. Eleanor Perényi, *Liszt* (London: Weidenfeld & Nicolson, 1975), 17.

26. Taylor, *Franz Liszt,* 15.

27. Norman Del Mar, *Richard Strauss: A Critical Commentary on His Life and Works,* vol. 1 (London: Barrie & Rockliff, 1962), 3.

28. Del Mar, *Richard Strauss,* 2.

29. See Denis Dille, *Thematisches Verzeichnis der Jugendwerke Béla Bartóks,* 2nd ed. (Kassel, Germany: Bärenreiter, 1976) for a complete list.

30. Paul Griffiths, *Bartók,* 2nd ed. (London: Dent, 1988), 4.

31. Griffiths, *Bartók,* 3.

32. Perényi, *Liszt,* 17.

33. R. Larry Todd, *Mendelssohn: A Life in Music* (New York: Oxford University Press, 2005), 65–66.

34. See, for example, Franklin B. Zimmerman, *Henry Purcell 1659–1695: An Analytical Catalogue of His Music* (London: Macmillan, 1963), 438.

35. Friedrich Chrysander, ed., *The Works of George Frederic Handel,* vol. 27 (Leipzig, Germany: German Handel Society Edition, 1879), preface. The sonatas are on pp. 58–90.

36. Otto Erich Deutsch, *Handel: A Documentary Biography* (London: Black, 1955), 3–4.

37. Malcolm Boyd, *Domenico Scarlatti* (London: Weidenfeld & Nicolson, 1986), 284.

38. Julie Anne Sadie and Rhian Samuel, eds., *The New Grove Dictionary of Women Composers* (London: Macmillan, 1994), xiii.

39. See, for example, Reese, *Music in the Middle Ages,* 388.

40. Leo Treitler, "Gender and Other Dualities of Music History," in Ruth Solie, ed., *Musicology and Difference: Gender and Sexuality in Music Scholarship* (Berkeley: University of California Press, 1993), 26.

41. Citron, *Gender and the Musical Canon,* 26.

42. Vitercik, *The Early Works of Felix Mendelssohn,* 3.

43. Vitercik, *The Early Works of Felix Mendelssohn,* 3.

44. Citron, *Gender and the Musical Canon,* 181.

• 4 •

Competence and Originality

*C*hildren's compositions are always in danger of being condemned from one of two directions. If they resemble existing works, they can be dismissed as merely derivative; but if they fail to comply with the standards of the day, child composers are often assumed to be incompetent. As Julian Rushton has said, "If a child in the eighteenth century composed in a markedly original way, differently from the adult composers whose music was heard all around, the result would probably have been taken as childish incompetence."[1] If a work is to be regarded as possessing originality, therefore, the difficulty is to demonstrate that any unusual features can be regarded as original rather than simply as an incompetent attempt to match existing norms. It is generally not difficult to point to any irregularities there might be in a child's compositions, but it is much harder to distinguish those that indicate originality from those that result from incompetence.

One approach to this problem is to consider how children learn to compose. Children in general learn by imitation; they learn to create by imitating either a single model or several similar ones, as is well known and has been noted by, for example, Rushton: "Precocious creativity results from a gift for mimicry (this certainly applies to Mozart)."[2] Often, however, the imitation is inexact, with the child imitating only superficial features of models, rather than their internal coherence. This can lead, for example, to a work with sound harmony but chaotic form that could be described as put together less than competently; alternatively, the form and harmony might be satisfactory, but the part-writing, which is a less obvious characteristic, might be full of grammatical errors (such as parallel fifths in eighteenth-century examples) because the child has failed to notice the nature of the part-writing in the model. Thus, if children learned purely by imitation, then any failure to imitate features that consistently recur in the models (such as correct part-writing) could be deemed incompetence, and certainly not a mark of originality.

Children do not learn only by imitation, however: they also learn by obeying instructions. If the instructions are well presented and dutifully observed, then satisfactory music can be composed—even by a computer or a child with no musical talent. But unfortunately it is difficult if not impossible to create original work merely by obeying instructions. On the other hand, if child composers fail to keep to instructions, perhaps simply forgetting them, or because the instructions are ambiguous or insufficiently clear, then the resulting irregularities will show incompetence rather than originality. Thus, whether children learn by mimicry or by instruction, there is no real scope for originality.

There is, however, a third method by which children learn—possibly the most important, but often overlooked: by trial and error, and by experimentation. Many children are extremely good at learning by this means, which is how they often manage to master technical and electrical gadgets such as recording equipment so quickly and easily—sometimes more quickly than adults. When applied to composition, this method of learning often leads to chance discoveries that can be called truly original: children may discover a musical possibility that works successfully and can be reused in later compositions, but that has not previously been noticed by other composers. Such discoveries may be entirely serendipitous, or they may require the composer to have used some imagination. Fortunately, many children have a very good imagination, as has often been observed, and so the likelihood of some new possibility being discovered is greatly increased in such cases. Such a previously undiscovered possibility may relate to any aspect of music, such as tonality, form, genre, texture, rhythm, or a particular combination of these elements. When this method of learning by discovery is borne in mind, it becomes evident that composers can create original work from a very early age. The assumption, so often unthinkingly held, that children's compositions could not show any originality, but must be entirely derivative until the composers find their own "voice" on reaching "maturity," is clearly erroneous, and the compositions of the children in the Checklist in Part 2 often do show striking originality. It is still not always easy for the onlooker to establish criteria that will reliably distinguish such originality from incompetence, but if the newly discovered possibility is used again in much later works, this provides a clear means of confirming that the idea resulted from true originality—though the converse is not true: if an irregular device is not reused later, it may nonetheless possess originality.

A notable illustration of originality through discovery is provided by Chopin's first polonaise, published at the age of seven, which is in G minor but ends "wrongly" in B flat major after the reprise of the opening section (ex. 4.1). The editors of the Chopin complete edition proceeded to correct what

Example 4.1. Chopin, Polonaise in G minor.

they evidently regarded as incompetence by arrogantly rearranging the piece to end in the tonic. As a seven-year-old, Chopin might not have known how unusual his ending was; but the fact that he approved of the effect is evident from his return to it many years later in his Fantasie Op. 49, which also ends in the relative major of its initial key. The reappearance of this idea therefore demonstrates that it results from originality rather than incompetence.

The same applies to other novel devices borrowed by adult composers from their childhood works, and the number of cases in which this has been observed is remarkable. So often, a composer has an original idea in childhood that then continues to resurface in works written many years later, and may become a hallmark of that composer's style. This style will, of course, continue to change and evolve in later life, but certain features that are not merely commonplace in the musical language of the time may keep recurring. Such features must be regarded as original since they become peculiarly associated with that composer (whether or not they may occasionally be found in the works of others).

Many examples of this process are mentioned in the Checklist, but it is helpful to see them all assembled together to demonstrate how common it is for a composer to continue exploiting ideas originally formed in childhood. Chopin, besides occasionally resorting to "wrong-key" endings, quickly developed an ornate chromaticism combined with strikingly idiomatic pianistic figuration. Mozart's love of opera, especially with plots that contain an element of forgiveness, is already apparent in his *Apollo et Hyacinthus,* written at the age of eleven, while his pupil Hummel quickly developed a characteristically light and graceful piano style. Weber's dramatic flair and his manner of using wind instruments became prominent at an early stage. For Beethoven, the idea of bursting from an oppressive C minor to a triumphant C major, so striking in his Fifth Symphony, appeared in his first known composition—a set of variations (WoO 63). Other characteristic features of his work can likewise be traced to his childhood compositions, such as intensive development of a small motif, use of long codas, and an unexpected reprise of a slow introduction within a sonata form (found in a sonata published at the age of twelve, but also in his late quartets). Schubert's first surviving work, a Fantasie for piano duet (D. 1), displays not only his characteristic lyricism and remarkable length, but also tonal variety and thematic transformation such as recur in later works.[3] Paganini's earliest work already exhibits unusual violinistic effects, while Rossini's contains typically energetic, mellifluous melody. With Mendelssohn, it is his polished counterpoint, general refinement, and delicate scoring that stand out, whereas Liszt at a similar age preferred bravura figuration or intense chromaticism (illustrated in examples 8.2 and 8.3 on page 130). Ouseley's fondness for remote modulations, which is clearly the result of experimentation at the piano rather than imitation of other composers, appears most strikingly in a march written at the age of six,[4] and similar progressions can be found in his two early operas, though rarely in his later works. Wolf quickly became absorbed in writing lieder whose most consistent feature, as in his later lieder, is paradoxically their enormous variety of approach and individuality. Strauss and Korngold both discovered rich orchestral effects in childhood, which served them well in later works with dramatic content (Strauss's operas and Korngold's film music), as did Korngold's distinctive chromatic but clearly tonal style. Grieg quickly showed a preference for short piano pieces built mainly out of two-bar phrases, often with characteristic harmony, whereas Scriabin displayed an early fondness for triple time, very unusual keys, and complex pianistic textures. Pianistic figuration also developed early in Rachmaninoff, but here it is combined with much greater lyricism and sheer melodic invention. Rheinberger and Busoni, meanwhile, not only concentrated on organ and piano music respectively from the start, but both adopted chromatic Bachian counterpoint as an important model from an early age, although Busoni blended this with Chopinesque techniques. Ives's fondness for borrowing hymn tunes, as well as his penchant for light-music styles, is already evident in his childhood works. Bartók, like Grieg, wrote numerous short piano pieces as a child, and their dance rhythms and characteristic textures clearly anticipate those found in his *Mikrokosmos,* even though the harmonic language is different. Prokofiev's early works already show a preference for ostinati and terrifying effects.

These stylistic links between a composer's childhood works and adult output have been noted by many writers, but only as applied to individual composers. Nobody seems previously to have observed just how prevalent the phenomenon is, but it seems to be almost the norm for a composer to discover as a child important ideas that remain a resource that could be called upon repeatedly in later works. Wordsworth's famous dictum, "The child is father of the man," applies very conspicuously in the field of composition, in which so many adult works have been "fathered" by childhood works that bear much of the same musical DNA. What is also noteworthy is the incredible variety of elements preserved and developed by different composers: some are rhythmic, some tonal, some relate to genre or texture, and some to yet other features. The only thing they all have in common is that something distinctive from their childhood compositions reappears in later works.

An even more important conclusion must follow. Whereas it has been widely assumed that children's compositions have no significance in the development of music history and can therefore be sidelined in any account of the evolution of musical style, it is now clear that in many cases these works were a major influence on the later output of the composers who wrote them. These influences were not just negative, in which composers learned what to avoid by making mistakes through trial and error as a child. In many cases these influences were thoroughly positive; composers made discoveries as children that continued to permeate their work for the rest of their lives. When this happens, the device may become so familiar that its origins in the work of a child composer are easily overlooked, as with Beethoven's use of C major to triumph over C minor in WoO 63, or Schubert's ingenious exploitation of thematic transformation in D. 1. Composers tend to learn by experience as much as by formal instruction, and good habits and good original ideas formed during childhood are almost bound to be exploited in some way as the composer develops in later years. These ideas might then infiltrate the work of other composers, thus having a much larger influence on the course of music history than has hitherto been realized. There are, therefore, plenty of cases in which children could after all, as suggested earlier, be regarded as "leaders in style change," initiating important stylistic developments that ought to be recognized as such by music historians. Such influence is in fact far more prevalent than the direct influence of a child's composition on other composers, though this phenomenon does occasionally occur too: The most notable example is probably Wieck's Piano Concerto, which contains features that reappear strikingly in the concertos of Schumann, Brahms, and Grieg.

There can be no doubt, therefore, that children's works sometimes display considerable levels of originality. Indeed, their degree of originality is often actually greater than that of adult composers, who tend to be so inhibited by the conventions of the time and by what is expected of them that they can have difficulty breaking free. Children have no such inhibitions (as demonstrated by the fable of the emperor's new clothes), and so child composers sometimes come up with surprising ideas that would not occur to adults, since children see the world from a different perspective. Thus their originality sometimes emerges in features that are not exploited in later works. An excellent example is Mozart's first known composition (K. 1a), which is only ten bars long but changes abnormally from 3/4 to 2/4 after four bars (refer to ex. 7.1 on page 88). Fortunately his father, Leopold, had the wisdom to write down the piece as it stood, rather than dismissing it as incompetent or adapting it to the norms of the period. Another notable example of originality that was not repeated is a forty-two-bar fantasia composed by Ouseley at the age of six that describes a recent illness.[5] Although it may derive some of its inspiration from other programmatic works of the period, such as the numerous battle pieces, the whole concept and structure are highly original, for there are no known models of any works portraying the full course of an illness. Its subtle interplay of tonality, tempo, and motivic material within a carefully organized structure is most imaginative, while its underlying poetic vision is vividly portrayed in the series of musical ideas presented. In both this work and in Mozart's K. 1a, the novel ideas appeared at a remarkably early age—six and five respectively—but they did not become absorbed into the composer's later style, remaining instead as singular instances of childhood originality.

In contrast to the many examples of originality noted previously, clear examples of incompetence in the works of child composers born before 1900 are extremely hard to find. There are occasional grammatical errors such as parallel fifths or octaves, slightly awkward progressions, or excessively static tonality. Nobody could possibly pretend that all these compositions are flawless masterpieces. Yet there is very little that would seriously mar one's enjoyment of a good performance of almost any of them, and the excerpts quoted throughout the present study illustrate the generally high levels achieved. Melodic lines are always well shaped, harmonies and bass lines are always sound, the textures are presentable, and the part-writing generally acceptable. Even the piece composed by Ouseley at the age of only thirty-nine months (see Ouseley in the Checklist), the youngest age yet discovered for any composer, is perfectly satisfactory as far as it goes, with a regular form (*A A' B B A A'*), "correct" harmony, and coherent motivic development; it does not differ greatly from numerous sixteen-bar marches and dance pieces that were being written in the 1820s. Thus children of even a very early age are sometimes capable of producing levels of competence that would surprise many, while their better works show considerable levels of imagination and thorough technical assurance. It seems that, before children were sufficiently confident to write down what they had invented, they had either undergone sufficient instruction or had sufficient talent to be able to produce music of at least passable quality. There are hardly any examples that could be described as incompetent or littered with grammatical errors. Among the weakest to survive are the earliest works of Prince Henry of England (later King Henry VIII; see Checklist), but even here there is a caveat: the works are assumed to be from his childhood because they are so weak, rather than being known to be from his childhood and then found to be weak. Britten's first known composition, "Do you no that my Daddy," mentioned previously, also stands out as being of much poorer quality than most children's compositions, while Vaughan Williams's first composition, *The Robin's Nest,* is so short at only four bars that it scarcely allows any scope for displaying compositional prowess; but these two works are not typical of the average standard achieved.

The relatively weak compositions from child composers of the past tend to exhibit individual flaws, rather than being generally incompetent. For example, Bartók's lengthy piano piece *A Duna folyása* (*The Course of the Danube*), though unfairly criticized by Griffiths (see chapter 3), is somewhat lacking in tonal variety within and between its many sections, and can scarcely be held up as a vivid portrayal of its subject matter. Nevertheless, published criticism of such works cannot always be taken at face value, since the critic is unlikely to be entirely impartial and may have some unconscious prejudices or some private agenda that impairs rational judgment. Any assessment of children's works using published criticisms needs therefore to be somewhat circumspect, as earlier examples demonstrate.

It seems, therefore, that the irregular features found in the compositions of children of the past generally represent originality rather than incompetence. Most of the obvious flaws, on the other hand, arise out of what has not been achieved in a work, rather than what has been. A common minor defect is for a work to be constructed mainly of short phrases that are not well linked, creating a disjointed effect. Other problems arise where material is not developed as well as it might have been or where there is too wide a range of ideas that do not show complete coherence. If flaws are caused by actual irregularities rather than by possibilities being overlooked, this is most often due to irregularities of part-writing, in which the composer has not mastered how the individual voices should move within the overall texture and harmony to create the desired effect. But this problem was usually avoided by composers keeping their part-writing simple and manageable, while the harmonic and melodic progressions themselves are almost always satisfactory. Thus, whatever the reasons are for the critical neglect of children's compositions, general incompetence or lack of originality is clearly not to blame. Originality must of course be coupled with good judgment to produce a great work, and it is here that actual instruction is most often beneficial. Instruction cannot teach originality, and able child composers scarcely need to be taught competence since they tend to acquire it through osmosis and mimicry; but they can sometimes have their judgment and taste refined by instruction, provided this is not so restrictive that it leads to dull conformity. Thus, as child composers develop, their music tends to become no more original and of only slightly greater competence; the main changes that may well be found seem to be in increased sophistication, greater awareness of possibilities, and better judgment of how to use them.

NOTES

1. Julian Rushton, *Mozart: An Extraordinary Life* (London: ABRSM Publishing, 2005), 26.

2. Rushton, *Mozart,* 26.

3. One cannot accept the description of the Fantasie as being "of little interest" and not at all Schubertian, as claimed in Philip Radcliffe, "Piano Music," in *The Age of Beethoven,* vol. 8, *The New Oxford History of Music,* ed. Gerald Abraham (London: Oxford University Press, 1982), 363.

4. Published in *The Harmonicon*, xi, part 2 (1833), 100. See Ouseley in the Checklist. See also Barry Cooper, "The Amazing Early Works of Frederick Ouseley," *The Musical Times* 147 (summer 2006): 49–58; the march is quoted in full on p. 53.

5. The piece is reproduced in full in John Stainer, "The Character and Influence of the Late Sir Frederick Ouseley," *Proceedings of the Musical Association* 16 (1889): 28–31. There is a detailed analysis in Cooper, "The Amazing Early Works," 55–56.

· 5 ·

Common Characteristics of Child Composers

$\mathcal{A}$ frequent objection to books on female composers in general is that each composer is a unique individual and to group them together on the basis of a nonmusical characteristic, their gender, seems arbitrary when their music has no obvious female characteristics. Observations that they are usually "not leaders in style change" (as noted earlier), or that their music, in common with that of large numbers of men composers of the past, has been largely neglected, are hardly justification for placing all women composers in a separate category, and some writers would argue that it is better to place individuals in the context of similar male composers (for example, by grouping Tailleferre among "Les Six"). The same objection might also be made regarding child composers, which may be one reason why they have not previously been singled out for separate treatment. A further objection might be that the children remain the same individuals after they become adults, and the idiosyncrasies of each composer may be more conspicuous than any specifically childlike features in their childhood compositions. Such idiosyncrasies do indeed often exist, as demonstrated earlier. Nevertheless, this does not invalidate treating children's compositions as a separate category for investigative purposes, and they are surely more likely than women's compositions to have common elements. Children's art is usually easier to recognize than women's art. The question is, then, whether children's compositions or the children themselves all exhibit, or tend to exhibit, certain characteristics. Such characteristics probably will not apply to every child in such a disparate group as those in the Checklist in Part 2, but there could be certain tendencies. In the same way that one might observe that women are smaller than men, and children smaller than women, without any suggestion that such characteristics are universal, there could be elements that occur disproportionately often with child composers—elements that have validity in terms of their preponderance rather than their universality.

Let us begin with family background, which is bound to be a far more important influence at an early stage of life than in later years. It is immediately evident that a strikingly large proportion of child composers had a professional musician as a parent. Some were music teachers, such as the fathers of Mozart, Czerny, Wieck, Bizet, Reger, and Langgaard, and Bruch's mother. Others were orchestral musicians (the fathers of Ries, Berwald, Rossini, Strauss, and Busoni) or singers (Beethoven's father and Rossini's mother). A few had some other musical occupation or were multitalented, such as the fathers of Weber, Sullivan, Elgar (piano tuner and music retailer), Ives, and Korngold (music critic). Many others had a parent who, though an amateur, was strongly inclined musically and probably had sufficient talent to develop as a professional. This often applied to the composers' mothers (such as those of Blahetka, Ouseley, Balakirev, Medtner, and Prokofiev), but it also applied to quite a few fathers (such as those of Liszt, Smetana, Paladilhe, Parry, Wolf, and Hindemith). Those fathers who were not professional musicians were almost always from the professional classes, though the occupations were quite varied. The most common occupations were teacher (Schubert, Chopin, Alkan, and Bartók) and doctor (Berlioz, Paladilhe, and Coleridge-Taylor), while the more unusual professions included carpenter (Crotch), diplomat (Ouseley), innkeeper (Verdi), pastor (Filtsch), and archaeologist (Furtwängler). Thus these parents had sufficient education and financial means to recognize and assist any exceptional musical talent in their children. Martinů's father was something of an exception, being a cobbler and bell-ringer.

Very few child composers had a composer as a parent; even when they did, the parent often had surprisingly little influence on the child's development. Bononcini's father died when the composer was eight; Mozart's son Franz Xaver lost his father when Franz Xaver was only four months; Mozart's own father, though undoubtedly a great teacher, seems to have abandoned composition by the time Mozart was born. The Boulangers' father was noted more as a singing teacher than as a composer, while Alexander Tcherepnin learned music mainly from his mother, rather than from his composer father, Nikolai. Linley and Domenico Scarlatti are unusual in that they developed as child composers alongside their fathers, though Strauss's father wrote a few fine works as well as being a conductor and prominent horn virtuoso. Beyond these, one finds one or two minor or amateur composers such as Pinto's mother and Bizet's father, but otherwise the tendency for children to follow in their parents' footsteps is conspicuously rare.

Even more exceptional is for a child composer to be the offspring of someone who had also been a child composer: Mozart's son is the only such person in the Checklist, although one could add Scriabin's son Julian (1908–

19), who composed several pieces before drowning at the age of eleven. Having two children compose within the same family is also rare: the only examples noted are Fanny and Felix Mendelssohn, and Nadia and Lili Boulanger, though neither Nadia nor Lili composed much as children. Schumann and his wife, Clara, were both child composers, but none of their children were. More typical is the Aspull or the Alkan family, in which several children developed as professional musicians, but only one actually composed as a child. George Aspull was one of ten brothers, all of whom were said to be above average musically,[1] but he was the only one to show an early inclination and flair for composition; only one other brother, William, composed a little at a later age. Alkan had four younger brothers and an elder sister who all became musicians, but again he was the only sibling to compose as a child, though two others did as adults. Other child composers' siblings who did not compose as children but became musicians and perhaps composers as adults include Daniel Purcell, Charles Wesley the younger, and Nannerl Mozart. More often none of the siblings composed (Medtner, for example, had four surviving siblings but none composed), and in some cases the composer was an only child or only surviving child.

A few children were lucky enough to have a musical older sister who could (and often did) provide help and encouragement. This applies to several notable child composers, whose elder sisters include Nannerl Mozart, Fanny Mendelssohn, Mary Jane Ouseley, and Nadia Boulanger, but it was not a particularly common pattern. An older brother sometimes helped instead, as with Schubert, Arriaga, and presumably Aspull, but this was also not very common. Thus the family backgrounds were quite varied, and Mozart was one of the few whose family background was ideal for nurturing a talented composer, with a father who had long been a music teacher and violinist as well as an occasional composer, and an elder sister who was already learning the keyboard before Mozart himself.

These facts and figures throw some light on the relative importance of environmental and genetic factors—the so-called nature–nurture debate, to use Shakespeare's phrase—in the development of the child composer. A child composer clearly needs a suitable environment to be able to flourish. Many children never had any opportunity to develop as composers, no matter what their ability, because there were no instruments available, or their parents could not read at all (let alone read music). Musically literate parents, however, would be likely to notice any exceptional gifts in their offspring, and any early inclination toward composition could be supported or at least tolerated. When this happened, these gifts were developed, as in the cases identified, and this helps explain why so many child composers had musicians for parents. Thus the right environment was an essential prerequisite for a child to develop as a composer. On the other hand, a suitable environment without exceptional innate gifts seems never to have produced a child composer. The ten Aspull brothers must have shared quite similar environments, yet only one, the ninth, showed early promise as a composer, and the same applies in nearly all other cases of composers belonging to large or small families. Thus these inherited gifts exhibited by child composers are not comparable to genetic inheritance of blue eyes or fair hair, for they are far too rare within families for this to be the case. If the ability and inclination to compose as a child had been the result of some specific genetic quirk, there would have been a much higher proportion of child composers whose parents or children were also child composers, but Mozart and Scriabin are the only examples so far identified. If child composers were, on the other hand, partly a product of parental pressure, there should be a much higher proportion who were siblings, rather than just the Mendelssohns and Boulangers (and in neither case is there evidence of significant parental pressure; indeed the Boulangers' composer-father died when the younger sister, Lili, was barely seven). The supposition must be that able child composers are not produced just by nature in the form of ancestral genetic connections, nor just by nurture in environments in which all siblings are encouraged by keen parents to compose, but only by a fortunate and rare conjunction of a group of innate individual characteristics and a suitable environment in which these can be developed. This hypothesis is supported by the fact that there has never been a great concentration of successful child composers in one place or time, but a rather random and sporadic appearance of individuals over many years. But this hypothesis needs to be further tested.

One thing that seems abundantly clear is that, although some children were forced or pressured to practice their instruments, none seems to have had any pressure from parents or others to compose. The initiative and the spark for composition seem always to have come from the children themselves, as far as can be ascertained, and any sense of pressure was internal. Beethoven explained the feeling at the age of twelve in a dedicatory letter published in 1783 in the original edition of his three early piano sonatas (WoO 47); he referred poetically to his Muse commanding him to write his music down: "My Muse wished it—I obeyed and wrote."[2] This sense of compulsion experienced by some composers provides further evidence for an innate, genetic predisposition to composition in a few rare children, rather than a response to an external incentive. Some of these children were then given full opportunity, resources, and encouragement that allowed them to flourish, as in the case of Mozart and Korngold. Others were merely allowed to develop as best they could, such as Samuel Wesley and Fanny Mendelssohn, and were perhaps given no instruction beyond the rudiments, as with Crotch and Ouseley. Czerny's condition seems to have been not untypical: he reports that as an only child he was somewhat isolated from the distraction of other children, but was given no particular encouragement to compose, even when he showed inclination in this direction. There is, however, no significant evidence of direct opposition by parents, who could be expected to view it as a harmless pastime; if there were opposition, it was presented when composition was suggested as a career, as with Wesley.

This absence of parental pressure distinguishes composition from some other fields in which prodigies have excelled, such as reading, mathematics, chess, or sport. In these fields there can be a danger of "hot-housing," with parents pushing their children to develop an early talent. This can result in a kind of burnout in which the child is eventually unable to cope and may abandon the activity. There is no evidence of this having happened with any child composers: composition was in general such an unusual activity that no parents would have expected their children to show great ability, and there was little incentive to develop it quickly if it did appear. Moreover, unlike in some fields such as reading or mathematics, the talent would not be exhibited in the form of an early achiever, doing at a young age what most cannot do until some years older. Competent composers are already exceptional, and competent child composers, who of their own volition sit down and write music, are doubly so; there was therefore no benchmark for what an average child composer might achieve.

Some of these conclusions might seem to be undermined by more recent cases in which whole classes of children have been encouraged to compose, sometimes at quite an early age. This is a different situation, however. Here, there is outside pressure on the child, in the form of incentives used to persuade the children to compose something. The results that are produced are in most cases far short of the competence exhibited in nearly all the surviving compositions by children of the past, who wrote out their works using proper notation that seems normally to have related closely to the sounds they intended. Some children in such classrooms do, of course, produce something noteworthy, and these may be children who simply needed the right environment to flourish as composers. Nevertheless, if they need to be instructed to compose before they start, the initial spark is missing, and they will probably not continue as composers outside the classroom.

By contrast, nearly all the child composers in the Checklist did continue as composers in later life—at least intermittently or for a time. This may to some extent reflect accidents of survival and the way in which the names were gathered; in the twentieth century several enthusiastic child composers have abandoned composition in favor of performance, musicology, or other occupations in later life. Nevertheless, it is probably true that nearly all child composers up to 1900—including any not on the list—continued to compose as adults, and became professional musicians. This continuity of composing activity in adult life is what might be expected if there was no "hot-housing" and the initial spark came from the child rather than some outside incentive: if the desire or sense of obligation to compose was innate, as appears to have been almost universally the case with the children identified, then it was unlikely to desert the child on reaching adulthood. It is significant that the main composers in the Checklist who did not compose beyond the age of twenty-one were Pinto, Arriaga, Aspull, and Filtsch, all of whom died before reaching that age. The complete disappearance of two others, Beaulaigue and Del Pomo, shortly after their first publications as child composers, may be due to the same reason. The only others who did not continue composing beyond the age of twenty-one were female. They include Riese and Weichsell, who seem deliberately to have abandoned composition despite their promising starts (though Weichsell continued as a singer using the name Mrs. Billington). But these are exceptions to the normal pattern of development.

It is also notable that child composers generally began composing without waiting to be taught how to do so. Crotch actually wrote a comment on the manuscript of his huge oratorio *The Captivity of Judah* (British Library, Add. MS 30388, f. 6r), which was composed between the ages of ten and thirteen: "The composer had never opened a treatise on the subject or received a single instruction concerning composition." Crotch, like other child composers, was at the outset untutored except in the rudiments. These composers began composing without waiting to be taught how, and their written compositions are analogous to children writing stories or drawing pictures without prior instruction, while their extemporizations can be likened to learning and then speaking a new language; extemporizing probably seemed to them to be just as natural. Subsequent teaching would result in modifications of style, increased sophistication, and greater skill in using notation, but true composition seems to come from within the child, spontaneously, and is merely filtered or shaped by the teaching, not initiated by it. These conclusions may need modifying in the light of further research, and the situation is doubtless more complex than this outline, but this is what current evidence seems to suggest.

Before starting to compose, nearly all child composers had begun learning the piano (or one of its precursors such as the harpsichord), even if they had already been learning some other instrument first. Some awareness of harmony gained through the practical experience of playing it seems to have been virtually essential as preparation for composition of more than single melodic lines, and here keyboard instruments have a great advantage over most others. Although some child composers later excelled on other instruments such as the violin (Spohr, Enescu) or as singers (Welsh, Weichsell), the keyboard was the main instrument for the majority, and indeed a remarkably large number became celebrated exponents in later life. Blow and Purcell were the two leading English organists of their day. Handel and Scarlatti were so highly regarded as keyboard virtuosos that a contest between them was arranged when they were in Venice; a similar keyboard contest was arranged later in the century for Mozart and Clementi, two other child composers who had developed as outstanding performers. Later examples of child composers who became formidable pianists include Beethoven, Czerny, Herz, Blahetka, Liszt, Chopin, Alkan, Wieck, Busoni, Scriabin, Rachmaninoff, Bartók, and, more recently, Glenn Gould. A notable exception to this pattern is Berlioz, who did not learn the piano, instead becoming aware of harmony through the guitar and through studying treatises while still a child; but the frequent connection between early attempts at composition and later success as a virtuoso pianist is worth further exploration.

Since almost all the child composers listed continued composing as adults, it is interesting to examine the extent of the correlation between their early success and their ultimate prominence as composers. It is difficult, of course, to find reliable means of evaluating different composers' overall achievements, but one way of investigating this problem is through the compilation of "league tables," ranking composers both as children and as adults, and examining the differences in rankings. The pitfalls of such league tables of perceived merit are well-known, for they have been widely debated since such tables were introduced extensively in the educational field—notably for schools and universities—around the 1990s. Unless there are objective means of measurement, any ranking can be challenged; even where the means appear to be objective, they can themselves be criticized as not wholly valid, for what are apparently objective figures may be based on subjective assessments such as inspectors' reports or other individual empirical evaluation. At best, such tables paint an incomplete picture. Nevertheless, the principle that league tables can provide useful evidence not readily obtainable by other means is generally accepted, thus justifying their introduction here, provided their potential drawbacks are recognized.

One possible method to create a league table of the listed composers' perceived standing as musicians in their lives as a whole is to measure the lengths of their entries in *The New Grove Dictionary*.[3] These lengths were determined by committees of expert scholarly opinion, who prescribed lengths within quite narrow limits on the basis of the perceived importance of each composer.[4] The lengths of their entries are therefore likely to be among the most reliable indicators available of composers' standing today. It is possible, of course, that the committees misjudged certain individual composers, who may have merited rather longer or shorter entries than they were allocated in the dictionary, and indeed the relative lengths of some of the articles have changed slightly in the second edition, published in 2001, from the previous edition, published in 1980. There is also probably a bias toward British composers, reflecting the origin of the dictionary itself. For the most part, however, the lengths found seem unexceptionable: well-known composers occupy many pages, whereas very obscure composers who wrote little are allocated only a few lines. This basis for measurement is by no means without problems, like any league table, and cannot be regarded as a wholly reliable indicator of standing. Nevertheless it does have the merit of being readily verified, and provides scope for direct comparisons with other lists using quantifiable means. Moreover, it is a method that has been employed with some success on several occasions, initially in 1903 by James McKeen Cattell; it is in fact sometimes known as the Cattell Space Method.[5]

Using this Cattell Space Method with *The New Grove Dictionary* and the composers in the Checklist, the league table emerges (table 5.1). For convenience, the table is split into four roughly equal "divisions," although the dividing lines could have been drawn elsewhere and some divisions are slightly larger than others (there are 27, 28, 31, and 29 composers respectively in the four divisions). A few of the entries, such as Korngold's, seem unduly brief, and the complete absence of an article on Eckert is surprising, while the extraordinary amount of space given to Liszt is due to an unusually long and detailed work list, rather than a direct reflection of his importance. Thus, as is to be expected, the table should be used cautiously and with circumspection; but it has some validity, for the composers near the top of the table are without exception far better known and more highly regarded than those near the bottom. One particular caveat is that some child composers—notably Welsh and Furtwängler—pursued a dual career in music later in life, and have been given more space in the dictionary than would be justified by their compositions alone. But this is of no consequence if one is investigating which child composers were most successful as musicians of some sort in later life.

One remarkable feature of the table is the huge range represented, from some of the longest composer entries in the entire dictionary to others occupying less than a column (half a page). This demonstrates clearly how some child composers developed into some of the greatest figures in the history of music, whereas others never lived up to their initial promise, composing quite worthy music that is nevertheless almost completely ignored today. Another striking feature is the complete absence of the names of several very great composers, such as Bach, Haydn, Wagner, Debussy, and Stravinsky, none of whom is known to have composed anything of significance before the age of sixteen. Even Schoenberg's childhood output, though he began composing at about the age of nine, is fairly small and insignificant.[6]

Table 5.1. Length of Entries in *The New Grove Dictionary* (2001)

Composer	Columns	Composer	Columns
Div. 1			
Liszt	121.5	Monteverdi	30.7
Schubert	74.1	Strauss	30.7
W. A. Mozart	71.0	Chopin	30.0
Beethoven	67.7	Schoenberg	27.3
Handel	65.5	Ives	27.2
Schumann	56.5	Elgar	22.8
Wolf	38.4	Purcell	22.6
Weber	37.2	Smetana	21.2
Verdi	36.6	C. P. E. Bach	20.7
Berlioz	35.4	D. Scarlatti	19.3
Felix Mendelssohn	34.4	Prokofiev	18.8
Rossini	34.0	Vaughan Williams	16.6
Telemann	33.2	Hindemith	16.0
Bartók	31.3		
Div. 2			
Bizet	14.7	Reger	7.2
Grieg	14.0	Fibich	7.1
Sullivan	12.4	Stanford	7.1
Scriabin	12.2	Clementi	6.8
Spohr	12.2	Busoni	6.3
Saint-Saëns	11.3	Martinů	6.2
Balakirev	11.2	Parry	5.4
Rachmaninoff	10.9	Bononcini	5.0
Kodály	10.4	Loewe	4.9
Hummel	8.2	Sessions	4.2
Franck	7.9	Crotch	4.0
Humperdinck	7.5	Wieck (Schumann)	3.9
Paganini	7.4	Medtner	3.8
S. Wesley	7.3	Fétis	3.7
Div. 3			
Bloch	3.5	Moscheles	1.8
Alkan	3.4	Stanley	1.8
Schulhoff	3.4	Ouseley	1.5
Castelnuovo-Tedesco	3.3	Pinto	1.5
Bax	3.2	Rheinberger	1.5
Czerny	3.1	Arriaga	1.3
Coleridge-Taylor	2.8	L. Boulanger	1.3
Enescu	2.8	Prince Henry	1.3
Furtwängler	2.8	N. Boulanger	1.2
Glazunov	2.8	Langgaard	1.2
Humfrey	2.6	F. X. Mozart	1.2
Kraus	2.1	A. Tcherepnin	1.2
Bruch	2.0	Korngold	1.1
Fanny Mendelssohn	1.9	Šebor	1.1
Ries	1.9	Neefe	1.0
Cowen	1.8		

(*continues*)

Table 5.1. *(continued)*

Composer	Columns	Composer	Columns
Div. 4			
Basiron	1.8	Salaman	0.9
Fiorè	1.8	Welsh	0.9
Fridman	1.8	King	0.8
Pistocchi	1.8	Parke	0.7
Linley	1.6	Aspull	0.5
Aubert	1.5	J. F. Berwald	0.5
Weichsell (Billington)	1.3	Del Pomo	0.5
Beaulaigue	1.2	Filtsch	0.5
Cardonne	1.2	Bergh	0.4
Paladilhe	1.2	Schroeter	0.4
Darcis	1.1	Darewski	0.1
Mornington (Wesley)	1.1	Bonwick	0.0
Blahetka	1.1	Eckert	0.0
Hurlstone	1.0	Riese (Liebmann)	0.0
Herz	1.0		

There is no comparable means for compiling a league table for these composers' childhood outputs, since there is not yet any scholarly consensus on the relative merits of child composers, and much of this music is still unpublished anyway, necessitating the need for further research. The present Checklist could have been used as a basis, but the lengths of entries in it are not intended to reflect the relative importance of the composers, even though a broad correlation is sometimes evident; a precise league table would therefore be premature at present. It is clear, however, that the child composers' outputs are far from equal in scope and size, in originality, in the age range at which each was composed, and in the attention each commanded at the time they were produced and since. And there are measurable criteria that do enable the composers to be grouped into different classes or divisions for comparison with table 5.1. One such criterion is the age at which each child began composing, and table 5.2 shows four groups based on this criterion. With a few composers it is completely uncertain when composing was begun, and these have been omitted, while in a few other cases the composer may have begun earlier than is at present supposed and therefore might be placed in a higher division if such details become known. In most cases, however, the data are secure. Within each group, the composers are listed in chronological order.

One of the most striking features of this table is the large number of children who began composing at the age of eight or younger. One might expect there to be relatively few such young composers, with most starting around the ages of twelve to fifteen, but research so far has not revealed this pattern,

Table 5.2. Composers' Ages at First Reported Composition

Age 3–8 (30 Composers)

Pistocchi	Schumann	Strauss
Purcell	Wieck	Busoni
W. A. Mozart	Eckert	Vaughan Williams
Weichsell	Smetana	Enescu
S. Wesley	Ouseley	Furtwängler
Crotch	Saint-Saëns	Prokofiev
J. F. Berwald	Rheinberger	Langgaard
Czerny	Cowen	Darewski
Herz	Stanford	Korngold
Chopin	Humperdinck	Fridman

Age 9–11 (37 Composers)

Del Pomo	Schubert	Elgar
Telemann	Arriaga	Glazunov
Händel	Felix Mendelssohn	Scriabin
Darcis	Blahetka	Schoenberg
Schroeter	Liszt	Coleridge-Taylor
Beethoven	Franck	Hurlstone
Hummel	Filtsch	Medtner
Welsh	Bruch	Bartók
Fétis	Bizet	Martinů
Weber	Grieg	Schulhoff
F. X. Mozart	Paladilhe	Castelnuovo-Tedesco
Rossini	Fibich	Hindemith
Bergh		

Age 12–13 (22 Composers)

D. Scarlatti	Paganini	Parry
Fiorè	Spohr	Rachmaninoff
Cardonne	Ries	Ives
Mornington (Wesley)	Loewe	Bax
Neefe	Verdi	L. Boulanger
Clementi	Alkan	Sessions
Kraus	Sullivan	A. Tcherepnin
King		

Age 14–15 (18 Composers)

Monteverdi	Riese	Wolf
Humfrey	Berlioz	Reger
Bononcini	Fanny Mendelssohn	Aubert
Bonwick	Aspull	Bloch
Pinto	Salaman	Kodály
Moscheles	Balakirev	N. Boulanger

Not Known

Basiron	Stanley	Parke
Prince Henry of England	C. P. E. Bach	Šebor
Beaulaigue	Linley	

and there seems to be no "typical" age for someone to start composing. The youngest so far recorded are Ouseley and Saint-Saëns, at the age of three, but there is always the possibility that an even younger composer remains to be discovered: Barber is said to have begun composing tunes at the piano when he was just two.[7]

Another noteworthy result that can be deduced from table 5.2 is that an early start provides little indication of later success, as can be seen by comparing tables 5.1 and 5.2. Of the thirty composers who began earliest, only eight are in the top division of table 5.1—Purcell, Mozart, Chopin, Schumann, Smetana, Strauss, Prokofiev, and Vaughan Williams—which is roughly the same number as would be expected in an entirely random sample. In fact the thirty very early starters are divided almost exactly equally across the four *Grove* divisions (8, 7, 8, 7 respectively). The largest proportion of later successes—composers from the top division of *Grove*—comes from the group who began composing between the ages of nine and eleven: twelve out of thirty-seven (Telemann, Händel, Beethoven, Weber, Rossini, Schubert, Felix Mendelssohn, Liszt, Elgar, Schoenberg, Bartók, and Hindemith) were successful in later life. But again, the figures are not far from the statistical norm. In fact this applies to all the figures from table 5.2. In other words, whatever the age at the time of the first composition, the composer is almost equally likely to finish in any of the four *Grove* divisions.

Another criterion for ranking child composers is by publications at the time of composition. This method has the drawback that printing of music became increasingly common only gradually over several centuries, and so early composers may be disadvantaged by such a criterion; but in other respects this method is useful in indicating child composers who actually made an impact at the time, having their works circulated well beyond their immediate environment. Publication also tends to be a guarantee of the quality of the output, since a poorly composed effort by a child is unlikely to be distributed in print, and indeed all the published works thus far studied do seem worthy of this accolade. If a child composer managed only a single published item, this might not indicate much, but if they had at least two publications, this is far more significant, for it suggests that the first one had had some success and that the child was already becoming recognized as a composer. Accordingly, it is worth compiling a list of composers who had achieved at least two publications by the time they were sixteen (table 5.3, again in chronological order). To these names might be added Monteverdi, whose second publication (*Madrigali spirituali*) was a substantial volume that appeared so soon after his sixteenth birthday that most or all of it must have been composed before then, and also Moscheles, who published several opus numbers in quick succession about the time he reached sixteen.

Table 5.3.   Composers with More Than One Publication before the Age of Sixteen

Beaulaigue	Welsh	Wieck
Purcell	Weber	Ouseley
Bononcini	J. F. Berwald	Filtsch
W. A. Mozart	F. X. Mozart	Fibich
Darcis	Riese	Cowen
Schroeter	Herz	Strauss
Weichsell	Felix Mendelssohn	Busoni
S. Wesley	Blahetka	Scriabin
Beethoven	Chopin	Aubert
King	Liszt	Darewski
Crotch	Alkan	Castelnuovo-Tedesco
Hummel	Salaman	Korngold

Here again there is little correlation between the composers listed and their future success, with only eight of the thirty-six being in the first division of the *Grove* list. In contrast, fourteen of them are in the fourth division, achieving so little later success that they were allocated less than one page in *Grove* (Beaulaigue, Darcis, Schroeter, Weichsell, King, Welsh, J. F. Berwald, Riese, Herz, Blahetka, Salaman, Filtsch, Aubert, and Darewski).

A third criterion for ranking child composers is by identifying which ones have written a major work such as a symphony, concerto, opera, or oratorio. Any child who can produce such a work is surely worthy of attention, and such an undertaking indicates a strong and serious commitment to composition, requiring much energy and perseverance. Most people can probably imagine a child composer producing the odd song or piano piece, but they may well be surprised by how many have produced a large-scale work, as indicated in table 5.4, which lists no fewer than forty such composers (again in chronological order).

Although many of the names are different from those in table 5.3, the same pattern applies once again: only one-quarter of the composers listed ended up in the first division of the league table based on *Grove*. A similar outcome emerges if all three criteria are used in combination: composers who began by the age of eight, and had at least two publications and at least one major work written before they were sixteen. Of the ten composers who fulfill these criteria (Mozart, S. Wesley, Crotch, J. F. Berwald, Wieck, Ouseley, Cowen, Strauss, Busoni, and Korngold), only Mozart and Strauss became really important in the eyes of the *Grove* committees, each of them having a *Grove* entry longer than the other eight composers put together. Clearly any early success, no matter what criteria are used for judging it, is no guide to later prominence in terms of general recognition by music historians. Whereas almost all the leading child composers continued as composers and professional musicians in

Table 5.4.   Child Composers Who Have Produced a Major Work

Telemann (opera)	Moscheles (symphony)	Cowen (opera)
Händel (cantata cycles)	Arriaga (opera, *Stabat mater*)	Humperdinck (singspiels)
Clementi (oratorio)		Strauss (orchestral serenade, symphony)
Mozart (operas, symphonies, masses)	Felix Mendelssohn (symphonies, concertos, singspiels)	Busoni (concerto, requiem)
Kraus (symphonies)		
Darcis (opera)	Liszt (opera, concerto)	Bloch (symphony)
S. Wesley (oratorios, concertos, symphony)	Wieck (concerto)	Enescu (symphonies)
	Eckert (opera, oratorio)	Prokofiev (operas, symphony)
Beethoven (concerto)	Franck (concertos)	
Crotch (oratorio, concerto)	Ouseley (operas)	Langgaard (symphony)
Hummel (concerto)	Filtsch (concerto)	Sessions (opera)
Fétis (concertos, symphonie concertante)	Saint-Saëns (symphony, incomplete oratorio)	Korngold (ballet, sinfonietta)
Spohr (concerto)	Bruch (symphony)	A. Tcherepnin (concertos, opera?)
Weber (operas, mass)	Šebor (symphony)	
J. F. Berwald (symphony)	Paladilhe (operas)	
Rossini (symphony)	Fibich (symphonies, opera)	

later life, relatively few became major historical figures receiving more than brief mention in general histories of music. Considered from the opposite direction, however, in order to identify the most significant works by child composers, one clearly cannot just turn to the childhood works of those who are considered the most important composers. Even some very minor composers whose names are largely forgotten today may have written substantial amounts of music in early life; in fact more than half the names in the bottom division of the *Grove* league table began early (at the age of eleven or younger) and more than half had publications and/or a large-scale work completed before they were sixteen. It is therefore very difficult to compile a comprehensive list of noteworthy child composers, since there are no reliable indicators; hence the present Checklist may be presumed to be far from complete.

These tables also throw light on the question of whether Mozart should be regarded as particularly exceptional compared with other child composers, and whether it is justifiable to continue singling him out as the most outstanding, or archetypal, child composer. He was not the youngest composer, having been surpassed in this respect by Ouseley, Saint-Saëns, Nyiregyházy, and possibly Enescu. He was also not the most prolific in terms of numbers of works, for his total of around 120 by the age of sixteen is surpassed by Mendelssohn (around 150), Ouseley (more than 200), and Busoni (more than 180), though these figures depend on how individual works and groups of works are counted; by some methods Mozart would score more highly. His longest work is probably no longer than Crotch's *The Captivity of Judah*, and he also did not compose for such large groups as Strauss and Korngold. Nevertheless, he is one of the ten composers who scored highly on all three criteria in tables 5.2 to 5.4, and he seems to have composed more large-scale works than any other child composer and possibly more in total length, as well as achieving a substantial number of publications, prestigious performances, and favorable reviews. One can conclude, therefore, that no other child composer can match him on all counts, and that in this respect he does indeed deserve to retain his reputation as the greatest of all child composers. He was also one of the few to excel as an adult composer in the eyes of music historians.

The reasons vary as to why some child composers did not develop later as far as might have been initially expected. Some simply died very young, such as Arriaga, Filtsch, and probably two sixteenth-century figures, Beaulaigue and Del Pomo. For Wesley, a head injury and lack of proper training prevented his achieving his full potential; Crotch became an extremely active musician and wrote some fine works, but became more interested in music theory, while Fétis turned to historical musicology. Ouseley, like Crotch, wrote some fine works (he "exercised" by composing a canon a day for twenty-five years, including some very difficult and abstruse ones), but was also a musicologist and had broad interests—he became a priest and read very widely.[8] Wieck became more notable as a pianist, and, after her marriage to Schumann, she put her main energy into supporting him and promoting his work by performing it in public. Several other girls seem to have lost interest in composing in adulthood (notably Weichsell, Riese, and perhaps Bonwick), as noted earlier, and the reasons here were perhaps more personal. Meanwhile Eckert developed mainly as a conductor, though he continued to compose intermittently, whereas Furtwängler composed very little after turning to conducting, although his few later works show he retained his capacity to do so. It is less clear, however, why certain other child composers achieved little prominence later and failed to live up to their initial promise, even though they gained reasonable levels of success as adult composers and showed little or no sign of having exhausted themselves through early exposure.

One phenomenon that may help to explain this lack of later prominence, at least in some cases, is quite striking. A high proportion of child composers became stylistically very conservative after reaching adulthood. This obviously does not apply to Beethoven, Liszt, or Bartók; but Crotch, Mendelssohn, Ouseley, Saint-Saëns, Bruch, Strauss, and Korngold, all of whom scored highly on the three criteria for outstanding child composers listed previously, are generally regarded as having been among the most conservative composers of their time. Several others also retained conspicuously conservative stylistic features in later life, as noted in the Checklist. Balakirev's style evolved hardly at all in his later years. Rheinberger was very little influenced by the more progressive composers of his day (notably Wagner), while Paladilhe deliberately kept well clear of what he regarded as the horrifying trends of the modernists. Langgaard, after a brief flirtation with modernism, reverted to a distinctly outmoded style from about 1925 onward. Although Scriabin does not follow this pattern in that his harmonic style developed considerably, verging on atonality, he remained very conservative in choice of genre and medium: all his childhood compositions are for piano, and throughout his life this same medium greatly dominated his output. His orchestral compositions can be seen as an outgrowth from this, and he wrote almost nothing else. Even Mozart, though by no means conspicuously conservative, has been praised for progressive innovation far less often than his contemporary, Haydn. Thus the tendency mentioned earlier for successful child composers to retain and develop in later life stylistic features that they discover or create very early on is often concomitant with a tendency to be somewhat resistant to newer trends emerging around them.

It seems likely that there is some psychological reason for this tendency to conservatism in former child composers. Their early facility and success with the musical language of the day may have dissuaded them from seeking out new styles once they had made their initial discoveries, so that innovation never became an important goal. When Saint-Saëns was twenty-eight he was described by Berlioz as knowing everything about music but lacking "inexperience"[9]—an intriguing concept with profound implications. The inexperienced composer needs to experiment, perhaps making mistakes but also sometimes chancing on something original that proves to be unusually successful, and the inexperience of child composers is one of the elements that makes study of their music so fascinating. Saint-Saëns, however, had quickly learned what worked and thereafter experimented little; his lack of inexperience may well have developed into a lack of desire for originality. The same seems to be true for surprisingly many notable child composers, who often show relatively little desire for innovation in later life. Thus here we have a possible explanation for why many outstanding child composers did not achieve exceptional distinction as adults. It is not that their composing skill diminished—far from it—but they did not perceive a need to be continually developing their style, or changing a formula that had been discovered early and worked successfully. Hence they did not become the leaders in style change who would significantly influence the next generation and attract the attention of music historians. By contrast, among the most progressive composers born in the nineteenth century, many produced little or nothing as children—for example, Wagner, Debussy, Schoenberg, and Stravinsky. Here it may be hypothesized that they did not take readily to the prevailing styles of their day, and tended to have difficulty inventing music until they had forged their own style or at least bent the current musical conventions into new forms that suited them better.

Progressive composers were also likely to neglect or even destroy their early works. C. P. E. Bach and Verdi, both of whom were continually innovating, are known to have destroyed their childhood compositions; several other composers are suspected of having done so where none survive. Grieg asked for his early piano pieces to be destroyed on his death, but thankfully some were preserved. A few composers, however, have shown more respect for their early works. Prokofiev described some of his and even quoted them in his autobiography, which he wrote much later in life. He was not afraid to point out the problems he had faced when composing his early works—often problems of rhythm, which he sometimes found difficult to notate—but he does not attempt to denigrate them or to conceal the existence of even the slightest of them, mentioning a waltz, march, and rondo composed at the age of six, and quoting the whole of his first composition, though it is only nine bars long.[10] In describing the second movement of the symphony he composed at the age of eleven (with some help from Glière), he states that the main theme was "in no way distinguished" but the second theme was "more interesting," and he quotes a few bars, showing an attractive melody for bassoons in parallel thirds in D flat major (though the main theme was in F).[11] Saint-Saëns was another composer who showed respect for his early works, observing many years after they were written that, even if they were unimportant, "it would be impossible to discover any faults in them."[12] Richard Strauss was even more positive about his early compositions, allowing some of them to be published many years later and presenting the autograph of one of them to some friends fifty years after it was composed.

Such attitudes suggest that there is plenty of good music to be found in children's compositions of the past, and although it would be foolish to pretend that they are all great works, there is indeed much that is of excellent quality and considerable intrinsic value, quite apart from what it can tell us about the social context in which composition was pursued, and about the early life of individual composers. It is clear from the Checklist and the preceding discussion that children made a considerable contribution to the repertory and to the development of musical style in the eighteenth and nineteenth centuries, even though most of this contribution has been neglected. And the contribution would be very much greater still if children up to the age of eighteen were included, or if present-day composers had made more effort to promote the childhood compositions that they are currently reluctant to recognize.

Identifying which works are of most outstanding quality from among those written by children is not an exact science, since it depends on aesthetic criteria and means of assessment that are imprecise. Although there is often a broad consensus about which music is of the best quality, tastes vary considerably from one era to another and even between different critics of the same era. Simplicity, for example, was a desirable aesthetic goal in the eighteenth century, but today is no longer so widely admired, the general preference tending toward greater complexity. If a work has been reviewed enthusiastically, however, as with Ayrton's assessment of Ouseley's opera *L'isola disabitata,* mentioned earlier, it probably possesses at least some outstanding qualities that make it worthy of attention. On the other hand, if the reviewer is dismissive, this may be caused by a failure to grasp the work's merits after a single hearing (or even, sometimes, with no hearing at all, as with Perényi's assessment of Liszt's *Don Sanche,* also mentioned earlier). But a preliminary survey reveals a strikingly high quality over a surprisingly wide range of composers. Those that seem most outstanding include Mozart's early operas, Crotch's *The Captivity of Judah,* Liszt's *Don Sanche,* Mendelssohn's string symphonies, Strauss's Symphony in D minor, and Korngold's early orchestral scores such as his *Schauspiel Ouvertüre*; but more thorough acquaintance with other, more obscure works would doubtless unearth plenty of other examples. Meanwhile some idea of the average quality of children's compositions of past centuries can be gained from the examples quoted in this book, since these examples were not selected on the basis of qualitative superiority. All show technical assurance, imagination, and musicianship to a level that, to judge from some of the dismissive comments cited earlier, many writers would not have thought possible; they exhibit no obvious signs that the composers in question had not yet grasped the principles of composition of the relevant period.

It seems, too, that children's compositions of the past cannot be readily distinguished from adults' music of a similar type. This is strikingly demonstrated, for example, with the fifty variations contributed by fifty different composers to part II of Diabelli's *Vaterländischer Künstlerverein* (Vienna, 1824),[13] in which it would surely be impossible to identify on stylistic grounds which one of the fifty was composed by the eleven-year-old Liszt. Thus it seems reasonable to adopt broadly the same critical approach for children's music as is used for similar music by adults, but unacceptable to regard any features such as lack of length or complexity as automatic defects, since relatively simple and short works can sometimes be of the highest quality.

There are, nevertheless, certain features that tend to occur more often in compositions by children than in those by adults. The most obvious is that children tend far more frequently to write very short works of perhaps sixteen bars or less, especially in their very earliest compositions (which is hardly surprising). This applies, for example, to the first known compositions by Mozart, Ouseley, and Prokofiev, and there are many other examples of very short compositions. But it is certainly not true of all children's compositions, and some are impressively long and ambitious, as is clear from table 5.4; Schubert's first surviving composition, though not fulfilling the criteria for table 5.4, is a Fantasie of more than a thousand bars. Conversely, some adult compositions are strikingly short, such as Beethoven's Bagatelle Op. 119 No. 10, written at the age of fifty, which consists of a mere twelve or thirteen bars. Thus brevity on its own is not a reliable sign that a work was written by a child.

Another noticeably common characteristic of children's compositions is a tendency to have a very consistent texture that hardly changes throughout the work or movement, but again there are many exceptions in which textural variety is employed and skillfully handled. With regard to form, several child composers favor a series of short, contrasting sections, often with little connection between them, strung together like beads on a necklace to produce a longer narrative. This is the form used in Schubert's previously mentioned Fantasie, and also in some descriptive pieces such as six-year-old Ouseley's work about illness[14] and *A Duna folyása* (The Course of the Danube) by Bartók. In such compositions a different texture is generally used and retained in each successive section. Even in works in which the music seems more continuous, as in a sonata-form movement, there is sometimes a slight tendency for child composers to think and compose in short sections that show relatively little sense of connection.

There is no consistent pattern in the harmonic style of child composers, for some compositions are fairly basic or traditional harmonically, while others are notably ambitious and original, such as the examples by Liszt (refer to ex. 8.3 and 9.2 on pages 130 and 166) and Busoni quoted in the Checklist. Appearances of grammatical "errors" such as parallel fifths or unresolved discords are slightly more common in the children's works studied than in adults' works of the same period, but the works are generally sound and "correct," with strong bass lines. Another very common feature is the use of four-bar phrases, which were so prevalent in music generally for much of the period in question that some child composers may have regarded this as the best way of building their phrase structures. In this context, Ena Steiner's suggestion that Schoenberg initially had to count out bars carefully to ensure he wrote four-bar phrases[15] seems implausible, since composers were likely to write them instinctively and perhaps make efforts to avoid them, as Schoenberg did later. It is doubtful, however, whether four-bar phrase structure was any more common with child composers than with adult composers of the same period, and Monteverdi, writing in the sixteenth century, does not show the same rigidity of phrase lengths. There are, then, no obvious and universal features that betray a work as a child's composition, but there are several features that have a tendency to be more common than in adults' compositions of the same period. This seems to be as far as one can go in establishing what makes a distinctively childlike style.

In sum, it is possible to go a long way toward answering the questions posed at the outset of this study. The main child composers born before the end of the nineteenth century have now been identified, though it is highly likely that a few have been overlooked, given that there is no reliable method of tracing them all. Nearly all continued as composers in adult life, though often with only limited success. Some child composers have emerged in every decade, at least from the 1750s onward, although for preceding periods they are often difficult or impossible to identify. From 1750 onward their distribution across different decades is remarkably consistent—not fewer than four and not more than ten are listed in any one decade, such as the 1750s. The works they produce are in general thoroughly competent and often highly imaginative and original, with elements of a personal style often appearing in these early works. Coherent music has been composed by children as young as three (Ouseley and Saint-Saëns). Whether any can be considered "masterpieces" depends on one's definition of this term, but there are certainly some outstanding works from several composers. Thus neglect of children's works seems clearly to be due more to prejudice and misguided presupposition than to deficiencies in the music itself. There is much popular music around that is not demonstrably superior to the works discussed in the Checklist. And although certain stylistic features tend to occur in children's music more often than in adults', it is normally not possible to identify a work as a child's composition on stylistic grounds. Only a few first attempts at composition, such as Vaughan Williams's *The Robin's Nest,* show by their brevity and stylistic uncertainty that they are unlikely to be the work of an adult.

It follows, therefore, that children's compositions of the past are fully worthy of study, and on the basis of their intrinsic merits deserve far more attention than they have been given. Those that were written by children who became major composers are of particular interest for the light they shed on the composers themselves and their early environments, and these childhood works often exhibit features that became prominent thumbprints in the composers' later music. There is also some benefit to be gained from studying the compositions of even the weakest of past child composers for the insights they may bring to our understanding of the role of music at the time, and of the position and role of the child in society. Such insights can feed into wider investigations of childhood in general. The present study is little more than a starting point in this context, and more research is clearly needed.

Wider questions about children and childhood in the history of music have also been neglected in the literature and need further definition and investigation. There is, for example, an excellent twenty-two-page article

on "Women in Music" in *The New Grove,* but the matching article of perhaps eleven pages on "Children in Music" is entirely absent.[16] The role of
children as performers in particular needs to be thoroughly appraised and
explored at this time of increasing interest in the social background in which
music is created. There is plenty of literature on cathedral choirs and choral
music, but not on the identity and role of choirboys in the shaping of and
performing the cathedral repertory.[17] Children have also played a prominent but often neglected role in the history of opera, either as characters
or sometimes as singers, and there is a long history, going back to Purcell's
Dido and Aeneas and beyond, of operas written specially for children or
performed exclusively by them, usually in a school context.[18] Other operas
include parts for children (often sung by sopranos) in a mainly adult context.
In some cases the presence of such children is merely incidental, for instance
the chorus of boy soldiers in Tchaikovsky's *The Queen of Spades.* In others
it is the main focus, as in Humperdinck's *Hansel and Gretel* and Britten's
The Turn of the Screw, to take two obvious examples. The child's role may
even be crucial although the child does not sing at all: in Puccini's *Madam
Butterfly,* it is Butterfly's impending loss of her child that prompts the final
tragic ending. And in Janácek's *Jenufa,* it is the baby boy who proves to be
the central character around whom the opera eventually revolves—the only
wholly innocent person, who yet is murdered as a sacrificial lamb on the
altar of adult self-interest.

A further possibility is for the history of music as a whole to be reinter-
preted along "childist" lines, imitating (critics might say, parodying) certain
feminist approaches to music. Bach could be perceived as attempting to rewrite
his childhood to include all the didactic works that he wished had existed, such
as *Das wohltemperirte Clavier* and the *Orgelbüchlein,* which were designed as instruction works especially for his children but also retrospectively for his own
childhood. Schumann's "cross-dressing" for works such as *Frauenliebe und-leben*
and *Carnaval* has been noted,[19] but it should be seen alongside his tendency to
don short trousers to fantasize as a child in *Kinderszenen* and *Album für die Jugend.*
Some of these lines of investigation will prove more fruitful than others, but it
is clear that a large amount of research needs to be done in a field whose very
existence seems to be unrecognized by many music historians.

NOTES

1. Muriel Silburn, "'The Most Extraordinary Creature in Europe,'" *Music & Letters*
3 (1922): 200.
2. "Doch meine Muse wollt's—ich gehorchte und schrieb."

3. Stanley Sadie and John Tyrrell, eds. *The New Grove Dictionary of Music and Musicians (NGD),* 2nd ed. (London: Macmillan, 2001).

4. Information kindly communicated by David Fallows, who was closely involved in the preparation of the dictionary.

5. See James McKeen Cattell, "A Statistical Study of Eminent Men," *Popular Science Monthly* 62 (1903): 359–77, in which Cattell measures eminence on the basis of relative amounts of encyclopedia space achieved. The Cattell method has been used more recently, for example, in Paul R. Farnsworth, "Elite Attitudes in Music as Measured by the Cattell Space Method," *Journal of Research in Music Education* 10 (1962): 65–68.

6. Ena Steiner, "Schoenberg's Quest: Newly Discovered Works from His Early Years," *Musical Quarterly* 60 (1974): 401–20.

7. Claude Kenneson, *Musical Prodigies: Perilous Journeys, Remarkable Lives* (Portland, Ore.: Amadeus Press, 1998), 285.

8. F. W. Joyce, *The Life of Rev. Sir F. A. G. Ouseley, Bart.* (London: Methuen, 1896), 116, 120. Joyce reports that, at his death, Ouseley owned more than 2,000 books and had read every one from cover to cover, except one—a large harmony treatise in Spanish, of which he had read only 1,700 pages!

9. James Harding, *Saint-Saëns and His Circle* (London: Chapman & Hall, 1965), 90.

10. Serge Prokofiev, *Prokofiev by Prokofiev: A Composer's Memoir,* ed. Francis King (London: Macdonald & Jane's, 1979), 10–11.

11. Prokofiev, *Prokofiev,* 36.

12. Harding, *Saint-Saëns,* 16.

13. Facsimile of Diabelli's *Vaterländischer Künstlerverein,* in *Denkmäler der Tonkunst in Österreich,* vol. 136, ed. Günter Brosche (Graz: Akademische Druck und Verlagsanhalt, 1983).

14. Published in Joyce, *Life of Ouseley,* 239–42.

15. Steiner, "Schoenberg's Quest," 404.

16. See, however, Alison Latham, ed., *The Oxford Companion to Music* (Oxford: Oxford University Press, 2002), in which an article on "Women in Music" is complemented by a somewhat shorter article on "Children in Music."

17. A new book on this subject appeared too late to be considered in the present study. See Susan Boynton and Eric Rice, eds., *Young Choristers, 650–1700* (Woodbridge, U.K.: Boydell Press, 2008).

18. John Rosselli, "Child Performers," and Hugo Cole, "Children's Opera," in *The New Grove Dictionary of Opera,* ed. Stanley Sadie, vol. 1 (London: Macmillan, 1992), 842–44.

19. Lawrence Kramer, "*Carnaval,* Cross-Dressing, and the Woman in the Mirror," in *Musicology and Difference: Gender and Sexuality in Music Scholarship,* ed. Ruth Solie (Berkeley: University of California Press, 1993), 305–25.

Part 2

ANNOTATED CHECKLIST OF
NOTABLE CHILD COMPOSERS

This Checklist includes all composers born before 1900 who have so far been identified as having composed a significant amount of music (which could still be quite small) before the age of sixteen. Since no previous list has ever been published that could be used as a starting point, there could well be several omissions, and some of the names included were identified only by chance or at a late stage. The composers are listed in chronological order of birth, but a composer index, complete with dates, will enable individuals to be found quickly. In this Checklist composers are presented with an indication of when they began composing and a brief account of what they composed before the age of sixteen. In most cases only the year of composition of particular works is given; the composer's age at the time of composition can be determined using the birth date. The lists of works generally include any lost works, since the aim of these lists is to show what the composers were capable of writing rather than what might have happened to their manuscripts in later years. Much of the information is derived from standard reference works, chiefly *The New Grove Dictionary (NGD), Grove Music Online (GMO), Die Musik in Geschichte und Gegenwart (MGG),* and occasionally the *Oxford Dictionary of National Biography (ODNB).* Additional specialist literature on individual composers is indicated at the end of their entries if it was used in compiling the entry or offers significant supplementary details. Often the basic information from these sources is supplemented by direct observation of the music itself, where scores or recordings are readily available. Recordings are noted where they are considered to be of particular significance or form a major collection, but there has been no attempt to include a comprehensive listing, especially with major composers whose early works may have been recorded several times.

· 6 ·

Composers Born before 1700

Philippe Basiron (c. 1449–May 1491)

There are no clear cases yet discovered of child composers from the fifteenth century or earlier. The most promising possibility seems to be Basiron, who showed exceptional ability as a young musician and from 1464 was instructing other boys in music. He is known to have composed four surviving three-voice chansons before the age of twenty, perhaps long before. Some of his other works could be equally early.

Higgins, Paula, "Tracing the Careers of Late Medieval Composers: The Case of Philippe Basiron," *Acta Musicologica* 62 (1990): 1–28.

Prince Henry of England (28 June 1491–28 Jan. 1547)

Later to become King Henry VIII, the prince may have begun composing around the age of ten, though none of his early compositions can be dated with any accuracy. His earliest work appears to be the chanson "Gentil prince de renom," which betrays signs of being an apprentice exercise, since it is a single voice added rather unskillfully to a preexisting three-part chanson. Three other extant French chansons that display increasing competence were probably composed by the time he was sixteen, and perhaps well before then. Some of his three-part English songs, such as "Pastyme with Good Companye," may also have been written at an early age. These are slightly more advanced than the French chansons in terms of contrapuntal technique but show nothing particularly exceptional. At the age of nineteen he composed two polyphonic masses (now lost), which suggests that he had by that time been composing less ambitious works for some years.

Fallows, David, "Henry VIII As a Composer," in *Sundry Sorts of Music Books: Essays on the British Library Collections, Presented to O. W. Neighbour on His 70th Birthday,* ed. Chris Banks and others (London: British Library, 1993), 27–39.

Barthélemy Beaulaigue (c. 1543–1559 or Later)

Beaulaigue was described as a choirboy of fifteen at Marseilles Cathedral when his first collection of thirteen chansons was published in 1558–59. Judging by their dedications, some were evidently written by 1554 and perhaps as early as 1551. These were followed by a collection of fourteen motets in 1559, when he was reportedly still only fifteen. The motets are for up to eight voices, and the last one, the five-voice "Vidi turbam magnam," incorporates an ingenious canon in the top two voices. Both publications survive complete in the Bibliothèque Nationale, Paris. The music in general (as well as the poetry of the chansons, which he also wrote) is so good that some authorities, typically, have doubted that he wrote it; but it seems highly implausible that such an elaborate account (including a woodcut portrait of the composer and details about the origin of some of the chansons) could possibly have been fabricated with no obvious benefit. It is significant that the authorship of many later children's compositions has been wrongly questioned because of the child's age at the time of composition, and the same has clearly happened here. Nothing is heard of Beaulaigue after 1559, so he may have died about that time. Works:

> *Chansons nouvelles . . . à quatre parties,* 1558–59
> *Motettz nouvellement mis en musique,* 1559

Auda, Antoine, *Barthélemy Beaulaigue, poète et musicien prodige* (Brussels: Antoine Auda, 1957?).
Dobbins, Frank, *Music in Renaissance Lyons* (Oxford: Clarendon, 1992), 231–51.

Claudio Monteverdi (15 May 1567 [Baptized]–29 Nov. 1643)

When Monteverdi began composing is unknown, but in 1582 he published a volume entitled *Sacrae cantiunculae,* consisting of twenty-three motets—three of them bipartite. The dedication of this volume is dated 1 August 1582, and therefore many of the motets were probably completed at the age of fourteen or younger. They display highly impressive skill in composition on a small scale, and it is surely inaccurate to claim that they were "probably written to acquire contrapuntal technique," with word setting that shows "some inexperience" (Arnold 1990, 527). Monteverdi had clearly acquired a sure contrapuntal technique before writing them. They also display great sensitivity to the meaning and rhythm of the words. These are mostly set syllabically, but melismas are sometimes used for expressive purposes, such as on the words *gaudium magnum* (great joy) in "Angelus ad pastores." His next collection of works, *Madrigali spirituali,* was published the following year in Brescia, with a dedication dated 31 July 1583, and so most were probably composed at the age of fifteen. There are eleven sacred madrigals, all but one bipartite, giving us effectively twenty-one pieces or movements. Unfortunately only the bassus partbook is known to survive. Works:

> *Sacrae cantiunculae,* 1582
> *Madrigali spirituali,* 1583

Arnold, Denis, "Monteverdi," *NGD* (1980), 12: 514–34.
Malipiero, G. F., ed., *Claudio Monteverdi: Tutte le opere,* vol. 14/1 (Vienna: Universal Edition, 1926–42).

Sound Recording

Sacrae cantiunculae, cond. Miklós Szabó. Hungaroton HCD 12921 (1977).

Francesco Del Pomo (sometimes wrongly given as Podio) (c. 1594–1605 or Later)

Del Pomo published a lost book of two-part ricercars in Palermo in 1604 at the age of ten, by which time he was known as an excellent singer and lutenist. There is no trace of him after 1605, however, and he may have died very young.

Chapel Royal Choirboys

Samuel Pepys records that on 22 November 1663 he heard an anthem composed by one of the choirboys at the Chapel Royal, and was told that there were four or five such boys who could compose anthems. That so many choirboys could compose anthems only three years after choirs had been re-established following the Restoration of the monarchy reflects well on the teaching skills of the Master of the Children, Captain Henry Cooke, but there was clearly much talent among the boys themselves. Those in question were most probably Pelham Humfrey (1647 or 1648–14 July 1674), Robert Smith (c. 1648–Nov. [?] 1675), John Blow (23 Feb. 1649 N.S.–1 Oct. 1708), Michael Wise (c. 1647–24 Aug. 1687), and William Turner (1651–13 Jan. 1740). Another possibility, a little younger, is Thomas Tudway (c. 1652–23 Nov. 1726). All six composed music in later life, and were old enough to have been composing by 1663 if they had had sufficient training (see entries for all six in Ashbee and Lasocki 1998). The anthem heard by Pepys is believed to be Humfrey's first setting of "Have Mercy upon Me" (Humfrey 1972, xiii, 140, and no. 4a). There is no confirmation of this suggestion, however.

Further evidence of the composing exploits of these choirboys appears in the second edition of James Clifford's *The Divine Services,* published in 1664. This volume includes the words of a large number of anthems, with three of the "children of his Majesties Chappel" represented: Humfrey, Smith, and Blow. Five anthems are by Humfrey, six are by Smith, and three by Blow. Unfortunately all except "Haste Thee O God" (Humfrey 1972, no. 3) are now lost.

The two early anthems by Humfrey that do survive show considerable sensitivity to word setting. "Have Mercy upon Me" in C minor is particularly remarkable for its change to C major in an almost Beethoven-like manner for the joyful final section. Such a change from C minor to C major to reflect a change of mood was very rare in the 1660s. Two other anthems by Humfrey, "Almighty God, Who Mad'st" and "Hear My Prayer" (Humfrey 1972, nos. 1 and 2), are strongly suspected on stylistic grounds to belong to Humfrey's earliest period (Dennison 1986, 57). Meanwhile in 1664 (or possibly earlier) three of the choirboys—Humfrey, Turner, and Blow—joined forces to produce the anthem "I Will Alway Give Thanks" (Humfrey 1972, no. 8), which has ever since been known as the "Club Anthem," with each composer contributing one section. The section by the young Turner is somewhat meager, but the other two show excellent craftsmanship, and the work as a whole is well planned and tonally unified. Works:

> Blow: "I Will Magnify Thee," "Lord Thou Hast Been Our Refuge," "O Lord Rebuke Me Not"
> Humfrey: "Bow Down Thine Ear," "Haste Thee O God," "Have Mercy upon Me," "It Is a Good Thing," "The Heavens Declare the Glory," "The Lord Declared His Salvation"
> Smith: "God Be Merciful," "O God My Heart is Ready," "O Sing unto the Lord a New Song, Sing unto the Lord," "O Sing unto the Lord a New Song, Let the Congregation," "Sing unto God," "When the Lord Turned Again"
> Humfrey, Turner, and Blow: "I Will Alway Give Thanks"

Ashbee, Andrew, and David Lasocki, *A Biographical Dictionary of English Court Musicians 1485–1714* (Aldershot, U.K.: Ashgate, 1998).

Clifford, James, *The Divine Services and Anthems Usually Sung in His Majesties Chappell and in All Cathedrals and Collegiate Choires in England and Ireland* (London: Nathaniel Brooke and Henry Brome, 1664).

Dennison, Peter, *Pelham Humfrey* (Oxford: Oxford University Press, 1986).
Humfrey, Pelham, *Complete Church Music* [part 1], in *Musica Britannica,* vol. 34, ed. Peter Dennison (London: Stainer & Bell, 1972).

Francesco Pistocchi (1659–13 May 1726)

Though born in Palermo, Pistocchi soon joined the renowned musical establishment at Bologna, where he published a collection of *Capricci puerili . . . in 40 modi sopra un basso d'un balletto,* Op. 1, as early as 1667. He remained active as a singer during the next few years, but no further compositions of his are known that date from earlier than 1679.

Henry Purcell (1659–21 Dec. 1695)

The earliest work ascribed to Henry Purcell is a part-song for three voices entitled "Sweet Tyranness" (Z S69), which was published by John Playford in *The Musical Companion* in 1667. Although dismissed as spurious by Franklin B. Zimmerman on the entirely unsound grounds of Purcell's age, it appears to be genuine, as does its later revision and arrangement as a solo for voice and bass (Z S70). This appeared in 1673 along with another Purcell song, the catch "Here's That Will Challenge" (Z 253). The solo version of "Sweet Tyranness" then reappeared in 1678 alongside five other songs ascribed to Henry Purcell. Some of these may also be very early works—particularly "More Love or More Disdain" (Z 397), for this appears in an earlier version, in E minor instead of D minor, in the Tabley Song Book (now in Manchester, John Rylands Library) (Holman 1994, 28). The most probable scenario, then, is that Purcell was composing from the age of eight or younger, and revised at least two of his early efforts for publication in the 1670s (both revisions show subtlety and skill, and are likely to be the work of the original composer, since it was more unusual to make minor revisions to other composers' works). Works:

"Sweet Tyranness," 1667, rev. and arr. 1673
"Here's That Will Challenge," 1673
"More Love or More Disdain," date unknown

Holman, Peter, *Henry Purcell* (Oxford: Oxford University Press, 1994)
Purcell, Henry, *Secular Songs for Solo Voice,* in *The Works of Henry Purcell,* vol. 25, ed. Margaret Laurie (Borough Green, U.K.: Novello, 1985).
Zimmerman, Franklin B., *Henry Purcell 1659–1695: An Analytical Catalogue of His Music* (London: Macmillan, 1963).

Giovanni Bononcini (18 July 1670–9 July 1747)

Bononcini's father, Giovanni Maria, also a composer, died when Giovanni was only eight years old, but the son quickly showed musical promise. He burst onto the scene as a composer in 1685, when he published three collections of instrumental music, Opp. 1–3, in very close succession. Their dedications are dated 10 September, 14 November, and 20 December of that year—a remarkable rate of productivity even by the standards of the time. Each collection consists of twelve works—chamber sonatas (entitled *Trattenimenti*), concertos, or symphonies—usually in four movements. Op. 3 is the most richly scored, with up to eight parts including one or two trumpets. At least one twentieth-century writer has doubted the authorship of these works on the grounds of Bononcini's age—an attitude to child composers that is all too prevalent—but there seems no question that they are genuine. They were followed by an Op. 4 the next year, and Opp. 5 and 6 in 1687. Works:

> *Trattenimenti da camera* (Op. 1), 1685
> *Concerti da camera* (Op. 2), 1685
> *Sinfonie a 5, 6, 7 e 8 istromenti* (Op. 3), 1685
> *Sinfonie* (Op. 4), 1686

Ford, Anthony, "Giovanni Bononcini," *The Musical Times*, 111 (1970): 695–99.

Georg Philipp Telemann (14 Mar. 1681–25 June 1767)

According to his own account, Telemann composed much vocal and instrumental music as a child, probably starting about the age of ten, and his most notable early work was the opera *Sigismundus,* written at the age of twelve. This is lost, however, and none of his surviving works can be dated before about 1697.

Georg Friedrich Händel, Later George Frideric Handel (23 Feb. 1685–14 Apr. 1759)

Händel studied music from an early age, despite some initial opposition from his father. According to his first biographer, John Mainwaring, "By the time he was nine he began to compose the church service for voices and instruments, and from that time actually did compose a service every week for three years successively" (Deutsch 1955, 4). This music would have been cantata-type works (though the term "cantata" was not then normally used for such works) for the Lutheran church in Halle, where he was living. Unfortunately all this music is completely lost. Mainwaring may have underestimated Händel's age here, as he did elsewhere, but the substance of the report is probably true.

Händel's earliest surviving works may be a set of six sonatas for two oboes and harpsichord (HWV 380-5), supposedly written at the age of about ten and preserved in an eighteenth-century copy formerly owned by the flautist Carl Weidemann and now in the British Library, London (R.M. 18.b.3). They were published in volume twenty-seven of Friedrich Chrysander's collected edition (1879, 58–90). According to one report, cited in the preface to that edition, these sonatas were shown to Händel in later life and he acknowledged them as his, declaring, "I used to write like the D---l in those days." Today they are generally regarded as spurious or at least doubtful. They seem too late in style for the supposed date of circa 1695, although they could have been revised at a later date. But they certainly exhibit characteristic melodic imagination and contrapuntal skill, along with Händel's renowned ability at developing whole movements out of two or three seemingly insignificant motifs.

None of Händel's other music can be shown to date from his childhood, though much of his early music is of uncertain date and some of it could be from before 1701. A likely case is his sonata for two violins and continuo, Op. 2, No. 2, which, according to one manuscript, was "Compos'd at the Age of 14." Certainly, if Mainwaring's report is correct, it seems highly probable that Händel continued composing regularly after he had ceased writing a weekly cantata for his local church in Halle. In this case, some of this music almost certainly survives in some form, if only in later versions, since he very often borrowed material from works he had written earlier.

Chrysander, Friedrich, ed., *The Works of George Frederic Handel*, vol. 27 (Leipzig, Germany: German Handel Society Edition, 1879).

Deutsch, Otto Erich, *Handel: A Documentary Biography* (London: A. & C. Black, 1955).

Domenico Scarlatti (26 Oct. 1685–23 July 1757)

Son of the famous opera composer Alessandro Scarlatti, Domenico must have been composing by his early teens, for he was appointed organist and composer to the royal chapel in Naples on 13 October 1701. Much early work is certainly lost, and until recently it was assumed that nothing of his had survived from this period. Now, however, several works have been identified that he may have composed before he was sixteen, namely four chamber cantatas and a piece of church music (see list of works). Of these works, which survive in manuscript in various libraries but are still unpublished, the first is probably by Scarlatti's uncle Francesco, since it is ascribed to him in one source and simply to "Scarlatti" in the others, but there is no good reason to doubt the authorship and date of the other works. Although *Vuoi ch'io spiri* and *Mi tormento* are ascribed to both Domenico and his father in different sources, it is far more likely that an early work of Domenico's would be misattributed to his well-known father than that a middle-period work of Alessandro would be misattributed to his young son. Domenico Scarlatti went on to write two whole operas as early as 1703—a further sign that he probably began composing considerable quantities of music well before he was sixteen. Works:

> *Belle pupille care* (cantata, probably by Francesco Scarlatti), 1697
> *V'adoro, o luci belle* (cantata), 1699
> *Vuoi ch'io spiri* (cantata), 20 Sep. 1699
> *Mi tormento il pensiero* (cantata), 10 Mar. 1701
> *Antra, valles, divo plaudeant* (motet), 1701

Boyd, Malcolm, *Domenico Scarlatti* (London: Weidenfeld & Nicolson, 1986).

Andrea Fiorè (1686–6 Oct. 1732)

Fiorè came to public attention with a set of twelve *Sinfonie da chiesa,* Op. 1, which were published in Modena in 1699 soon after he reached his thirteenth birthday. He is also reported to have composed an opera, *L'Innocenza difesa,* in Milan in 1700, but this has not been confirmed. In later life he composed many more operas, chiefly for Milan and Turin.

· 7 ·

Composers Born between 1700 and 1800

John Stanley (17 Jan. 1712–19 May 1786)

Blinded at the age of two, Stanley showed early promise and studied the organ with Maurice Greene. By 1731 he had composed several organ voluntaries, and at least one of these probably dates back to the mid-1720s.

Cooper, Barry, *English Solo Keyboard Music of the Middle and Late Baroque* (New York: Garland, 1989), 351.

Carl Philipp Emanuel Bach (8 Mar. 1714–14 Dec. 1788)

Bach probably wrote several compositions as a child, but later destroyed all his works from before 1733 on the grounds that they were "too youthful."

Wolff, Christoph, "Recovered in Kiev: Bach et al. A Preliminary Report of the Music Collection of the Berlin Sing-Akademie," *Notes* 58 (2001): 259–71, esp. 266–68.

Jean-Baptiste Cardonne (26 June 1730–1792 or Later)

Cardonne composed a motet for large choir in 1743, and it was performed before the king of France the same year. The achievement was repeated in each of the two following years, but all three motets are lost. (The same fate has befallen a single motet composed for the same purpose at a similar age by François-André Philidor [1726–95], who is not otherwise known as a child composer.) Cardonne also wrote an air entitled "Etrenne de l'Amour et de Bacchus," which was published in February 1746, but no other childhood works of his are known.

Garret Wesley, later Lord Mornington (19 July 1735–22 May 1781)

Wesley is reported to have begun composing, without any instruction, about the age of thirteen, writing three little pieces that he stuck together and called a serenata. Nothing of his is known to survive from this period, however, though he later became a widely respected composer.

Barrington, Daines, *Miscellanies by the Honourable Daines Barrington* (London: J. Nichols, 1781), 319–20.

Christian Gottlob Neefe (5 Feb. 1748–26 Jan. 1798)

Neefe claims in his autobiographical notes that he began composing at the age of twelve, but nothing is identifiable as having been composed by him as a child. In later life he taught Beethoven and was responsible for arranging publication of some of Beethoven's childhood compositions.

Muzio Clementi (23 Jan. 1752–10 Mar. 1832)

The earliest work Clementi is known to have composed is a full-scale oratorio, *Martirio de' gloriosi Santi Giuliano, e Celso,* the libretto of which survives in a printed source from Rome dated 1764, although the music is lost. A three-movement keyboard sonata in the then-unusual key of A flat, with the middle movement in D flat, dates from the following year and survives in the Bibliothèque Nationale, Paris (MS 1706). No other compositions of Clementi are known to date from before 1768 (the date of an early version of Op. 1, No. 2), but it seems certain that there must have been several, for an oratorio is most unlikely to be the first thing he ever wrote. The sonata is a well-constructed work in which each movement explores the structural distinction between binary form and sonata form in a different way. The finale is particularly successful, with broken-chord motifs exploited in a variety of ways. Works:

> *Martirio de' gloriosi Santi Giuliano, e Celso* (oratorio), 1764
> Keyboard Sonata in A flat major, 1765

Clementi, Muzio, *Opera Omnia*, vol. 51, ed. Andrea Coen (Bologna, Italy: Ut Orpheus Edizioni, 2004), 74–85.

Tyson, Alan, *Thematic Catalogue of the Works of Muzio Clementi* (Tutzing, Germany: Schneider, 1967), 13, 97.

Sound Recording

Sonata in A flat in Muzio Clementi, *Piano Sonatas,* Pietro Spada. Arts Music 472232 (1983).

Wolfgang Amadeus Mozart (27 Jan. 1756–5 Dec. 1791)

Mozart is the most celebrated of all child composers, both today and in his own lifetime. His father, Leopold Mozart (1719–87), was also a composer, writing a substantial number of vocal, orchestral, chamber, and keyboard works; his famous violin treatise, *Versuch einer gründlichen Violinschule,* was published in the same year as Wolfgang's birth. His sister, Nannerl (1751–1829), excelled on the harpsichord from an early age and doubtless gave Wolfgang much help in his early years, but she was not noted for composing as a child—she seems to have left that entirely to her brother—and the few works she composed later (such as a song mentioned by Wolfgang in 1770) are now lost. Young Wolfgang was one of only very few child composers whose father was also a composer; on the other hand very many composers have had children who did not compose, or became notable as composers only later in life (e.g., some of Bach's sons). Thus it was far from likely that young Mozart would show any early talent for composition; but when he did, he had an advantage over most other child composers, and partly for that reason was able to develop more quickly and fully. Leopold gave his son enormous amounts of help in such matters as theoretical instruction, sometimes writing out and editing his early compositions, and taking him and Nannerl from their native Salzburg on long concert tours across Europe, where the boy's compositional development could be advanced through exposure to a very wide range of music.

Mozart is said to have begun composing at the age of four, but his earliest known works appear to be six very short keyboard pieces, K. 1a–f, written at the age of five (the K. numbers refer to Köchel 1862; some K. numbers have been revised in the sixth edition to reflect an updated chronology, in which case the revised number is given here in parentheses). The six pieces of K. 1 were followed by K. 2–5, also short keyboard pieces, written when Mozart was six, and all are published in the Mozart collected edition (*Neue Ausgabe sämtlicher Werke,* IX:27/i, ed. Wolfgang Rehm). The very first piece, K. 1a in C major, probably composed at the keyboard when Mozart had only just turned five, is particularly intriguing. Though only ten bars long, it changes from 3/4 to 2/4 after four bars (ex. 7.1). Thus it displays a childlike originality and disregard for convention, and is something that any adult composer of the time would have been most unlikely to do. To compose a piece of two equal halves would be perfectly normal, but Mozart gave the two halves a different metrical structure, cleverly manipulating the simple formula $4 \times 3 = 6 \times 2$. It was written down by his father, who fortunately had the wisdom to leave it as it was, rather than persuading young Mozart to "improve" it by making it more regular. This has not prevented the editors of the *Neue Mozart Ausgabe* from adding a spurious and

Example 7.1.   Mozart, Andante in C, K. 1a.

inappropriate editorial flat to the last bass note of bar 7, with the result that Mozart's clever manipulation of tonality through the cross-relation between B flat and B natural is seriously undermined. Another interesting feature of the piece is his striking use of register, with the top note of the last chord being a whole octave lower than the bottom note of the first chord. This, too, is something that an adult composer might well have avoided as too risky a strategy. Yet melodically, rhythmically, and harmonically, the piece is perfectly sound and well organized. Thus the whole piece, despite its brevity, is an excellent demonstration of a fertile imagination coupled with secure technique at a very young age.

Before long, Mozart was composing more ambitious pieces. Two pairs of violin sonatas (K. 6–9) were composed during the period 1762–64, and were published in Paris as his Opp. 1 and 2 in 1764. These were followed by six more violin sonatas, with optional cello (K. 10–15), published in London in 1765 as Op. 3, and another set of six (without cello) composed and published in The Hague as Op. 4 the following year. His first symphony (K. 16), like his Op. 3, dates from his visit to London in 1764 and 1765, and is a three-movement work scored for oboes, horns, and strings, like many other symphonies of the time. It was quickly followed by several more symphonies in three or four movements, with similar or slightly larger scoring, so that by the time Mozart turned sixteen, he had composed at least fourteen symphonies, and possibly several more whose authorship cannot be confirmed, such as K. 97 (73m) in D major (Eisen 1989). His earliest concertos (K. 37, 39–41), of 1767, are less adventurous, being mere adaptations for keyboard and orchestra of a number of solo keyboard works by other composers such as Raupach and Honauer, and he did not compose an original concerto until as late as 1773.

Meanwhile, however, he had turned to many other genres including vocal music, especially of the more dramatic kind. It was in early 1767, shortly after returning to Salzburg from a tour that had lasted some two and a half years, that he revealed his extraordinary skills in this area, in three works written in quick succession. These were the first act of a three-act sacred singspiel with allegorical characters, *Die Schuldigkeit des ersten Gebots,* performed on 12 March (the second and third acts, by Michael Haydn and Adlgasser, are lost); a cantata for Holy Week known as *Grabmusik,* probably performed on 7 April; and a three-act comic opera, *Apollo et Hyacinthus* (strictly speaking this was an intermezzo, performed between the five acts of the tragedy *Clementia Croesi*), which was presented on 13 May. Each of these works consists of a series of musical numbers, mostly arias, alternating with passages of recitative as in conventional opera of the day.

Considered together, these three works are remarkable in many ways—not least for their size and scope. All three are fully worked out with voices and orchestra, and are on a substantial scale. *Grabmusik* consists of four main numbers totaling around 500 bars; *Die Schuldigkeit* is more than twice as long, with an introductory sinfonia and eight numbers; and *Apollo* consists of around 2,000 bars of music, plus recitatives, lasting more than an hour in performance. Also striking is Mozart's speed and fecundity of composition. *Apollo* appears not to have been begun until after *Die Schuldigkeit* had been successfully performed, and it must therefore have been completed in less than two months to allow time for singers to learn their parts before the performance. The other two works were probably composed with comparable rapidity. Yet there is nothing slapdash about the music, and many touches of originality and imagination can be found that enhance the musical settings in these three works. Mozart displays mastery in a great variety of moods and styles, and shows himself extremely sensitive and responsive to characterization, the meaning and rhythm of the words, the dramatic situations (especially in the accompanied recitatives), and the overall structure of the works. A few examples will bear this out.

Apollo provides a good illustration of Mozart's awareness of dramatic structure. For the nine numbers, he chose eight different major keys, ranging from E on the sharp side to E flat, but in a skilfully distributed order that tended to maximize contrast between successive numbers. Contrast was also achieved through a variety of meters and tempos, so that each number contrasts strongly with the others. In addition, Mozart created tonal variety within a single number in places where the text was suitable. A particularly striking example is the first aria in *Grabmusik*. This is a standard *da capo* aria in which the main section is in bravura style in D major, but in the middle section, where thunder and lightning are called upon, the music moves from D minor through C minor to E flat major, before ending with a half-close in the unlikely key of E minor, evoking something of the tortured anguish of Soul contemplating the death of Christ.

Mozart's handling of orchestration is also very imaginative in places. In the third number in *Apollo,* the opening motif is played by violins and horns accompanied by the lower strings; it is then repeated by the violas playing *forte,* accompanied just by violins playing the bass line *piano* beneath them, in a reversal of normal roles. In *Die Schuldigkeit* a trombone makes a dramatic appearance with a solo in F sharp minor, as the Christian recalls the warning about the Last Judgment, "Du wirst von deinen Leben genaue Rechnung geben" ("You will give an exact reckoning of your life"). The trombone then has a longer obbligato role in a later aria (No. 5) that is characterized by some large leaps of a ninth or tenth for the voice (ex. 7.2), anticipating a feature that Mozart often used in later works. Another striking passage in *Die Schuldigkeit* is in an accompanied recitative between Nos. 2 and 3, where the upper strings have semiquaver triplets that clash rhythmically with a dactylic ostinato figure in the bass strings, all accompanied by sustained chords for oboes, bassoons, and horns.

The three works consistently reveal Mozart as a fully-fledged composer of dramatic music. To describe them as mere apprentice works, as has occasionally been done, is misleading unless one accepts that composers are always capable of learning from the works they have composed, and that every work is in this sense "apprentice." After hearing them, one can no longer be surprised at the quality of the works Mozart produced in the next few years, as he continued with the same level of invention and fecundity. A large-scale *Missa solemnis* in C minor (K. 139 [47a]) was composed in 1768 and performed in Vienna on 7 December that year. Three other mass settings date in 1768–69 (K. 49 [47d], 65 [61a], and 66), and he composed several other sacred works around that period, some of them with a sizable orchestral accompaniment, such as the Litany K. 109. He also continued in the field of dramatic music,

Example 7.2.   Mozart, "Jener Donnerworte Kraft" from *Die Schuldigkeit des ersten Gebots.*

Table 7.1.   Dramatic Works Written by Mozart between 1768 and 1771

No.	Title	Date
K. 51 (46a)	*La finta semplice*	1768, performed 1 May 1769 (?)
K. 50 (46b)	*Bastien und Bastienne*	Performed autumn 1768
K. 87 (74a)	*Mitridate, rè di Ponto*	Performed 26 Dec. 1770
K. 111	*Ascanio in Alba*	Aug.–Sep. 1771, performed 17 Oct. 1771
K. 118	*La Betulia liberata*	Summer 1771
K. 126	*Il sogno di Scipio*	Summer 1771, performed May 1772

with five more operatic works and an oratorio before his sixteenth birthday, as listed in table 7.1.

The oratorio *La Betulia liberata* seems not to have been performed during Mozart's lifetime, but it is a very impressive work with powerful choruses and well-characterized arias. *Bastien und Bastienne* is a singspiel displaying a wide range of influences and an unusually large proportion of through-composed music, rather than regular formal patterns as in most similar works of the period. It also exhibits skillful characterization, with the three singers having different types of music that admirably suit their characters (Tyler 1990). The other four works are Italian operas, two of them very long and in three acts: *La finta semplice* and *Mitridate*. They are among his most outstanding achievements of the period.

Thus Mozart's output as a child is truly remarkable, with about 120 works (mainly K. 1–120) completed before 1772, in a great variety of genres, and it is impossible to do full justice to it in the present context. His success was widely recognized at the time, and it may well have prompted a surge in the number of active child composers, which certainly increases significantly around this time. It would seem that Mozart's reputation as the most successful child composer in history is well deserved, despite the great wealth of music composed by other children in the past. Yet for all his fame as a composer and his renown as a child genius, very little of his early music is much performed. Although some of it has airings from time to time, and his Menuett in F for piano, K. 2, is popular with learners, his earliest composition that appears regularly on concert programs and in recordings is the Divertimento in D (K. 136) written in 1772. Similarly, there has been relatively little detailed study of this music, compared with the numerous books on his later works, and there is certainly scope for more detailed appraisal. Short studies of these works have sometimes been included in more general accounts of Mozart's music (especially Landon 1990), but studies of Mozart's early period tend to concentrate on biographical factors rather than the music itself. This is true, for example, even in Stanley Sadie's highly detailed *Mozart: The Early Years* (2006), which discusses some of the works but tends to focus on their biographical context. It seems that the music of even the greatest child composer has gained less admiration and appreciation than it deserves. Works:

Symphonies

> K. 16 in E flat, 1764–65
> K. 19 in D, 1765
> K. (19a) in F, 1765
> K. 22 in B flat, Dec. 1765
> K. (45a) in G, Mar. 1766
> K. 43 in F, 1767
> K. 45 in D, Jan. 1768
> K. 48 in D, Dec. 1768
> K. 73 in C, 1769–70
> K. 74 in G, 1770
> K. 110 in G, July 1771
> K. 120 in D, Oct.–Nov. 1771
> K. 112 in F, Nov. 1771
> K. 114 in A, Dec. 1771
> Several others of doubtful authenticity (see Eisen 1989)

Sacred Drama/Oratorio

> *Die Schuldigkeit des ersten Gebots* (allegorical drama, K. 35), 1767
> *Grabmusik* (cantata, K. 42), 1767
> *La Betulia liberata* (oratorio, K. 118), 1771

Operas

> *Apollo et Hyacinthus* (K. 38), 1767
> *La finta semplice* (K. 51 [46a]), 1768
> *Bastien und Bastienne* (K. 50 [46b]), 1768
> *Mitridate, re di Ponto* (K. 87 [74a]), 1770
> *Ascanio in Alba* (K. 111), 1771
> *Il sogno di Scipio* (K. 126), 1771

Other Works: Miscellaneous keyboard music, chamber music, masses, etc.

Eisen, Cliff, "Problems of Authenticity among Mozart's Early Symphonies: The Examples of K. Anh. 220 (16a) and 76 (42a)," *Music & Letters* 70 (1989): 505–16.

Köchel, Ludwig Ritter von, *Chronologisch-thematisches Verzeichniss sämmtlicher Tonwerke Wolfgang Amade Mozart's* (Leipzig, Germany: Breitkopf & Härtel, 1862; 6th ed., ed. Franz Giegling [Wiesbaden, Germany: Breitkopf & Härtel, 1964]).

Landon, H. C. Robbins, ed., *The Mozart Compendium* (London: Thames & Hudson, 1990).

Mozart, Wolfgang Amadeus, *Neue Ausgabe sämtlicher Werke*, ed. Internationale Stiftung Mozarteum Salzburg (Kassel, Germany: Bärenreiter, 1955–2007); also available on-line at http://dme.mozarteum.at.

Sadie, Stanley, *Mozart: The Early Years* (New York: Oxford University Press, 2006).

Tyler, Linda, "Bastien und Bastienne: The Libretto, Its Derivation, and Mozart's Text Setting," *Journal of Musicology* 8 (1990): 520–52.

Sound Recordings

All works in Mozart Edition, various performers. Philips 422 501-2PME6 *et seq.* (1990–91).

Thomas Linley the Younger (5 May 1756–5 Aug. 1778)

Son of the composer Thomas Linley Sr. (1733–95), Linley Jr. became prominent as early as 25 July 1763, when he sang and played a violin concerto in a concert at Bath. It is unclear whether he himself composed the concerto, but he did compose several altogether, of uncertain date, although only one of them survives. He also composed a set of six violin sonatas in 1768 and a seventh sonata the following year, but all but one of them are lost. The surviving one, in A major in three movements, is in the British Library, London (R.M. 21.h.10). It displays considerable compositional skill, while its emphasis on technical virtuosity and brilliance indicates Linley's already outstanding abilities as a violinist. He died in a boating accident at the age of only twenty-two.

Beechey, Gwilym, "Thomas Linley, Junior. 1756–1778," *The Musical Quarterly* 54 (1968): 74–82.

Joseph Martin Kraus (20 June 1756–15 Dec. 1792)

Four short, rather Italianate symphonies appear to date from 1769 to 1772, while Kraus was in Mannheim (see Van Boer's [1998] thematic catalogue). Two (VB 37 and 38) are described as pantomimes rather than symphonies, suggesting they may have originated in some ballet or other theatrical entertainment. The first of these is a three-movement work in D; the second, in G, has two short middle movements—a Tempo di marcia in C and an Adagio in F, creating a rather unusual key scheme. Of the other two symphonies, a

Sinfonia buffa in F (VB 129) has three movements, and the symphony in A (VB 128) is the longest of the four, consisting of a full four movements with minuet and trio placed third, as was to become the norm later. Works:

Symphony (Pantomime) in D
Symphony (Pantomime) in G
Sinfonia buffa in F
Symphony in A

Van Boer, Bertil H*., Joseph Martin Kraus (1756–1792): A Systematic-Thematic Catalogue of His Music* (Stuyvesant, N.Y.: Pendragon, 1998).

François-Joseph Darcis (c. 1760–c. 1783)

Viennese by birth, but with a French father, Darcis became prominent as a keyboard player in Paris from about the age of ten. Nearly all of his compositions date from the six-year period 1770 to 1776 (see list of works). Most were published in Paris; *Le bal masqué* is preserved only in a manuscript in the Bibliothèque Nationale, Paris (Rés. F 308). Two further airs, probably from the same period, are found in the same library (Rés. F 482).

Darcis fled to Russia in 1777 and wrote little thereafter. Thus he is one of the few composers to have attained greater prominence as a child than as an adult. His style displays attractive melodic writing and has been compared with early Mozart. His stage music seems to have pleased the public well enough, for both *Le bal masqué* and *La fausse peur* were performed several times. Music critics were generally less favorable toward these works, although the airs in *La fausse peur* were praised as "agreeable and effective." There has been no detailed study of Darcis's music in recent times, however. Works:

Six keyboard sonatas (Op. 1), c. 1770
Le bal masqué, one-act comedy with ariettes, first performed on 31 March 1772
Six keyboard sonatas with violin ad. lib. (Op. 2), 1773
Petits airs de Lucile et de Julie arrangé pour le clavecin (Op. 3), 1773
La fausse peur, opéra comique, first performed on 18 July 1774
Quintetto concertant, piano, bassoon, and string trio, 1775

Johann Heinrich Schroeter (c. 1762–After 1784)

Younger brother of the more famous Johann Samuel and Corona, Schroeter's date of birth may be somewhat earlier than his father's suggestion of 1763. He first came to attention as a violinist in 1770, before moving with his family to London, where he published a set of *Six duetts for two violins* in 1772. Only two later works are known, both dating from the 1780s.

Wolff, Konrad, "Johann Samuel Schroeter," *The Musical Quarterly* 44 (1958): 338–59.

Elizabeth Weichsell or Weichsel (later Billington, then Fellisent) (27 Dec. 1765–25 Aug. 1818)

Later famous as the singer Mrs. Billington, Weichsell played the piano from an early age, and composed two sets of keyboard pieces that she published at the time: *Three Lessons for the Harpsichord or Piano Forte . . . by Elizabeth Weichsell, a child eight years of age* (c. 1775); and *Six Sonatas for the Piano Forte or Harpsichord . . . composed by Elizabeth Weichsel in the eleventh year of her age. Opera 2da* (1778). Since she was born at the end of 1765, she was probably aged nine and twelve respectively when the two collections appeared in print, but they were probably composed some months earlier, in which case the stated ages may well be correct. One of the sonatas (Op. 2, No. 6) has been issued in a modern edition (Schleifer and Glickman 1998, 181–92). It is curious, however, that this sonata is included in a volume devoted to "women composers," considering that the sonata was written long before Weichsell reached womanhood; this illustrates the loose thinking that so often occurs regarding age as opposed to gender. Weichsell later gave up composition and concentrated on building a career as a singer of international repute.

Schleifer, Martha F., and Sylvia Glickman, eds., *Women Composers: Music through the Ages* (New York: G. K. Hall, 1998).

Samuel Wesley (24 Feb. 1766–11 Oct. 1837)

Son of the prolific hymn writer Charles Wesley, and father of the composer Samuel Sebastian Wesley, Samuel showed outstanding abilities from the age of about three, and for a time was promoted as a child musician, like his brother Charles (1757–1834). But whereas no compositions by the brother are known from before 1776, Samuel appears to have been one of the most prolific and gifted of all child composers, and composed more than one hundred works by the age of sixteen. The only substantial works published at the time were a set of eight keyboard sonatas that appeared around the end of 1777, but most of the unpublished works are preserved in manuscript in the British Library, London. A few survive in other libraries, while a few are lost.

The most remarkable of these numerous compositions is surely the oratorio *Ruth,* which Wesley wrote out at the age of only eight, during the period

Example 7.3.   Wesley, "Preserve Thy Soul Untainted" from *Ruth*.

8 September to 26 October 1774. It is even reported that much of it was composed up to two years earlier still, at a time when he had not sufficiently mastered notation to be able to write it down. In the oratorio, Wesley shows that he had already developed a fluent and mature style of composition, as can be seen from the opening of Orpah's aria "Preserve Thy Soul Untainted" (ex. 7.3), in which the violin part anticipates the first two vocal phrases before rounding off the ritornello into a standard but not entirely predictable cadence. The short-breathed character of this passage is fairly typical, but by no means invariable during the work. From about the same period, two arias survive from what appears to be an otherwise lost oratorio, *Gideon,* and these were followed by yet another oratorio, *The Death of Abel,* completed in 1779. The influence of Handel is still unmistakable, but with some more modern features such as expressive appoggiaturas.

Many of Wesley's other very early compositions are preserved in British Library Add. MS 34998, which dates from 1774 and 1775 and includes songs; anthems; chamber music; more than a dozen hymn tunes; five canons; three Anglican double chants (KO 171); an Overture in F (KO 401); the keyboard parts of two concertos (KO 410–11); four fugues for organ (KO 628) written in November 1774; five keyboard sonatas (KO 745–49); and other organ, harpsichord, and vocal music. His first publication, a set of eight sonatas for harpsichord or piano (KO 701), appeared in late 1777, and during the period 1778–81 he composed four violin concertos (KO 418–21), a *Sinfonia Obligato* in D, at least three violin sonatas (KO 502–4) and a string quartet in G (KO 523). From about 1780, however, he became increasingly drawn to music of the Roman Catholic Church, and contributed more than a dozen such works before he was sixteen—mainly short motets preserved in British Library Add. MS 31222.

Thus by the age of sixteen Wesley had a formidable basis for developing into a truly great composer, having by that time successfully tackled many of the principal genres of the day. Unfortunately, he did not fulfill his potential, and the reason may be largely his own fault. He once wrote to his sister Sally that his worst fault was not his intemperance, nor his disastrous marriage, nor saying his prayers in Latin, but his neglect of his outstanding abilities (see letter in Manchester, John Rylands Library, DDWes 6/40). A serious head injury incurred in 1787 may also be to blame for his relative lack of success as an adult composer. Moreover, his father, who had done much to promote Samuel as a performer during the 1770s and early 1780s, was somewhat opposed to him becoming a professional musician, and consequently Wesley lacked the kind of support that had so benefited Mozart in his early years as a composer. His relatively modest achievements in later years, however, should not be allowed to function as a disincentive to detailed investigation of his early works, which are mostly still unpublished and in need of much more thorough appraisal. A promising start has now been made through a full catalogue of his output (Kassler and Olleson 2001), while an early account of his childhood composing activity appears in Barrington (1781). Works:

> Approximately fifteen hymn tunes, c. 1773–75
> Six keyboard sonatas, 1774
> Twelve organ voluntaries, c. 1774
> *Ruth* (oratorio), 1774
> Two harpsichord concertos, 1774
> Overture in F, 1774–75
> *Gideon* (fragment of oratorio), c. 1775
> Overture in G, 1775
> Approximately twelve anthems, 1775–76
> *Eight Sonatas for the Harpsichord or Piano Forte*, 1777
> Overture in D, 1778
> *The Death of Abel* (oratorio), 1779
> String quartets in C and G, c. 1779
> Violin concertos in C, A, D, and E flat, 1779–81
> Overture in C, 1780
> Approximately fifteen Latin church works, 1780–81
> *Sinfonia Obligato* in D, 1781
> Anglican chants, canons, songs, partsongs, further chamber music, organ
>   music, and keyboard music, 1774–81

Kassler, Michael, and Philip Olleson, *Samuel Wesley (1766–1837): A Source Book* (Aldershot, U.K.: Ashgate, 2001).
Barrington, Daines, *Miscellanies by the Honourable Daines Barrington* (London: J. Nichols, 1781), 291–309.

Sound Recording

Violin Concerto No. 2 in D in *English Classical Violin Concertos*, Elizabeth Wallfisch. Hyperion CDA 66865 (1996).

Ludwig van Beethoven (16 Dec. 1770–26 Mar. 1827)

Beethoven began learning music from his father, a professional singer, at about the age of five, and was reportedly soon extemporizing at the piano. It is uncertain when he first began writing his improvisations down as compositions, but his earliest known work is a set of variations in C minor on a theme by Ernst Dressler. This was published about the end of 1782, and is remarkable for bursting from C minor to C major for the final variation—a tonal scheme that was very unusual at the time, but one that anticipates several later works by Beethoven, notably the Fifth Symphony. He followed the Dressler Variations by publishing two songs, two rondos, and an impressive set of three piano sonatas (WoO 47) that show many original features. Particularly noteworthy is No. 2 in F minor, which begins with a slow introduction that is recalled during the main allegro—a procedure not previously known but one that he reused several times in later life, including in his late quartets. All these works were published in 1783 or early 1784.

Beethoven also wrote other compositions from the period before 1787 that were not published at the time. Probably many are lost, while others were published only posthumously, but those that are known are listed in the following list of works. The largest of them is a piano concerto in E flat, which contains a highly elaborate piano part, although the orchestral parts are missing. The Romance, which is also incomplete, with most of a central section in E major missing, is evidently the slow movement of a lost concerto for flute, bassoon, and piano. The three piano quartets, though showing some similarities to three violin sonatas by Mozart, transcend their models in several significant ways, such as being more tonally adventurous and having generally more energetic rhythms and figuration. The one in E flat, composed second but now known as No. 1, is particularly outstanding. The first movement is an adagio with an exceptionally ornate piano part, and it leads into a stormy allegro for the second movement in the extraordinary key of E flat minor. This movement has tremendous energy and dynamism, with driving rhythms and intensive motivic development that generate a power very characteristic of Beethoven's later minor-key movements. The finale, a set of variations, is back in the major, but it includes one dramatic variation in the minor that recalls the mood of the previous movement. Many of the most characteristic features of Beethoven's later music can already be found in these very early works from his childhood. Works:

Dressler Variations (WoO 63), 1782
"Schilderung eines Mädchens" (WoO 107), 1783
Rondo in C (WoO 48), 1783
Three piano sonatas (WoO 47), 1783

Fugue in D for organ (WoO 31), 1783
Rondo in A (WoO 49), 1784
"An einen Säugling" (WoO 108), 1784
Piano concerto in E flat (WoO 4), 1784
Three piano quartets (WoO 36), 1785
Minuet in E flat (WoO 82), 1785
Trio for piano, flute, and bassoon (WoO 37), 1786
Romance in E minor (partly lost, Hess 13), 1786

Beethoven, Ludwig van, *Ludwig van Beethovens Werke*, 25 vols. (Leipzig, Germany: Breitkopf & Härtel, 1862–65, 1888).
Cooper, Barry, "Beethoven's Childhood Compositions: A Reappraisal," *The Beethoven Journal* 12 (1997): 2–6.
Johnson, Douglas, *Beethoven's Early Sketches in the "Fischhof Miscellany": Berlin, Autograph 28* (Ann Arbor, Mich.: UMI Research Press, 1980).

Sound Recording

The Complete Beethoven Edition, vols. 2, 6, 14, 16, various performers. Deutsche Grammophon 453 707-2GCB5; 453 733-2GCB8; 453 772-2GCB6; 453 782-2GCB3 (1997).

Sarah Bonwick (c. 1770–?)

Bonwick's only known childhood work is "Sophia. A new song, the words and music by Miss Bonwick, fourteen years of age." This was published by Longman & Broderip, supposedly circa 1790 (see *Lbl*), but it must have been earlier, since she became an organist at St. Bartholomew's, London, in 1784 and could hardly have been younger than twelve then. She continued composing until at least the 1790s.

Cooper, Barry, "'Miss Bonwick' Identified: An Eighteenth-Century Composer and Organist," *The Musical Times* (forthcoming).

Maria Frances Parke (26 Aug. 1772–15 Aug. 1822)

Parke is often confused with Maria Hester Park (née Reynolds) (29 Sep. 1760–7 June 1813), leading to suppositions that she began composing at an early age. The only possible childhood work by either composer seems to be the song "I Have Often Been Told," by M. F. Parke, dated 1787 in *NGD* (2001), but more probably written about 1797 (Tolley 2001).

Tolley, Thomas, "Haydn, the Engraver Thomas Park, and Maria Hester Park's 'Little Sonat,'" *Music & Letters* 82 (2001): 421–31.

Matthew Peter King (c. 1773–Jan. 1823)

In his first publication, the song "Haste, a Rosy Wreath Prepare," King is described as "Master M. P. King," implying that he was still a child; it was probably published about 1785. His *Six Sonatas for the Piano Forte or Harpsichord, with an Accompaniment for a Violin . . . Op. Prima* may have appeared not long afterward, but his other early works, from Op. 2 onward, are thought to date from 1789 or later.

William Crotch (5 July 1775–29 Dec. 1847)

Son of a carpenter, Crotch began showing extraordinary aptitude at an extremely early age, and could play "God Save the King" with harmony on the organ at the age of two. His talents were displayed in public tours from the age of three, and at about that age he began extemporizing compositions at the keyboard. The first compositions to be written down were a set of variations and a minuet, which were notated in Carlisle by Thomas Greatorex from Crotch's playing when Crotch was about six. Soon Crotch had learned to write music down himself. Many of his earliest works are probably lost, including those notated by Greatorex, but some might yet be identified in some musical notebooks by Crotch that are preserved in the Norfolk Record Office, Norwich. Among his early works that do survive, the first may be a keyboard concerto with accompaniment for two violins and bass, performed on 27 May 1785 and published shortly afterward, dedicated to Charles Burney "by Master Crotch, the self-taught musical child, aged 9 years."

Other works quickly followed. By far the most remarkable is a large-scale oratorio, *The Captivity of Judah,* which took nearly three years to compose. Begun in 1786, it occupies more than 400 pages of manuscript (British Library, Add. MS 30388), and was finally performed on 4 June 1789. The libretto was prepared from the Bible mainly by the Reverend Alexander Schomberg, who had befriended the Crotches in 1783 and taken much interest in the development of William. The manuscript of *The Captivity of Judah* gives much interesting detail about the composition of the work. The first 221 pages were written while Crotch was in Cambridge, but most of the rest was written after he had moved to Oxford in 1788, while the final Hallelujah chorus and the symphonies to Acts II and III were added in the Isle of Wight in September 1789, a few months after the first performance. Several musicians are mentioned as having helped in the composition, though one can be fairly certain that the main invention is pure Crotch; they likely helped in such matters as layout, notation, and scoring. Two men in particular, Pieter Helendaal and Thomas Twining, subjected the work to an intense critique, enabling some technical faults to be eliminated. Crotch himself also later went through the score annotating several passages that were faulty or overly derivative. The lack of technical perfection, however, is perhaps better viewed today not as faulty but as a characteristic of the style, and the flaws could easily be overlooked by a less severe critic, for they are no worse than might be found in some other music of the period.

It is fascinating to see what was achieved by a composer who "had never opened a treatise on the subject or received a single instruction concerning composition" (Add. 30388, f. 6r). The general sound of the oratorio is thoroughly Handelian, with hardly a sign of more modern Classical styles, but there is plenty of imaginative invention. Particularly striking is a fine eight-voice double chorus in which the Babylonian captors address their Jewish captives in the words of Psalm 137: "Sing us one of the songs of Zion." They are answered by the Jews: "How shall we sing the Lord's song in a strange land?" (ex. 7.4 shows the vocal parts only). The Babylonians sound suitably merry, taunting the Jews with their quick-fire phrases from all directions in well-crafted counterpoint; the Jews, by contrast, sing in a plaintive manner, mainly in timid single voices or in block chords, huddling together to show both fear and solidarity. Crotch here combines extraordinary psychological

Example 7.4.   Crotch, "Sing us one of the songs" from *The Captivity of Judah.*

insight with skill at musical interpretation of the feelings of the two groups (as well as differing interestingly from Handel, who had tended to use homophonic choruses mainly for pagans rather than Jews or Christians, in works such as *Belshazzar* and *Alexander's Feast*).

Crotch composed many shorter works as a child, including some lost sonatas published about 1786, a brief work for string quartet (1788–90), and some songs and choral music. A double chant in D minor for psalms (British Library, Add. MS 30392, f. 23), composed on 5 February 1791, became widely circulated in printed collections during the nineteenth century and is still in regular use today in some cathedrals and churches. He quickly made up for his early lack of training, studying with professors at both Cambridge and Oxford, gaining a B. Mus. degree in 1794 and becoming professor of music at Oxford while still only twenty-one. In later life he was noted as an organist, conductor, scholar, lecturer, and composer, but his works tended to be conservative and never achieved the international fame that his early promise might have suggested. A provisional list of his early works is provided, based mainly on *NGD* and Rennert (1975). Rennert also provides much information about Crotch's early life (which was documented at the time by several observers), but he says little about the music itself. Works:

Minuet, keyboard, c. 1781, lost

Variations on *God Save the King*, keyboard, c. 1781, lost

Sonata, keyboard, 1783, lost

Concerto, keyboard, with acc. for two violin and bass, c. 1784, Norfolk Record Office, MS 11246; publ. London: Holland, 1785; only known copy is in Oxford, Christ Church

Music for the farce *Transformation*, 1786, lost

Two sonatas, keyboard (or violin and keyboard), publ. London, c. 1786, lost

"Liberty, A New Song," London: Holland, 1786; only known copy is in the Royal College of Organists Library

"Sycamore Vale," song, 1787 (lost)

"The Rose Had Been Washed," song, c. 1787, publ. London: Holland, c.1790; only known copy is in the British Library

The Captivity of Judah, oratorio, 1786–89, British Library, Add. MS 30388.

Two fugues, organ or pianoforte, 7 Oct. 1790, British Library, Add. MS 30392, ff. 3r–3v

String quartet, June 1788 and 8 Oct. 1790, ibid., ff. 4r–5r

Cantata, part of *Messiah* (words by Pope), 23 Oct. 1790, ibid., ff. 5v–17v

Te Deum in B flat, 28 Oct. 1790, incomplete, ibid., ff. 17v–22v

Two double chants, 5 Feb. 1791, ibid., f. 23r

Chorus to Humanity, 30 Oct. 1790–25 May 1791, ibid., ff. 23v–30r
God is Our Hope, anthem, 1 May 1791–1 Oct. 1791, ibid., ff 30v–39v
Various early works in manuscript notebooks in Norfolk Record Office

Rennert, Jonathan, *William Crotch 1775–1847* (Lavenham, U.K.: Dalton, 1975).

Johann Nepomuk Hummel (14 Nov. 1778–17 Oct. 1837)

Hummel studied with Mozart for a time between the ages of eight and ten, and began composing about then. His earliest works were for piano, and he performed an original set of variations in Munich in March 1789. Further sets soon followed, and after moving to London, where his piano playing made a considerable impact, his compositions began to be published. A collection of three of sets of variations appeared in London on 23 April 1791 as his Op. 1, and two more appeared the same year as Op. 2. The following April he published three sonatas for piano or harpsichord (Op. 3), two of them with violin or flute accompaniment and one of these also having a cello part. By early 1793 Hummel was back in Vienna, where he published a different Op. 3, consisting of two new sets of variations plus a revised version of Op. 2, No. 1 (variations on "The Lass of Richmond Hill"). His earlier Op. 3—the three sonatas—soon became known confusingly as Op. 2, and the set is often listed nowadays as Op. 2a. The Viennese Op. 3, which describes Hummel as "aged 14" and was therefore probably published in 1793, attracted a huge number of subscribers from London, Vienna, Prague, and numerous other cities: the subscription list includes more than 500 people, who ordered nearly 700 copies altogether—a remarkable total by any standard, and far in excess of the total of 123 subscribers for 245 copies that was achieved by Beethoven's Op. 1 two years later.

Several more works by Hummel date from the 1790s, including further sets of piano variations, two piano concertos, a piano quartet, some songs with piano, and some partsongs, but in most cases a precise date of composition has not been established (for a complete list, see Sachs "Checklist" [1973–74], although this, like *NGD,* gives incorrect information about the contents of Op. 3). These other works remained unpublished, but most of the manuscripts are preserved in the British Library. All Hummel's surviving piano compositions are now available, edited by Joel Sachs. In general those he wrote as a child are well-constructed works that exhibit the light, decorative, fluent, and graceful style commonly associated with his later music. There are, however, more profound moments in the slow movements and minor-key variations, as well as occasional striking chromaticism of which Mozart would surely have approved. Works:

Three Sets of Variations (Op. 1), 1791
Variations to the Lass of Richmond Hill, and Jem of Aberdeen (Op. 2), 1791

> *Three Sonatas* (Op. 3 [or 2a; nos. 1 and 2 are trios]), 1792
> *Trois airs variés* (Op. 3), 1793
> Other sets of variations, S1, S2, S16, S18, S19

Hummel, Johann Nepomuk, *The Complete Works for Piano: A Six-Volume Collection of Reprints and Facsimiles,* ed. Joel Sachs (New York: Garland: 1989–90).

Kroll, Mark, *Johann Nepomuk Hummel* (Lanham, Md.: Scarecrow Press, 2007).

Sachs, Joel, "A Checklist of the Works of Johann Nepomuk Hummel," *Notes* 30 (1973–74): 732–54.

Sound Recording

Piano Sonata No. 1 in Johann Nepomuk Hummel, *Piano Sonatas,* Dana Protopopescu. Koch DICD 920237 (1995).

Thomas Welsh (1781–24 Jan. 1848)

Welsh's mother was a sister of Thomas Linley the younger (see earlier entry), and he first attracted attention as a singer in Wells Cathedral Choir, which he joined at the age of six. In 1792 he began singing solos in stage works in London. By this time he had already begun publishing songs he had written, although it is unclear precisely when he began composing. Four such songs, all "composed by Master Welsh," are preserved in The British Library and elsewhere. Their titles and dates, as given in the library catalogue (*Lbl*), are in the following list of works. A fifth song, "The Death of Poor Cock Robin" (3 pages), also "composed and sung by Master Welsh," is preserved in the library at Tatton Park (Pargeter 1977). Unlike the other four, which were issued by recognized publishers, this was printed "for the Author" and could therefore be his first publication. The phrase "Master Welsh" indicates that the composer was still perceived as a child, and was probably younger than sixteen. He later became a celebrated bass singer and teacher, but never developed far as a composer. Works:

> "The Death of Poor Cock Robin," c. 1790?
> "O Tommy Tommy," 1791
> "The Gentle Shepherdess," 1794
> "Fair Mary," 1796
> "This Is the House," 1797

Pargeter, Shirley, *A Catalogue of the Library at Tatton Park, Knutsford, Cheshire* (Chester, U.K.: Cheshire Libraries and Museums, 1977).

Nicolò Paganini (27 Oct. 1782–27 May 1840)

Paganini's earliest known work is a set of variations for violin and guitar entitled *Carmagnola,* composed at the age of twelve, which employs some unusual
violinistic effects—a feature that was to become a hallmark of his later style.
He continued composing in the following years, but no other works have yet
been confirmed as dating from his childhood.

François-Joseph Fétis (25 Mar. 1784–26 Mar. 1871)

Fétis composed and performed his first concerto at the age of nine (whether
for piano or violin is unclear; he played both instruments). This and another
concerto also dating from before 1800 are both lost, but three unpublished
string quartets from the same period survive in the Brussels Conservatoire
(Wotquenne 1898–1912, no. 6567). Fétis is also reported to have composed
some piano sonatas, divertissements, pots-pourris, and a symphonie concer-
tante before 1800. He continued composing in later life, but became more
notable as a musicologist.

Huys, Bernard, *François-Joseph Fétis et la vie musicale de son temps, 1784–1871* (Brussels:
  Bibliothèque Royale Albert I, 1972).
Wangermée, Robert, *François-Joseph Fétis: musicologue et compositeur* (Brussels: Palais des
  Académies, 1951).
Wotquenne, Alfred, *Catalogue de la Bibliothèque du Conservatoire Royal de Musique* (Brus-
  sels: Coosemans, 1898–1912).

Louis Spohr (5 Apr. 1784–22 Oct. 1859)

Spohr's mother was an able pianist, while his father, a doctor, could play the
flute. Spohr began learning the violin about the age of five, and his earliest attempts at composition were made about 1796 or perhaps even earlier.
They consist of three duets for two violins (WoO 21), which his father carefully preserved. Another duet (WoO 22) was written shortly afterward, and
a violin concerto in G (WoO 9) was composed about 1799. The autograph
score of this is in the Bayerische Staatsbibliothek, Munich, but the concerto,
like the earlier duets, seems never to have been published. Spohr composed
many more works during this period, according to his own account, including
the first three numbers (overture, chorus, and air) for an unfinished singspiel
(WoO 140), another violin concerto (WoO 144), and six string trios (WoO
141), but all are now lost. Thus Spohr's early works have suffered more than
their fair share of neglect and it is difficult to assess how capable a composer
he was as a child. His duets show some awkward part-writing and limited

harmonic variety, while the concerto, though far more advanced and complex, still has occasional infelicities; but he clearly developed considerable facility in composition well before he was sixteen. Works:

> Three violin duets, in F, C, and E flat (WoO 21), c. 1796–97
> Three nos. for unfinished singspiel (WoO 140), c. 1796–97
> Violin duet in E flat (WoO 22), c. 1797
> Violin concerto in G (WoO 9), c. 1799
> Six trios (WoO 141, two violins and cello?), c. 1797–1801
> Violin concerto (WoO 144), c. 1797–1801

Brown, Clive, *Louis Spohr: A Critical Biography* (Cambridge: Cambridge University Press, 1984).
Göthel, Folker, *Thematisch-bibliographisches Verzeichnis der Werke von Louis Spohr* (Tutzing, Germany: Schneider, 1981).

Ferdinand Ries (28[?] Nov. 1784–13 Jan. 1838)

Ries learned music initially from his father, the noted violinist Franz Ries, who also taught Beethoven for a time. Ries's first known composition was a set of three string quartets (WoO 1) dated 31 October 1798, which is described on the autograph score as "Oeuvre première," suggesting it may have been his first actual composition. On the other hand these quartets are substantial works in four movements (though in one quartet a movement is missing), and so it seems likely that he had previously dabbled in composition. The following year saw the completion of a sonata for cello and piano (WoO 2) and a set of variations for violin and piano (WoO 3). The cello sonata was one of the first works in this genre, composed only two years after Beethoven's pioneering cello sonatas Op. 5 had been published in 1797. Two more works (WoO 4–5) were written in 1800. Like much of Ries's output, none of these works is available in a modern edition, although WoO 4, a set of eight waltzes for piano, was published in Vienna in 1810. Works:

> Three string quartets (WoO 1), 1798
> Cello sonata (WoO 2), 1799
> Variations for violin and piano (WoO 3), 1799
> Eight waltzes (WoO 4), 1800
> Violin sonata in A flat (WoO 5), 1800

Hill, Cecil, *The Music of Ferdinand Ries: A Thematic Catalogue* (Armidale, Australia: University of New England, 1977).

George Frederick Pinto (25 Sep. 1785–23 Mar. 1806)

Pinto was a remarkably talented and original composer who died at the tragically early age of 20. His mother, Julia, composed and published at least one work, and he himself studied the violin with Johann Peter Salomon from the age of eight. Most of his compositions were written during his last three years, but a waltz and rondo for pianoforte date from about 1800 to 1801 and have been published in an edition by Nicholas Temperley (1985). In addition, a set of three divertimentos Op. 1 was advertised on 5 November 1801, but no copy is now known.

Pinto, George Frederick, *Complete Works for Solo Piano,* in *The London Pianoforte School,* vol. 14, ed. Nicholas Temperley (New York: Garland, 1985).

Carl Maria von Weber (18[?] Nov. 1786–5 June 1826)

Weber was the son of Franz Anton Weber, a musician and occasional composer. Weber began composing in 1798, his first known composition being a set of six fughettas for piano (J. 1-6), which he wrote in Salzburg while studying with Michael Haydn. The fughettas were published there with a dedication dated 1 September 1798. Each one is thirteen bars or less, but they mostly show adequate skill in four-part counterpoint, and they were praised in a review in the newly established Leipzig journal the *Allgemeine musikalische Zeitung.* Several more piano works followed in the next two years, including three sonatas and four sets of variations, but all are lost except one set of variations, Op. 2. This set is notable particularly for showing skilled handling of the instrument and its sonorities, and again it was favorably reviewed in the *Allgemeine musikalische Zeitung.* Other lost works from this period include some partsongs (J. Anh. 9), canons (J. Anh. 10), three string trios (J. Anh. 11–13), and probably three more (J. Anh. 24–26).

A few more piano works were composed between 1800 and 1802, but far more significant are Weber's first efforts at writing music for voices and orchestra. The first was a now-lost opera, *Die Macht der Liebe und des Weins,* written not long after the six fughettas but clearly a far more substantial work. It was followed in 1800 by his second opera, *Das Waldmädchen,* performed in Freiburg just after his fourteenth birthday. Most of this opera is also lost, but his third opera, *Peter Schmoll und seine Nachbarn,* does survive. Composed in 1801 and perhaps finished the next year, it was performed in Augsburg in early 1803. This is a truly impressive and substantial work, in twenty separate numbers, and shows that Weber's natural aptitude for theater music was already abundantly evident at the age of barely fifteen. John Warrack describes it as exhibiting "considerable dramatic flair," although his criticism that the harmony is "seldom more than merely correct" seems unfair (Warrack 1976, 41–42). One of the most striking features in the work is Weber's handling of the orchestra and especially the wind instruments. Here he even had the idea of employing some unusual or archaic instruments, and one number includes parts for two recorders and two basset horns, creating some very remarkable sonorities.

Weber's other notable early work is a mass in E flat (sometimes known as his *Jugendmesse* to distinguish it from a later work in that key). This was apparently completed before the turn of the century, and a fair copy that may incorporate some revisions is dated 3 May 1802. Warrack singles out for special comment the work's unusual symmetrical structure built around a central Credo in E flat, with the same music used for the Kyrie and Dona. Some of the other movements use surprisingly remote keys such as A minor and G major. At times, a somewhat operatic style prevails, as one might expect from a composer who was already confident at writing music for the stage. Thus Weber made rapid progress as a composer from his six fughettas written at the age of eleven. By the time he was sixteen his works had made a considerable impact, and his music was already showing many characteristic features of his later style. Works:

> Six fughettas (J. 1–6), 1798
> Three piano sonatas (Anh. 16–18), 1798–1800
> Four sets of variations (Op. 2, Anh. 14, 15, 19), 1798–1800
> *Die Macht der Liebe und des Weins* (opera), 1798
> *Das Waldmädchen* (opera), 1800
> Twelve allemandes for piano (J. 15–26), 1800–01
> *Peter Schmoll und seine Nachbarn* (opera), 1801–02
> Two three-voice canons, 1802
> "Die Kerze" and "Umsonst" (songs, J. 27–28), 1802
> Six ecossaises (J. 29–34), 1802
> Other lost works

Jähns, Friedrich Wilhelm, *Carl Maria von Weber in seinen Werken: chronologisch-thematisches Verzeichniss seiner sämmtlichen Compositionen* (Berlin: Schlesinger, 1871).

Warrack, John, *Carl Maria von Weber,* 2nd ed. (Cambridge: Cambridge University Press, 1976).

Sound Recordings

Six fughettas in *Salzburg Organ Landscape*, Florian Pagitsch. Dabringhaus und Grimm MDG 319 0990-2 (1999). Several recordings of overture (only) of *Peter Schmoll*.

Johan Fredrik Berwald (4 Dec. 1787–26 Aug. 1861)

Berwald was a cousin of the more famous Franz Berwald, and his father, Georg, was an orchestral bassoonist and violinist who was living in Stockholm when Johan Fredrik was born. After making his debut as a violinist at the age of barely six, Berwald first published compositions, three "polonoises" for violin and piano named Op. 1, appeared in 1796. They must have been composed when he was no more than eight. They were shortly followed by two large orchestral works, published in Berlin as an *Ouverture périodique* in C and a *Simphonie périodique* in E flat. Both works were probably composed in 1797 and published in 1798, with the overture being dated 13 April 1797 (Brook 1983, 83), although some authorities suggest the symphony was composed and published in 1799. The symphony in particular is an extremely impressive work in the late Classical style, scored for oboes, horns, trumpets, timpani, and strings. A modern edition has been printed in *The Symphony 1720–1840* (Brook 1983). In three movements (though the published versions incorporate a minuet and trio by Johan Wikmanson), it exhibits plenty of drama and contrast, notably at the start of the development section of the first movement, where fortissimo outbursts alternate with whole-bar rests and carry the music sequentially from G minor through to B flat minor in the course of ten bars.

Berwald's other principal early works are some string quartets. Three appeared as Op. 2 in Berlin in 1799; three more were published as Op. 3 and a seventh as Op. 5. He continued composing for many years, and in later life also became notable as a conductor, but in recent times he has been almost entirely neglected except in a few small-scale studies in Swedish and some unpublished research. Thus, in a situation unusual for a child composer, a work written at the age of nine or ten has become better known today than his adult compositions. Principal works:

> Three polonoises, violin and piano (Op. 1), 1796
> *Ouverture périodique* in C, 1797
> *Simphonie périodique* in E flat, 1797–98
> Three string quartets (Op. 2), 1799
> Three string quartets (Op. 3), 1801–04
> String quartet in G (Op. 5), 1802

Brook, Barry S., ed. *The Symphony 1720–1840, Reference Volume* (New York: Garland, 1986).
Brook, Barry S., ed., *The Symphony 1720–1840*, Series F, vol. III (New York: Garland, 1983).

Carl Czerny (21 Feb. 1791–15 July 1857)

Czerny's father settled in Vienna in 1786 and earned his living as a piano teacher. The main source of information about Czerny's childhood is his own reminiscences, written in 1842 and published in English in 1956. Here he recalls that he began composing at the age of seven, without any special encouragement from his father, and that his compositions were sufficiently correct that, on looking back at them years later, he found "little occasion to change anything." His first significant work was a set of twenty variations for violin and piano on a theme of Wenzel Krumpholz, which was published as Op. 1 in 1806 and achieved good sales. The variations were so skilfully written that, although Czerny had had little instruction in theory at the time, "nobody would believe that I had composed them without assistance." (Czerny 1956, 312). No other works from his childhood are known.

Czerny, Carl, "Recollections from My Life," trans. and ed. Ernest Sanders, *The Musical Quarterly* 42 (1956): 302–17.

Franz Xaver Wolfgang Mozart (26 July 1791–29 July 1844)

Son of Wolfgang Amadeus Mozart, and sometimes also known as Wolfgang Amadeus himself, Franz Xaver never managed to show the same exceptional talent as his father, but nevertheless became a composer and pianist in his own right. His earliest works, an unpublished rondo in F for piano and a substantial piano quartet in G minor (a key much favored by his father), were apparently written in 1802, but it was not until 1805 that he began to achieve prominence as a composer. In that year he composed a cantata (now lost) for Haydn's birthday; his piano quartet was published as Op. 1 (it may have appeared before 1805); and several other piano works appeared: seven variations on a minuet from his father's *Don Giovanni* (WoO 1), seven variations on a march from the opera *Aline* (WoO 8), and a *Rondeau favorit* (WoO 13). Other early works include *Eight Variations on a Russian Theme* (WoO 11) and eight lieder, but his most substantial early work is a piano concerto in C, Op. 14, which dates from 1807 but was not published until 1809 or 1810. Franz Xaver Mozart was one of very few child composers whose father had achieved significant success as a composer, and yet ironically the elder Mozart died when young Franz was only four months old and therefore had no direct influence on his musical training. Works:

> Rondo in F (piano), 1802
> Piano quartet in G minor (Op. 1), 1802
> *Rondeau favorit* (piano, WoO 13), 1805

Seven variations (piano, WoO 1), 1805
Seven variations (piano, WoO 8), 1805
Cantata for Haydn's birthday, 1805
Eight variations (WoO 11), 1806–07
Eight deutsche lieder (WoO 5), 1807
Piano sonata (Op. 10), 1807 (publ. 1808)
Piano concerto in C (Op. 14), 1807 (publ. 1809–10)

Hummel, Walter, *W. A. Mozarts Söhne* (Kassel, Germany: Bärenreiter, 1956).

Gioachino Rossini (29 Feb. 1792–13 Nov. 1868)

Both of Rossini's parents were professional musicians; his father was known chiefly as a horn player and his mother as an opera singer. One of his first works, the song "Se il vuol la molinara" for soprano and piano, may have been written as early as 1801, and in 1802 he began composing the first of a substantial number of sacred compositions for voice or voices and orchestra, while studying with Giuseppe Malerbi in Lugo. Some twenty-one such works are known from the period 1802–09; most are not precisely datable, but two of the latest are the Ravenna Mass of 1808 and the Rimini Mass of 1809.

Rossini's most notable contribution from his childhood, however, is undoubtedly a set of six sonatas, each in three full-sized movements, for the unusual combination of two violins, cello, and double bass (Rossini 1954). They were composed in the summer of 1804, and are among the most successful works ever written by any child. Five were published in a version for string quartet in the 1820s, and they are still popular today as a regular part of the string repertory. Although Rossini was already familiar with the works of Mozart and Haydn, these sonatas only occasionally show their influence; at times they bear the unmistakable stamp of Rossini's own personal style, foreshadowing his later operas in various ways. Commentators have observed typical Rossinian features in their melodic style, use of crescendos, their occasional use of the double bass as a kind of buffo character (notably in the finale of No. 3), and perhaps the appearance of a storm in the finale of No. 6. The sonatas do, however, also show some surprisingly inventive and unusual features. No. 1 in G major, for example, has a slow movement in the unexpected key of E flat; still more unexpected is the opening of the finale, which begins on an E major chord before working round to the tonic key of G. In No. 5, the second theme is heard first in the tonic before reappearing in modified form in the dominant. It combines energetic and mellifluous melody with simple but effective harmony and four-bar phrases in typical Rossinian manner, but it is spiced up with striking "percussive" cross-relations between E flat in the

Example 7.5.   Rossini, Sonata No. 5 in E flat, first movement.

melody and E natural in the bass-line (ex. 7.5). The acerbic clash, emphasized by the articulation marks for the double bass and contrasting with the jaunty scale that follows in the first violin, is a strikingly original effect and is much exploited in the rest of the movement, which is nearly 250 bars long.

Other instrumental music that Rossini composed as a child includes five duets for two horns and a symphony known as the Sinfonia "al Conventello," both dating from circa 1806. The symphony is scored for full orchestra (minus timpani and second bassoon), and is in one movement—thus more an overture than a symphony. It begins with a solemn largo in D minor, which leads into a vivacious allegro in D major. Rossini was also heavily involved with music for the theater by that time, usually as keyboard player and occasionally as a treble singer. At times, too, he was able, following the custom of the time, to contribute an aria for insertion in an existing opera, though the only documented case from this period is his tenor aria "Cara, voi siete quella" (written in 1806 for a performance of Joseph Weigl's opera *L'amor marinaro*). Thus he had already established himself as a significant composer long before his first opera was written at the age of eighteen. Works:

"Se il vuol la molinara" (song), 1801 (?)
Cavatina, 1802–03
Six sonatas, 1804
"Cara, voi siete quella" (insertion aria), 1806
Sinfonia "al Conventello," c. 1806
Five duets in E flat for horns, c. 1806

Gallo, Denise P., *Gioachino Rossini: A Guide to Research* (London: Routledge, 2002).
Rossini, Gioacchino, *Sei sonate a quattro,* in *Quaderno Rossiniani* 1, ed. Alfredo Bonaccorsi (Pesaro, Italy: Fondazione Rossini, 1954).

Sound Recordings

Many recordings of the six sonatas.

Gertrude van den Bergh (21 Jan. 1793–10 Sep. 1840)

Although van den Bergh is absent from most reference works, she was a respected pianist and composer in her day who apparently published a piano sonata at the age of nine: The evidence is a catalogue from 1802 by the publisher J. J. Hummel, which lists this work (a later catalogue circa 1814 lists this and two other works by her). There is no reason to suppose the sonata was written by an older relative, even though Hummel does not indicate her first name.

Johannson, Cari, *J. J. & B. Hummel Music-Publishing and Thematic Catalogues* (Stockholm: Library of the Royal Swedish Academy of Music, 1972).

Ignaz Moscheles (23 May 1794–10 Mar. 1870)

Moscheles began composing at least as early as 1808, and actually had a symphony performed in Vienna on 12 March 1809. This does not survive, however, and his earliest published works date from around 1810. These consist of several sets of piano variations (Opp. 1, 2, and 5–7), some dances (Op. 3) and a sonatina (Op. 4), all of which were printed in quick succession.

Helene Riese (later Liebmann) (16 Dec. 1795–1835 or Later)

It is uncertain at what age Riese began composing, but she developed quickly as both a pianist and a composer, publishing three piano sonatas (Opp. 1–3) in 1811. These were favorably reviewed in the *Allgemeine musikalische Zeitung,* as was her song "Kennst du das Land" (Op. 4). After her marriage in 1813 she published compositions under her married name, but ceased doing so in 1817, having published at least sixteen opus numbers, and there is little sign of her activities thereafter. Works:

> Piano sonatas in D, E flat, and C minor (Opp. 1–3), 1811
> "Kennst du das Land" (song, Op. 4), 1811 (Jackson 1987)

Jackson, Barbara Garvey, ed., *Lieder by Women Composers of the Classic Era*, vol. 1 (Fayetteville, Ark.: ClarNan Editions, 1987).

(Johann) Carl (Gottfried) Loewe (30 Nov. 1796–20 Apr. 1869)

Loewe was initially taught music by his father, Adam Loewe. He sang in the choir at Cöthen for a time before moving to Halle about 1809. There he was taught by the noted theorist and composer Daniel Gottlob Türk, and began composing about that time. His earliest known works are a group of eight so-called *Jugendlieder* (Songs of Youth), written about 1810. Around late 1812 he wrote two further songs, "Klotar" and "Das Gebet des Herrn," which were published the following year as his Opp. 1 and 2, though these opus numbers were later suppressed and used for other works. All ten compositions (except "Klotar") are printed in volume one of the collected edition of Loewe's songs, edited by Max Runze (1970). For reference to two other works from the same period (fragments of a lament for Queen Luise and a cantata for his teacher Türk), see volume one of Runze's edition (1970, v).

Five of the *Jugendlieder* are simple strophic settings with no preludes and only short postludes; but "Das Blumenopfer" and "Die Jagd" have more unusual structures. In the former, stanzas 1, 2, 4, and 5 have the same setting (G minor, 6/8), but the remaining three stanzas have a different setting in contrasting mood and meter (G major, 2/4, and faster). Similarly in "Die Jagd," the middle two stanzas are in A minor but the outer two in C major. This alternation of major and minor, with different but recurring music, is distinctly unusual. "Heimweh" is perhaps even more striking. It is through-composed, slow, and highly expressive, with a very wide vocal compass of almost two octaves. As with the unusual structures in the other two songs, this feature to some extent reflects the poetry, but is introduced mainly for musical rather than pictorial reasons.

Although in later life he composed in many other genres, Loewe is today remembered almost exclusively as a composer of songs. It is therefore striking that he had already developed a strong penchant for this genre by the age of sixteen, and was displaying both melodic fluency and imagination in his settings. Works:

Eight lieder, c. 1810:
"An die Natur"
"Die treuen Schwalben"
"Das Blumenopfer"
"Romanze"
"An die Nachtigall"
"Die Jagd"
"Heimweh"
"Sehnsucht"
Two lieder, c. 1812: "Klotar" and "Das Gebet des Herrn"
Lament for Queen Luise, c. 1810–12
Cantata, c. 1810–12

Runze, Max, ed., *Carl Loewes Werke: Gesamtausgabe der Balladen, Legenden, Lieder und Gesänge für eine Singstimme*. . . . (Leipzig, Germany: Breitkopf & Härtel, 1899–1904; reprint Farnborough, U.K.: Gregg, 1970).

Franz Schubert (31 Jan. 1797–19 Nov. 1828)

Schubert's father was a schoolteacher and music lover who, though not a professional musician, was able to give Schubert some early instruction in music. Schubert is reported to have begun composing short lieder, string quartets, and piano pieces as early as 1807 or 1808 when he began studying music theory, but his first surviving composition dates from 1810. He quickly became so fast and fluent at composing that he had written about fifty more works by the time he was sixteen, including D. 1–15, 17–37, 39, 44, 128, and 642, though some are incomplete or lost (the standard numbering for his works derives from Otto Erich Deutsch's thematic catalogue). These works include two full-sized string quartets, D. 18 and D. 32, while two others are lost (D. 19 and D. 19A).

Schubert's first known work (D. 1) is a fantasie for piano duet, composed between 8 April and 1 May 1810. It seems impossible to believe that this was his first composition, however, since it is a very large-scale work extending to 1,195 bars. It is interesting that he should choose fantasie rather than sonata, and piano duet rather than piano solo, as if deliberately setting out to compose something decidedly uncommon, for this is what he certainly achieved. The work, in fact, seems to subvert Classical norms of structural regularity, cohesion, and formal patterns, as embodied in the main instrumental genres of sonata, quartet, and symphony, with Schubert choosing the one Classical genre that was overtly wild and unpredictable. The leading composers of the day had, of course, occasionally composed instrumental fantasies (Beethoven's single example, Op. 77, had been written only a few months earlier and was still unpublished); but Schubert's D. 1 sounds quite different from any of theirs. In this work he announces that music does not have to be written in the conventional way, and that there is another way of composing beautiful music. Whereas Beethoven's earliest works already show evidence of either fantastic elaborations or intensive development, Schubert's fantasie avoids both these typically Beethovenian devices. Instead it displays endless lyricism; extraordinary fecundity of invention; a great range of imagination; wide tonal variety; originality in modulation; a delight in repetition of good ideas; and a reluctance to draw to a conclusion, resulting in the "heavenly length" that is often associated, like the other features mentioned, with the later Schubert style (as is the piano-duet medium, which he used frequently in later life). Indeed this fantasie is arguably more purely Schubertian than most of his later instrumental music such as his symphonies and quartets, where he perhaps felt duty-bound to address the main compositional issues of the day by conforming more closely to recognized norms and genres.

Schubert's fantasie is sometimes divided into three movements in modern editions, but it actually consists of around twenty sections, each with a different tempo mark from the adjoining ones. Some sections lead into the next without a break, while others may pause on a half-close or even come to a complete stop with a full close. The longest is the finale, an allegro maestoso of 232 bars, while a few adagio linking passages are so short that they cannot really be described as a proper section. Another section is a self-contained march and trio, with *da capo* to the march. Eight different key signatures are employed during the course of the work, which begins in G major and ends in C major, but the actual keys being used do not always match the written signatures. Initially the overall impression is of a series of unrelated fragments and movements that are joined side by side into a rhapsodic structure like beads on a string, making an attractive display of contrasting miniatures but not much more. Closer inspection, however, reveals some fascinating cases of thematic transformation between sections a long way apart. This is particularly significant in view of Schubert's use of this device in later works, notably his "Wanderer" Fantasie (D. 760). Versions of the opening adagio theme appear transformed at the first allegro (bar 23), the march in F (bar 315), and a vivace in B flat minor (bar 613). Meanwhile a light, jaunty theme that first appears in a presto in B flat major (bar 284) returns in an agitated B flat minor section (bar 527) and majestically in C major in the finale (bar 964). Thus Schubert did make use of large-scale planning, and gave the work an overall cohesion that becomes apparent only with

Example 7.6. Schubert, Fantasie, D. 1, bars 575–80.

greater familiarity. As in his later music, his harmony is often very conventional but at times is most extraordinary. At bars 575–80 he executes a most
unusual modulation (ex. 7.6). The procedure of introducing the notes of a
chord individually is reminiscent of the opening of Mozart's "Dissonance"
Quartet (K. 465), but the actual notes used by Schubert are quite different,
and the modulation relies on treating the D flat as an enharmonic C sharp
to move from a D flat major chord into D minor. What is not visible in the
example is what precedes the D flat chord: the first time, this is the key of
B flat minor, close to D flat major, but at the repeat it is A minor, resulting
in two extraordinary modulations in quick succession. Schubert's treatment
of dissonance is at times equally astonishing, as in the introduction of an
unexpected G flat against a B flat minor triad in bar 726 (ex. 7.7), while the
rapidly throbbing semiquavers above seem an anticipation of the throbbing
triplets in his famous song *Erlkönig*.

   This detailed account of the fantasie shows that Schubert already had
a well-developed and highly original style at the age of thirteen, and it was
quickly employed in other works. Most are somewhat shorter and perhaps less
striking, but in addition to the two string quartets mentioned earlier, there
is an important one-movement piano trio in B flat (D. 28), a further string
quartet (D. 36) written around the time of his sixteenth birthday, two more
fantasies (D. 2e and 9, for piano solo and piano duet respectively), and several
lieder, the first of which (*Hagars Klage*, D. 5) is dated 30 March 1811. None

Example 7.7.   Schubert, Fantasie, D. 1, bars 723–31.

of these works was published during Schubert's lifetime, but his importance and ability as a child composer can now be fully attested. Works:

> Fantasies for piano duet (D. 1, 9), 1810–11
> Fantasie for piano solo (D. 2e), 1811
> Three string quartets (D. 18, 19, 19a), 1810–11
> Six minuets for wind (D. 2d), 1811
> Overture for string quintet (D. 8), 1811
> Three orchestral overtures (D. 4, 12, 26), 1811–12
> *Der Spiegelritter* (incomplete singspiel, D. 11), 1811–12
> Piano trio in B flat (D. 28), 1812
> *Salve regina* (D. 27), 1812
> Kyrie (D. 31), 1812
> String quartets in C and B flat (D. 32, 36), 1812–13
> Songs with piano (D. 5–7, 10, 15, 17, 23, 30, 33, 35, 39, 44), 1811–12
> Partsongs (D. 17, 33–35, 37–38)
> Various short piano pieces and dances; many fragments and unfinished works

Deutsch, Otto Erich, *Franz Schubert: thematisches Verzeichnis seiner Werke in chronologischer Folge*, 2nd ed. (Kassel, Germany: Bärenreiter, 1978).
Schubert, Franz, *Neue Ausgabe sämtlicher Werke*, eds. Walther Dürr and others (Kassel, Germany: Bärenreiter, 1964–).

Sound Recordings

Fantasies, D. 1 and 9, in Franz Schubert, *Piano Duets,* vol. 4, Yaara Tal and Andreas Groethuysen. Sony Classical SK68243 (1995).
Early quartets including fragments in Franz Schubert, *String Quartets,* vols. 1–3, 8–9, Leipzig Quartet. Dabringhaus und Grimm MDG 307 0601-2 (n.d.). Many recordings of the Piano Trio D. 28.

· 8 ·

Composers Born between 1801 and 1850

Hector Berlioz (11 Dec. 1803–8 Mar. 1869)

The son of a doctor, Berlioz had little chance to develop his musical abilities during his early childhood, but made rapid progress from about the age of twelve, when he began learning the flute. He then encountered Rameau's *Traité de l'harmonie,* from which he gained sufficient knowledge to begin composing at about the age of fourteen. His first work was probably a *Potpourri concertant sur des thèmes italiens,* for a sextet of flute, horn, two violins, viola, and bass, which most likely dates from early 1818, with the flute part intended for himself and the horn part for his teacher's son. He also composed two quintets for the same instruments minus the horn, a combination possibly explained by the suicide of his teacher's son in the summer of 1818. Berlioz later claimed that the quintets had been written when he was twelve and a half, but a date in the latter half of 1818 seems far more likely. In 1819 he offered the sextet and some songs, and probably also the quintets, to some Parisian publishers, but all were rejected and are no longer extant except for one song, *Le Dépit de la bergère,* although two melodic fragments were incorporated into his later works. The surviving song is a simple romance, but the piano part is rather unsophisticated and contains some awkward part-writing. Works:

> *Potpourri concertant* (sextet), 1817–18
> Two quintets, 1818–19
> Romances (voice and piano), including *Le Dépit de la bergère,* 1818–19

Holoman, D. Kern, *Catalogue of the Works of Hector Berlioz* (Kassel, Germany: Bären-reiter, 1987).

Fanny Mendelssohn (later Hensel) (14 Nov. 1805–14 May 1847)

Fanny Mendelssohn was the elder of two sisters of Felix (see "Felix Mendelssohn"); their father, Abraham, was a wealthy banker. His own father, Moses Mendelssohn, was a noted philosopher. Thus the family background, which combined wealth, intellect, and a musical mother, was an excellent environment for Fanny and Felix to develop their creative talents. Both children began studying music theory with Carl Friedrich Zelter in 1819, and both soon turned to original composition. Fanny's first known work was a song, "Ihr Töne, schwingt euch fröhlich," written in 1819 for her father's birthday on 11 December; it may have been Felix's first efforts in composition, probably made during the previous two months, that encouraged her to take up this activity. The song exhibits the "spontaneity and melodic inspiration" that were characteristic of her later style (Tillard 1996, 67), and during the next two years she continued composing energetically. Unfortunately the manuscript containing the works written during 1820 and 1821, which is said to include thirty-eight songs in French, eleven piano pieces, and a few other pieces, is in private hands and unavailable for study. Thus it is impossible at present to provide an adequate account of Fanny Mendelssohn's childhood output. Works:

> "Ihr Töne" (song), 1819
> Other songs, arioso and recitative; chorus; four choral arrangements and eleven piano pieces; mostly preserved in privately owned manuscript, 1820–21

Tillard, Françoise, *Fanny Mendelssohn,* trans. Camille Naish (Portland, Ore.: Amadeus Press, 1996); originally published as *Fanny Mendelssohn* (Paris: Belfond, 1992).

Henri Herz (2 Jan. 1806–5 Jan. 1888)

Herz's date of birth is sometimes given as 1803, but there is no documentary evidence to support this; his age may have been exaggerated to make him more acceptable at the Paris Conservatoire. He began composing about the age of eight, and his works appeared in print in very quick succession from 1818 onward. His most common form at this stage was the set of variations; some of the sets included additional sections such as an introduction or rondo. All his works are for piano, though some have orchestral or other accompaniment, and this continued to be the case throughout his long career. By 1822 he had reached about Op. 12, although the precise date of each publication is uncertain. These early works are shown in the following list (based on Pazdírek 1957). Works:

Sets of variations (Opp. 1, 3, 4, 6–10)
Fantasies (Opp. 5, 12)
Rondos (Opp. 2, 9, 11)

Pazdírek, Franz, *Universal-Handbuch der Musikliteratur* (Vienna: Franz Pazdírek, 1904–10; reprint Hilversum, Netherlands: F. Knuf, 1957).

Juan Crisóstomo Arriaga (27 Jan. 1806–17 Jan. 1826)

Arriaga's father was a merchant, but his elder brother played the violin and guitar, and both seem to have encouraged Arriaga to develop his outstanding musical talents. He showed such striking ability as a child that he is sometimes referred to as the Spanish (or Basque) Mozart—partly because he was born exactly fifty years to the day after Mozart himself. His first known composition, entitled *Nada y mucho,* dates from 1817—a trio for three violins that later had a text and a bass part added. It was followed by an overture for nine instruments in 1818; this is known as Op. 1, although none of his childhood works were published during his lifetime.

His most notable work before he moved to Paris in September 1821 was his opera *Los esclavos felices,* probably composed mainly in 1819 and premiered in Bilbao in 1820. Most of it is lost, but the overture survives. It begins with a very lyrical introduction, with a graceful, flowing melody decorated by occasional expressive chromatic appoggiaturas and some delicate countermelody. This slow introduction is followed by a well-constructed allegro in modified sonata form, in which the end of the exposition merges into the development section without a clear division. The development section itself spends a long time in the key of the flattened seventh—a risky strategy since this key, more than any other, tends to undermine the tonic, but the ploy is brought off successfully. The style is inevitably somewhat indebted to Italian opera, with echoes of Rossini, particularly in the coda, in which there is a humorous false ending before a final reprise of the main theme.

Altogether Arriaga appears to have composed about twenty works before moving to Paris, but many of them are either lost or not precisely datable—sometimes both. They include two patriotic hymns and several sacred works. Among these, the most successful may be a *Stabat Mater* for three male voices and orchestra, which is thought to have been composed by 1821 while Arriaga was still in Bilbao. The most notable of his instrumental works is a set of variations for violin and piano, *La Hungara,* Op. 22, also probably dating from 1821, which he arranged for string quartet (Op. 23) the following year. In its original form it contains an astonishingly virtuosic violin part with a fairly simple accompaniment, and it suggests that he may have been as skilled on the violin as he was as a composer. The fast variations have rapid and complex figuration, while the slow ones make use of some ingenious double stopping, and the climax comes in the final variation, which combines both double stopping and rapid figuration. Arriaga continued composing prolifically after moving to Paris, but his career was tragically terminated by his early death before he reached the age of twenty. Works:

> *Nada y mucho* (violin trio), 1817
> Overture (Op. 1), 1818
> *Romanza* (piano), 1819 (?)
> *Los esclavos felices* (opera), 1819–20
> Variations for string quartet (Op. 17), 1820
> March (military band), 1820–21 (?)
> Two patriotic hymns, 1820–21 (?)
> *Stabat Mater* (voices and orchestra), 1821
> *La Hungara* variations (violin and piano, Op. 22), 1821

Arriaga, Juan Crisóstomo, *Obra completa 1*, ed. Christophe Rousset (Madrid: Instituto Complutense de Ciencias Musicales, 2006).

Sound Recording

Overture Op. 1 and Overture *Los esclavos felices* in Juan Crisóstomo Arriaga, *Orchestral Works,* cond. Jordi Savall. Auvidis Astrée E8532 (1995).

Felix Mendelssohn (later Mendelssohn Bartholdy) (3 Feb. 1809– 4 Nov. 1847)

Although Mendelssohn did not begin composing until he was more than twice old as Mozart was when he began, he made much more rapid progress once he started, and altogether he composed more than 150 surviving works before he was sixteen. His childhood compositions have together received more attention than those of any other child composer, with the possible exception of Mozart. Four books in particular may be recommended for further reading (see the following references). Many of the works themselves have been published in the Mendelssohn complete edition begun in 1960 by the Internationale Felix-Mendelssohn-Gesellschaft and resumed in 1997 by the Sächsische Akademie der Wissenschaften; a few others were published in Julius Rietz's earlier attempt at a complete edition. Some, however, have still never been published, notably most of the early works for the stage.

Like his sister Fanny, who was born in November 1805 (see "Fanny Mendelssohn"), Felix Mendelssohn began composing toward the end of

1819, probably a month or two before her, and his earliest surviving composition is now thought to be a sonata in D major for two pianos—apparently composed in October or November and perhaps intended for himself and his sister to play. His first precisely dated composition, however, like his sister's, is a song for their father's birthday on 11 December 1819, "Ihr Töne, schwingt euch fröhlich." Both children had already shown great aptitude for music by the time they began studying theory with Carl Friedrich Zelter in summer 1819, and Felix in particular made extraordinarily rapid progress during the next few months and years. His natural ability and diligence were greatly helped by the excellence of Zelter's teaching of counterpoint, so that Mendelssohn quickly gained a contrapuntal mastery that was inaccessible to most other child composers.

From about the beginning of 1820, Mendelssohn became extremely prolific in his output of new works. Well over a dozen chamber works date from that year, nearly all scored for violin and piano. Some are fugues that could be regarded as exercises in counterpoint as much as original compositions, but others are more substantial, including a trio in C minor for violin, viola, and piano. At the same time, he was also writing an even larger number of solo piano (or occasionally two-piano) works, approximately thirty of which can be dated to 1820, and a few songs. Again some works are very short, but others are substantial multi-movement sonatas. His most outstanding works of this year, however, were those written for the stage. Two shorter works, the dramatic scene *Quel bonheur pour mon coeur* and the *Lustspiel* entitled *Ich, J. Mendelssohn* in three scenes, were followed by the substantial singspiel or comic opera *Die Soldatenliebschaft,* which consists of an overture and eleven numbers. It was composed during a period of roughly ten weeks and was completed in full score on 30 November in Berlin according to the date on the autograph. It was tried out with piano accompaniment on his father's birthday (11 December), and with full orchestral accompaniment on Mendelssohn's own birthday (3 February 1821). The work displays great skill not only in counterpoint but, more surprisingly, in orchestration. Although he had had little or no formal teaching, he had clearly learned much from the numerous scores he had studied, and his orchestration, according to his mother, "for a first attempt borders on the incredible" (Todd 2005, 65). His orchestration is in fact not merely competent but actually quite imaginative, such as in his use of pizzicato strings along with horn, bassoon, and piccolo (Todd 2005, 66), and it effectively helps to portray the individual characters and the scenes in general.

During 1821 Mendelssohn continued composing fast and fluently, producing many more works. These included two more singspiels: *Die beiden Pädagogen* and *Die wandernden Komödianten,* the first of which was composed in only six weeks. It has been published in the *Leipziger Ausgabe* (vol. 5/1,

1966), and, like its predecessor, is a substantial work with overture and eleven numbers, interspersed with spoken dialogue. It is more comical than *Die Soldatenliebschaft,* however, and contains some hilarious moments, unusual in Mendelssohn, such as in No. 8, in which the preceptors Luftig and Kinder-schreck express support for two different educational reformers of the past by simply chanting their names for a time, sometimes very loudly ("Basedow" in bars 53–54) or repetitively ("Pestalozzi, Pestalozzi, Pestalozzi, Pest, Pest, Pest," etc. in bars 55–61). This number is also notable, however, for Mendelssohn's use of rapid staccato pianissimo strings (bars 84 ff.)—an effect he later put to good use in works such as the overture to *A Midsummer Night's Dream.* Other numbers also have striking orchestral sonorities, such as the unusual combination of flutes, bassoons, horns, and strings in No. 3, with interesting accompaniment figures punctuating the vocal lines.

In 1821 Mendelssohn also began a remarkable series of string sinfonias (or symphonies, as they are often called) that extended to the end of 1823. Although the first sinfonia is a bit primitive in places, the later ones are astonishingly well crafted and sophisticated, with rich and highly skilled part-writing and inventive scoring. There are thirteen altogether, though Nos. 10 and 13 are single movements preceded by a slow introduction, in the manner of a Baroque overture. The others are mostly in three movements (fast-slow-fast), sometimes four, while No. 11 has five. This work also has a highly original tonal design: the slow introduction is in F major, but the main allegro is in F minor, as is the finale; the second movement is in D minor, with added percussion, and is followed by an adagio in E flat and a menuet in F minor (with trio in F major). This design somewhat anticipates that of Mendelssohn's string quartet in A, Op. 13, in which again the slow introduction is in the major, but the main allegro, the penultimate movement, and the finale are in the minor, although the key structure in the rest of the quartet is less adventurous than in the sinfonia.

Some of the other sinfonias also have imaginative tonal organization, which might be combined with unusual scoring. Notable here is No. 9 in C minor/major, in which the slow movement begins in E major for violins alone, divided into four. By contrast, a central *minore* section is scored for two viola parts and bass, while in the reprise the four violins resume unaccompanied before being joined by the two violas and, eventually, the cellos and basses for the last few bars. The slow movement of No. 8 is scored for three viola parts and bass, but shortly after its completion Mendelssohn rearranged the entire sinfonia for full orchestra. This was not simply a matter of adding wind parts to the existing strings, but involved an entire reworking of the whole texture throughout. Nevertheless, he was clearly pleased with the opening of the slow movement, in which the unusual scoring and harmonic progression (which is slightly reminiscent of Mozart's "Dissonance" Quartet) remained unaltered.

Mendelssohn continued to compose with equal facility and imagination during the following few years, and by the beginning of 1825 he had finished many more works. Particularly substantial is a full-scale, three-act singspiel, *Die beiden Neffen* (1823); in the orchestral field his thirteen string sinfonias were supplemented by five concertos and his so-called First Symphony, plus a very unusual overture for wind instruments. He also continued composing chamber and piano works, together with some organ pieces; more than a dozen songs; and some shorter and longer sacred works, including a Gloria and a Magnificat. His music was also starting to be published. Three piano quartets composed during the period October 1822 to January 1825 appeared in print as Opp. 1–3 not long after they were composed, and his First Symphony was published a little later. Much was left unpublished, however, and Mendelssohn apparently came to regard his early works as insufficiently mature to be worth preserving, although this was obviously not his view when he first wrote them. Thankfully, he did not destroy them, and the manuscripts are preserved mainly in Berlin. Most of these works are actually very fine, beautifully crafted, and well worth hearing. Moreover, their style is unmistakably Mendelssohnian. The fluency and facility that one associates with the later Mendelssohn, the delightful refinement and regularity in which every note seems perfectly placed, the imaginative orchestral effects and delicate scoring, the rich textures in which accompanying parts often have much melodic interest, and the conservative approach in which tradition is valued far more highly than novelty, are all conspicuously present in these early works. Without the experience of composing them, Mendelssohn could never have brought his later works to such perfection. His childhood compositions laid a very solid foundation for his celebrated string octet of 1825, his overture for *A Midsummer Night's Dream* of 1826, and all the masterpieces that followed in the next twenty years or so, besides anticipating specific features of individual works such as the quartet Op. 13. Works:

Stage works: *Quel bonheur*, Mar. 1820; *Ich, J. Mendelssohn*, Aug.–Dec. 1820; *Die Soldatenliebschaft*, Dec. 1820; *L'homme automate*, Feb. 1821; *Die beiden Pädagogen*, Mar. 1821; *Die wandernden Komödianten*, Dec. 1821; *Die beiden Neffen*, Nov. 1823

Orchestral: thirteen sinfonias for strings, 1821–23; five concertos, 1822–24; Symphony No. 1 in C minor, 1824; wind overture, 1824

Violin and piano: at least three sonatas and twelve shorter pieces, 1820–24

Other chamber music: three piano quartets (Opp. 1–3), 1822–25; piano
  trio, 1820; string quartet, 1823; viola sonata, 1824; clarinet sonata,
  1824; sextet, 1824; shorter works
Piano music: six sonatas (including one for two pianos), 1819–23; many
  shorter works
Organ music: ten pieces
Sacred and choral works (about twenty)
Eighteen songs, etc.

Leipziger Ausgabe der Werke Felix Mendelssohn Bartholdys (Leipzig, Germany: Internationale Felix-Mendelssohn-Gesellschaft, 1960–77; Sächsische Akademie der Wissenschaften, 1997–).

Rietz, Julius, ed., *Felix Mendelssohn Bartholdy's Werke: kritisch durchgesehene Ausgabe*,
(Leipzig, Germany: Breitkopf & Härtel, 1874–77).

Seaton, Douglas, ed., *The Mendelssohn Companion* (Westport, Conn.: Greenwood,
2001). See especially the list of works compiled by John Michael Cooper (701–85).

Todd, R. Larry, *Mendelssohn: A Life in Music* (New York: Oxford University Press,
2005).

———, *Mendelssohn's Musical Education* (Cambridge: Cambridge University Press, 1983).

Vitercik, Greg, *The Early Works of Felix Mendelssohn: A Study in the Romantic Sonata
Style* (Philadelphia: Gordon & Breach, 1992).

Sound Recording

Die beiden Pädagogen, cond. Heinz Wallberg. CPO 999 550-2 (1998). Also many
recordings of thirteen string symphonies, early concertos, and some early piano
music.

(Anna Maria) Leopoldine Blahetka (15 Nov. 1809–17 Jan. 1885)

Until recently Blahetka was thought to have been born in 1810 or 1811, but
her baptismal certificate shows she was born in Vienna in 1809 (Köhler 1968,
vol. 4, 364). Her father was a friend of Beethoven, while her mother was
an accomplished pianist from the Traeg family, Viennese music publishers.
Blahetka herself began composing by the early 1820s—probably about 1821,
having made her public debut as a pianist in 1818. Her first published composition appeared in 1822 and her published output had reached as high as Op.
11 by spring 1825, but many details about her early works are uncertain. On
2 March 1823 she gave a concert in Vienna in which she played a piano concerto by Ries and her own Piano Variations with Orchestra (Köhler 1968, vol.
3, 440). Later that year she intended to dedicate a work to Beethoven (Köhler
1968, vol. 4, 195). She continued composing in later life, and achieved even

greater success as a pianist. Her Op. 6, *Variations sur un thême [sic] original,* of circa 1825, was reprinted in 1992 in a selection of her piano music. The theme itself contains several ingenious harmonic surprises, while the five highly decorative variations and coda that follow demand great technical virtuosity almost throughout.

Blahetka, Leopoldine, *Music for Piano,* ed. Lydia Hailparn Ledeen (Bryn Mawr, Pa.: Hildegard Publishing, 1992).
Köhler, Karl-Heinz, and others, eds., *Ludwig van Beethovens Konversationshefte,* vols. 3 and 4 (Leipzig, Germany: Deutscher Verlag für Musik, 1983, 1968).
Rössl, Elisabeth, "Leopoldine Blahetka: Eine Pianistin und Komponistin der Bieder-meierzeit," in *Biographische Beiträge zum Musikleben Wiens im 19. und 20. Jahrhundert: Leopoldine Blahetka, Eduard Hanslick, Robert Hirschfeld,* ed. Friedrich C. Heller (Vi-enna: Verband der Wissenschaftliche Gesellschaft Oesterreichs, 1992), 112–211.

Fryderyk (Frédéric) Chopin (1[?] Mar. 1810–17 Oct. 1849)

Son of a teacher, Chopin spent most of his childhood in Warsaw, and his first published composition appeared there in 1817. This was a polonaise, a genre to which he returned many times during his life, and it was one of two he composed that year. In G minor, with a trio section in B flat major, the piece is particularly interesting in that, if the first section is played again as a normal *da capo,* it ends in the relative major. This so astounded the editors of the Chopin complete edition in the twentieth century that they proposed concluding the piece with just the first half of the first section, so that it would end in the tonic (Chopin 1949, 153). The piece would then, however, be hopelessly unbalanced structurally, and the B flat ending is surely what Cho-pin intended. He used a similar tonal structure years later in his fantasie in F minor, Op. 49.

During the next few years Chopin wrote several more piano works, but the exact total is unclear since many appear to be lost (for a full list of those known to have existed, see Krystyna Kobylańska's thematic catalogue). At least two more polonaises survive, however, from 1821 and circa 1822 to 1824, as well as two mazurkas that were published in 1826. Also dating from the mid-1820s are a set of variations (1824) and his rondo in C minor, published as is Op. 1 in 1825. Thus a list of his extant works up to 1826 is provided here (opus numbers from Kobylańska).

The polonaises already show inklings of the later Chopin style, with their firm and fairly basic harmonic foundation embellished by incidental chromaticism and often ornate melodic lines. The rondo in C minor con-tinues this trend with some very Chopinesque features. The unison opening on tonic and dominant, answered by a rising right-hand phrase with chordal

accompaniment, anticipates similar features in the previously mentioned fantasie. Meanwhile, a highly sectional structure using contrasting keys is combined
with other typical Chopin procedures that once again blend highly ornate em-
bellishment of lyrical melody, broken-chord accompaniment, and interesting
chromatic decoration of what would otherwise be straightforward harmonies.
A chromatically descending series of decorated chords in bars 41–46 seems a
particularly characteristic Chopin thumbprint, with the tonality so disorientated
that it is almost lost completely before being quickly restored (see ex. 8.1). This
rondo and his other childhood works show Chopin to be already a master of
the keyboard, with much effective and original use of its potential in both piano
technique and overall sonority. Extant works:

> Polonaise, G minor (Op. IIa/1), 1817 (publ. 1817)
> Polonaise, B flat (Op. IVa/1), 1817 (publ. 1834)
> Polonaise, A flat (Op. IVa/2), 1821 (publ. posthumously)
> Polonaise, G sharp minor (Op. IVa/3), 1824 (publ. posthumously)
> Introduction and variations (Op. IVa/4), 1824 (publ. posthumously)
> Rondo, C minor (Op. 1), 1825 (publ. 1825)
> Mazurka, G or B flat (Op. IIa/2), 1825–26 (second version publ. 1826)
> Mazurka, B flat (Op. IIa/3), 1825–26 (second version publ. 1826)
> Polonaise, B flat minor (Op. IVa/5), 1826 (publ. posthumously)

Chopin, Frédéric, *Complete Works*, vol. 8, ed. Ignacy Paderewski and others (Warsaw:
    Fryderyk Chopin Institute, 1949).
Kobylańska, Krystyna, *Frédéric Chopin: thematisch-bibliographisches Werkverzeichnis* (Mu-
    nich: Henle, 1979).
Chopin's First Editions Online: http://www.cfeo.org.uk/apps.

Example 8.1.   Chopin, Rondo in C minor.

Robert Schumann (8 June 1810–29 July 1856)

Schumann began composing piano dances as early as 1818, but these are lost, and the only two works surviving from his childhood are two choral items dating from 1822: a setting of Psalm 150 and an overture and chorus, both with orchestral accompaniment. Although ambitious in scope, neither work has yet been printed, as far as can be ascertained, and there is little evidence of further compositions before about 1827.

Franz Liszt (22 Oct. 1811–31 July 1886)

Liszt first took piano lessons from his father, Adam, at the age of six. Adam was a clerk by profession, but an able amateur musician who had come to know Haydn in Eisenstadt before Franz Liszt's birth. Liszt quickly showed extraordinary talent, and moved to Vienna in 1821, studying the piano there with Carl Czerny. It was in Vienna that he composed his first published work, a variation on Diabelli's celebrated waltz, which appeared alongside variations by forty-nine other composers in July 1824 in a collection entitled *Vaterländischer Künstlerverein* (Beethoven's set of thirty-three variations on the same theme had appeared the previous year). During this period Liszt composed several other works in quick succession, culminating in the one-act opera *Don Sanche*. The overture to this was performed in Manchester on 16 June 1825, and the complete opera was premiered in Paris on 17 October 1825, five days before Liszt's fourteenth birthday. The Diabelli Variation shows Liszt to be already thoroughly competent at composition, and it is written in a fluent, technically demanding style that sounds and looks impressive, with its frequent hand-crossing and wide compass (see ex. 8.2). Nevertheless the figuration falls well under the fingers, like so much of Liszt's later piano music, and it clearly owes something to his piano teacher, Czerny.

Florid piano writing continued in Liszt's next few works for piano, of which the most significant are the *Etudes* of 1826. These were later adapted as the basis for the better known *Transcendental Studies* (*Etudes d'exécution transcendante*) of 1837. Another side of the later Liszt's style, his intense chromaticism, is evident in his scherzo of 1827. Here the music modulates rapidly at the beginning from G minor to F sharp minor, without even establishing the tonic at the outset (ex. 8.3; Watson 1989, 20).

Liszt's most notable work from this period, however, is surely his opera *Don Sanche,* which lasts nearly ninety minutes. According to all three catalogues cited in table 8.1, this work is still unpublished; but *NGD* claims that it was published in Paris by Chantavoine in 1912. If this is so, this edition must be extremely rare, and no copy of it has been located for the present study. A recording is available, however, with extensive notes by András Batta. As Batta

Example 8.2.   Liszt, Diabelli Variation.

indicates, opinions about this work have varied, with some thinking it so good that they "questioned whether the child could have written it," while others have dismissed it without apparently ever becoming properly acquainted with it. In actual fact it displays much imagination, resourcefulness, and a thorough command of compositional technique. A great variety of moods is evoked by Liszt to suit the changing dramatic situations, and throughout the work the melodic charm is particularly noteworthy. The orchestration is also very skillful, but it appears that Liszt had some assistance with this from Paër, with

Example 8.3.   Liszt, Scherzo in G minor.

whom he had been studying in Paris since late 1824. The extent of this assistance is not wholly agreed upon by scholars. Yet any assumption that this assistance was necessary on the grounds that Liszt had not learned to orchestrate seems highly questionable. Preparations for the premiere had to be made at considerable speed once the work had been accepted (by a jury that included Cherubini), and any assistance by Paër was therefore probably given in order to save time, rather than to cover for Liszt's supposed inexperience. (Liszt was anyway by that time familiar with the operatic world, having already published two works based on opera excerpts.) One outstanding passage occurs in which Alidor summons up a storm with a highly dramatic recitative followed by an aria in which Liszt cleverly intertwines E minor and E major. The aria also incorporates some vivid word-painting, including a downward leap of an eleventh on the word "ombres," referring to the shades of night. As the *Gazette de France* reported at the time, "The opera contains several numbers that our most popular composers would not disown" (Taylor 1986, 15).

A complete catalogue of the works Liszt is known to have composed by 1827 is provided in approximately chronological order (see table 8.1). Several are lost, and some from 1824 are known only through a reference in a letter by Liszt's father dated 20 March 1824. There is no single standard system of

Table 8.1.   List of Works by Franz Liszt

Work	AW	DW	HS
Tantum ergo (lost), 1822	717	2	702
Variation on a theme of Diabelli, 1822–23 (publ. Vienna, 1824)	12	232	147
Huit Variations (Op. 1), c. 1824 (Paris, 1825)	13	238	148
Sept variations brillantes (Op. 2), c. 1824 (Paris, 1824)	14	237	149
Impromptu brillant (Op. 3), 1824 (Vienna, 1825)	15	234	150
Allegro di bravura, 1824 (Paris, 1825)	16	235	151
Rondo di bravura, 1824 (Paris, 1825)	17	236	152
Lieder (lost), 1824	—	—	—
Rondo (lost), 1824	740	233	724
Fantasia (lost), 1824	740	233	724
Waltz in A, by 1825 (publ. London, 1832)	—	240a	208a
Trio (lost), 1825	733	393	717
Quintet (lost), 1825	734	393	718
Three sonatas (lost), 1825	741	239	725
Piano concerto (possibly two, lost), 1825	729	223	713
Sonata for piano duet (lost), 1825	772	—	755
Opera *Don Sanche*, 1825 (perf. 17 Oct. 1825)	173	1	1
Etude en 48 [12] exercices, c. 1824–26 (publ. Paris, 1826)	1	240	136
Piano concerto, A minor (lost, different from 1825, perf. 9 June 1827)	729	223	713
Scherzo, G minor, 27 May 1827	18	241	153

AW: Walker, pp. 392–459; *DW:* Watson, pp. 333–64; *HS:* Searle, pp. 51–71

numbering Liszt's works, but several systems have been devised, and three are referred to in the present list. Another list of early works is in Emmerich Horvath (1978).

Horvath, Emmerich, *Franz Liszts Kindheit (1811–27)* (Eisenstadt, Austria: Nentwich, 1978).

Searle, Humphrey, "Liszt," in *The New Grove Dictionary of Music and Musicians,* ed. Stanley Sadie (London: Macmillan, 1980), 11: 51–71.

Taylor, Ronald, *Franz Liszt: The Man and the Musician* (London: Grafton, 1986).

Walker, Alan, ed., *Franz Liszt: The Man and His Music* (London: Barrie & Jenkins, 1970).

Watson, Derek, *The Master Musicians: Liszt* (London: Dent, 1989), 333–64.

Sound Recordings

Franz Liszt, *Don Sanche,* cond. Tamás Pál, with notes by András Batta. Hungaroton, LP: SLPD 12744/5; or CD: HCD 12744/5, 1986.

Piano works in Franz Liszt, *Piano Works,* vol. 26, Leslie Howard. Hyperion CDA 66771/2 (1994).

George Aspull (June 1813–19 Aug. 1832)

A child of astonishing ability and promise, Aspull died of tuberculosis at the age of only nineteen. His father, Thomas, a violinist and music teacher, published a posthumous account of George's career along with three of the boy's compositions in 1837. According to this account, Aspull was born in Manchester in June 1813, but other evidence suggests it could have been a year later (he was baptized at Bolton in September 1814, though late baptism was not unusual). He was not introduced to the piano until 1821, but made such rapid progress on the instrument that, less than three years later, Rossini hailed him as "the most extraordinary creature in Europe." Similar praise was bestowed by Clementi and Kalkbrenner. He was extemporizing compositions in public from 1822 onward, and was noted mainly as a pianist. None of his compositions were published in his lifetime—the only ones to survive are the three published by his father. The earliest of these is an impressive 325-bar fantasia in F minor composed in Whitby in September 1830, which shows much merit, combining intensity of expression with notable motivic cohesion and a carefully balanced structure, somewhat like a grand sonata form. His father's plans to publish a second volume, which might well have included earlier works, unfortunately never came to fruition. Among George's eight older brothers, William (1798–1875) later published more than thirty compositions, but he was not known as a composer when he was a child.

Aspull, George, *The Posthumous Works of G. Aspull . . . Edited by His Father* (London: Thomas Aspull, 1837).
Silburn, Muriel, "The Most Extraordinary Creature in Europe," *Music & Letters* 3 (1922): 200–05.

Giuseppe Verdi (9 or 10 Oct. 1813–27 Jan. 1901)

The son of an innkeeper, Verdi played the organ regularly from the age of nine, and by his own account composed a great deal of music from the ages of thirteen to eighteen: "marches by the hundred for the band, perhaps hundreds of little works to be played in the church, in the theater, and in private concerts; five or six concertos and variations for piano, which I played myself in private concerts; many serenades, cantatas (arias, duets, many trios), and several religious compositions" (Phillips-Matz 1993, 30). At the age of about fourteen Verdi composed an overture for Rossini's *Il barbiere di Siviglia,* which attracted much public applause when it was performed. None of this early music is known to survive, however, and Verdi appears to have taken some trouble to destroy much of it himself.

Phillips-Matz, Mary Jane, *Verdi: A Biography* (Oxford: Oxford University Press, 1993).

Charles Valentin Alkan (real name Morhange) (30 Nov. 1813– 29 Mar. 1888)

Alkan belonged to an extremely musical family, for his four younger brothers and an elder sister all became musicians (their father ran a small school in Paris). Some of his siblings published compositions as adults—notably Maxime and Napoléon—but it was Charles Valentin who made by far the most rapid progress as a child, and he is the only one of the siblings known to have composed at an early age. His public debut as a composer took place on 2 April 1826, when he took part in a concert, performing works that included "un Air varié de sa Composition" (Smith 1976, 18). This could well have been a version of a work later performed in Liège in March 1827 and published in 1828 as Alkan's Op. 1: a set of variations on a theme of Steibelt, which was reviewed very favorably by Fétis. In 1829 another set of variations for piano appeared in print, *Les Omnibus,* Op. 2, shortly followed by a rondoletto, Op. 3. These works, written about the age of twelve to fifteen, are impressively challenging for pianists, and Op. 2 has been described as "a worthy youthful virtuosic essay exploring contemporary piano sonorities: that is, broken-octave figuration, *alla polacca* rhythms and multiple use of glissandi which are really the unifying narrative points of this set of variations" (Eddie 2007, 30). Like Liszt, Alkan soon became well known in several countries as a virtuoso pianist-composer. Works:

> Steibelt variations (Op. 1), 1827–28
> *Les Omnibus* variations (Op. 2), 1829
> Rondoletto (Op. 3), 1829–30

Eddie, William A., *Charles Valentin Alkan: His Life and His Music* (Aldershot, U.K.: Ashgate, 2007).
Smith, Ronald, *Alkan Volume One: The Enigma* (London: Kahn and Averill, 1976).

Charles Kensington Salaman (3 Mar. 1814–23 June 1901)

Salaman made his public debut as a pianist in 1828, and that year he also published two songs ("Oh! Come Dear Louisa" and "Trip It Gentle Mary") and an *Original Theme with Variations for the Pianoforte, Op. 1,* all listed in the British Library catalogue (see *Lbl*). In 1830 he performed his own *Rondo brillant* for piano and composed an ode for a Shakespeare commemoration, which was performed at Stratford-on-Avon on 23 April 1830. Although now largely forgotten, he was quite prominent in his day as a pianist, composer, and writer on music.

Clara Wieck (later Schumann) (13 Sep. 1819–20 May 1896)

Both of Wieck's parents were able pianists, and her father earned his living as a piano teacher and a seller of instruments. Clara soon developed her own skills as a pianist, and by the age of twelve was well on the way to becoming a renowned virtuoso on the instrument. Meanwhile she had begun composing at least as early as 1828, when she wrote a waltz for piano. Several of her earliest works mentioned in various documents, including her first waltz and a scherzo for orchestra, are now lost, but others were published during the 1830s. Her Op. 1, a set of four polonaises, appeared in print in 1831 after being composed during the previous two years, and several more piano works were composed and published as Opp. 2–6 between 1832 and 1836. They range from the virtuosic to the more poetic and introspective, and were generally well received. The crowning achievement among her early works, however, was a piano concerto in A minor, begun in January 1833. One movement, the finale, was completed later that year, and was performed at least twice in 1834, in May and September. The first two movements were added by 1835, and a complete performance of the three-movement work took place on 9

November 1835. The concerto was then revised in 1836 and published the following January.

A detailed examination of the concerto can be found in Lindeman (1999, 129–40). Lindeman notes that the first movement has a very unusual structure, consisting of an exposition and a developmental section but no proper recapitulation. Use of sonata form without recapitulation had occasionally appeared before (in Beethoven's Overture *Leonore No. 2,* Schubert's "Wanderer" Fantasie, and Berlioz's *Symphonie Fantastique,* for example), but the absence of any tonic recapitulation is probably unprecedented in a piano concerto. Instead the opening movement modulates near the end to E major and then leads without a break into a slow movement, a "Romanze" in the remote key of A flat major. The outer two movements have close thematic links, and the middle movement also has some thematic similarity, though this is less conspicuous. The finale was orchestrated by Clara's husband-to-be, Robert Schumann, who had by then known her for some years. But this should not be taken as an indication that she was incapable of orchestration; she apparently orchestrated the first two movements herself. Particularly striking is her use of a solo cello in the slow movement. This was one of several features of her concerto that were later to appear in Schumann's own piano concerto in A minor, and it can also be found in the slow movement of Brahms's Second Piano Concerto. Whatever defects Clara's concerto has (and she was well aware of them), it shows much originality and is unusual for having been a direct influence on other composers. Works:

> Waltz for piano, 1828
> Four polonaises (Op. 1), 1829–30 (publ. 1831)
> Three sets of variations, 1830–31
> Scherzo for orchestra, 1830–31
> Songs, including "Der Traum" and "Alte Heimath," 1831
> Etude in A flat, c. 1831
> Caprices (Op. 2), 1831–32
> Romance variée (Op. 3), 1831–33
> Lost piano pieces, 1832–33
> *Valses romantiques* (Op. 4), 1835
> Four *pièces caractéristiques* (Op. 5), 1833–36
> Piano concerto in A minor, 1833–35 (revised 1836)
> *Soirées musicales* (Op. 6), 1834–36

Chissell, Joan, *Clara Schumann: A Dedicated Spirit* (London: Hamilton, 1983).
Lindeman, Stephan D., *Structural Novelty and Tradition in the Early Romantic Piano Concerto* (Stuyvesant, N.Y.: Pendragon, 1999).
Reich, Nancy B., *Clara Schumann: The Artist and the Woman* (London: Gollancz, 1985).

Sound Recordings

Early piano works in Clara Schumann, *Complete Piano Works,* Jozef de Beenhouwer.
CPO 999 758-2 (1991). Several recordings of Piano Concerto in A minor.

Carl (Anton Florian) Eckert (7 Dec. 1820–14 Oct. 1879)

Eckert began composing by the age of five, as is indicated in the *Berliner allgemeine musikalische Zeitung* of 7 December 1825. When aged seven, having already composed a setting of *Erlkönig* (although he was unfamiliar with Schubert's at the time), he met Goethe and set Goethe's poem *Der König des Thule.* He became quite celebrated as a child composer, writing his first opera, *Das Fischermädchen,* at the age of ten and a two-act oratorio, *Ruth,* at the age of thirteen, which was performed in Berlin in 1834. In later life, however, he achieved only limited success as a composer, and became far more prominent as a conductor in Vienna, Stuttgart, and finally Berlin. Nearly all his childhood works appear to be lost, though some may survive among his manuscripts in Berlin.

Blume, Friedrich, ed., *Die Musik in Geschichte und Gegenwart, Supplement* (Kassel and
  Basel, Germany: Bärenreiter, 1949–68).
Gibbs, Christopher H., "'Komm, geh' mit mir': Schubert's Uncanny 'Erlkönig,'"
  19th-Century Music 19 (1995): 115–35, esp. 116.

César Franck (10 Dec. 1822–8 Nov. 1890)

The son of a clerk of no great distinction, Franck enrolled at the Liège Conservatoire in 1830, and began studying harmony in 1833. In 1834 he began a remarkable series of extended compositions, a series that continued when he moved to Paris in 1835. Many of these early works can be found in manuscripts in the Bibliothèque Nationale in Paris, and most were given opus numbers at the time. Unfortunately they have remained unpublished and consequently have received very little attention. Laurence Davies opines, "It scarcely seems necessary to say much about Franck's unpublished efforts" (1973, 65), and he makes only a few brief comments about them, even omitting them altogether from the list of works included in his appendix. This dismissive attitude, so typical of writings about children's compositions, seems inappropriate, for there is here a substantial body of works that deserves proper examination. Many of these works are typical show pieces of the period—"brilliant" variations and fantasies were a very common genre among pianist-composers of the period, especially those associated with Paris. Other works, however, suggest a more elevated conception, such as two sonatas, some fugues, and a lost cantata.

The opus numbers that Franck used for these early works suggest there were at least nineteen of them, but a few works and numbers are missing and seem not to have survived. One of the earliest works that does survive is entitled *Variations brillantes sur un thème original,* Op. 4, for piano and orchestra, occupying thirty-five pages in full score (Ms 8552). This is dated 1834, with the date supported by a note indicating that the composer was aged eleven. Op. 5 (Ms 8547) is a similar set of variations on a theme by Hérold, also dated 1834, with the composer noting on the manuscript that he was now eleven and a half. Op. 6 (Ms 8553) is a Grand Trio for piano, violin, and cello, dated 22 November 1834, and consists of a twenty-four-page score plus parts for strings. The opus numbers appear to have been assigned as usual in chronological order as the works were completed; thus the approximate dates of several that are undated can be deduced from their opus numbers. A complete list of Franck's early works that have so far been identified or located is given in table 8.2, and shows that his total output from the years 1834–38 is quite impressive. Although the list is heavily dominated by music for solo piano, as with several other child pianist–composers of the time such as Chopin and Wieck, Franck soon branched out into other fields and was composing music with orchestra from an early stage (probably Op. 2). A volume of compositional exercises written in 1835 through 1836 under the tutelage of Antoine Reicha also survives (Ms 1831).

Davies, Laurence, *Franck* (London: Dent, 1973).

Table 8.2. Works Identified for César Franck

Work	Date
Concerto (Op. 2; Davies 1973, 116; lost?)	1834 (?)
Grand rondo, piano (Op. 3)	1834
Variations brillantes sur un thème original, piano and orchestra (Op. 4)	1834, aged 11
Variations brillantes sur l'air du Pré aux clercs [by Hérold], piano and orchestra (Op. 5)	1834, aged 11½
Grand Trio, piano, violin, cello (Op. 6)	22 Nov. 1834
Variations brillantes sur la ronde favorite de Gustave III (by Auber), piano and orchestra (Op. 8)	1835, aged 12
O salutaris, chorus and piano (not organ)	19 Feb. 1835
Première grande sonate, piano (Op. 10)	[1836] aged 13
Deuxième grand concerto, piano and orchestra (Op. 11)	[1836]
Première grande fantaisie, piano (Op. 12)	[1836]
Fantaisie (Op. 13; Davies 1973, 65; lost)	[1836]
Deuxième fantaisie, piano (Op. 14)	[1836]
Two mélodies, piano (Op. 15)	c. 1837
Deuxième sonate, piano (Op. 18)	c. 1837
Troisième fantaisie, piano (Op. 19)	c. 1837
Seven fugues	Dec. 1837–July 1840
Notre Dame des orages, cantata (lost)	c. 1838

Sound Recordings

César Franck, *Piano Concerto No. 2, Op. 11,* Martijn van den Hoek. Naxos 8 553472 (1997).

Variations brillantes Op. 5 in César Franck, *Piano Music,* Marios Papadopoulos. Meridian CDE 84206 (n.d.).

Bedřich Smetana (2 Mar. 1824–12 May 1884)

Although Smetana began composing at an early age, nearly all of his childhood compositions are lost, though some are mentioned in his diary. At the age of four he began learning music in general, and the violin in particular, from his father, a master brewer and amateur violinist. From about the age of six he learned piano and violin from a local musician, Jan Chmelík, who wrote down Smetana's first compositions, a waltz and a galop (both now lost). His first surviving work is a thirty-two-bar galop in D for piano, written in his own hand but perhaps incomplete. It is dated 1832, though this date may not be accurate, as it was added later. Further piano compositions were written in the 1830s, as well as a few short pieces for string quartet, but the next works that survive complete date from 1840. Most notable of these is his *Louisen-Polka* in E flat; there is also a *Georginen-Polka* in D and a *Galopp di Bravoura* in B flat, all written for piano about the same time. The main importance of Smetana's childhood compositions is that they demonstrate that he felt an urge to compose from an early age and quickly reached a reasonable level of competence; but his works of this period made no significant impact in the public sphere.

Clapham, John, *Smetana* (London: Dent, 1972).

Frederick Arthur Gore Ouseley (12 Aug. 1825–6 Apr. 1889)

Ouseley is possibly the youngest child ever to compose a complete and coherent piece of music that still survives, and is certainly the youngest composer listed in the present study. His father, Sir Gore Ouseley, had been ambassador to Russia and Persia, while his mother and his two sisters, Mary Jane (who was about eighteen years older than him) and Alexandrina Percival, were capable amateur musicians who gave him much help and encouragement; but the desire to invent compositions seems to have stemmed entirely from Ouseley himself, at an extremely early age. A fuller account of his childhood compositions can be found in Cooper (2006) and also in Joyce (1896).

Ouseley's first work (refer to ex. 2.1 on page 15) is dated 18 November 1828, when he was aged three years and ninety-eight days. It was published many years later by Stainer (1889); it reappeared in Joyce (1896, 242), and again in Cooper (2006, 51). Stainer's source is preserved in Oxford, Bodleian Library, Tenbury MS 660, a collection of 243 pieces by Ouseley, dating from 1828 to 1840. The pieces are numbered 1–276, plus four unnumbered pieces, though some numbers are missing (these may represent compositions that were withdrawn). They were apparently written down by his sister Mary Jane, for he began composing long before he learned to write; but his sisters appear not to have attempted to "correct" his music in any way. Individually the pieces are not particularly substantial—mostly marches or waltzes, often of only sixteen bars—but collectively they amount to a very impressive achievement. Nearly all the major keys are used, and occasional minor keys, with a striking penchant for A flat major and minor.

Two pieces in particular from this manuscript are worth singling out. The first is No. 197, composed on 9 January 1832, a march in C major. This begins conventionally with a statement in the tonic followed by a modulation to the dominant, as if to assert that Ouseley knew perfectly well how to keep within the norms of the day, but it then contains extraordinary modulations through C minor, A flat major, E major, and E minor, and thence back to the tonic (ex. 8.4).

Such wide-ranging modulations in such a short piece would be most remarkable in any music written as early as 1832, and he must have discovered

Example 8.4.   Ouseley, March in C.

them through experimenting at the piano and skilfully assembling them into a coherent and well-structured piece, rather than by imitating existing models or instruction books. Ouseley's originality in this respect so impressed his admirers that the march was published the following year in *The Harmonicon* (vol. 11/2, 1833, 100; see also Cooper 2006, 53). A second noteworthy piece is No. 207, also published by Stainer (1889) and reprinted in Joyce (1896). This was composed two months after the march, when he was still only six, on 22 March 1832, and is a programmatic piece in A flat major and minor depicting Ouseley's experiences in a recent illness, in a vivid but thoroughly musical way. The six sections all have programmatic inscriptions, portraying gradual descent to extreme illness and back to full health. Thus the work has an almost mythic quality of descent to some underworld and back.

Later in 1832, Ouseley composed his first opera, *Tom and His Mama.* The *maestoso* introduction in C major contains some striking modulations, similar to those in the previously mentioned march, and again the key of A flat is involved—Ouseley seems to have had a special fascination for this key. His second opera, written the following year, is based on a libretto by Metastasio, *L'isola disabitata* (The Deserted Island), and William Ayrton, sometime-editor of *The Harmonicon* and a man thoroughly acquainted with Italian opera, compared it favorably with Haydn's setting of the same text. A short excerpt from an aria in this opera is quoted in Gatens (1996, 150).

Ouseley produced many other works during his childhood, and it appears that most of them still survive, albeit only in manuscript. The main sources are listed in Cooper (2006), while a fuller description of some of these sources is given in Edmund Fellowes's catalogue of the Tenbury manuscripts (1934). Further investigation of these sources would surely unearth some more treasures. Works:

243 short piano pieces (Tenbury MS 660), 1828–40
Tom and His Mama (opera), 1832
L'isola disabitata (opera), 1833
Two Italian duets, 1834 and 1836
Waltzes for piano duet, Feb. 1839
Various chamber works and a Te Deum (Tenbury MS 759), 1839
Various small compositions (Tenbury MSS 1370–73), 1833–43

Cooper, Barry, "The Amazing Early Works of Frederick Ouseley," *The Musical Times* 147 (summer 2006): 49–58.
Fellowes, E. H., *The Catalogue of Manuscripts in the Library of St. Michael's College, Tenbury* (Paris: Editions de l'Oiseau-Lyre, 1934)

Gatens, William, *Victorian Cathedral Music in Theory and Practice* (Cambridge: Cambridge University Press, 1996).

The Harmonicon: A Journal of Music, 11 vols. (London: Pinnock, 1823–33; reprint Farnborough, U.K.: Gregg, 1971).

Joyce, F. W., *The Life of Rev. Sir F. A. G. Ouseley, Bart.* (London: Methuen, 1896).

Stainer, John, "The Character and Influence of the Late Sir Frederick Ouseley," *Proceedings of the Musical Association* 16 (1889): 25–39.

Carl (Károly) Filtsch (28 May 1830–11 May 1845)

Filtsch's enormous promise was cut short by an untimely death from tuberculosis at the age of only fourteen, making him one of the shortest-lived of all child composers listed here. He learned the piano from the age of three, taught by his father, a Protestant pastor, and he later studied with Sechter, Liszt, and especially Chopin. His earliest known composition dates from 1839, and nearly all of his works are for piano solo. Several were published during his lifetime, including a group of three that were issued in Vienna as *Premières pensées musicales* in 1843 and reissued in London in 1844. Three more were published shortly after his death as *Oeuvres posthumes*. An account of his life is in *MGG* (second edition), with a somewhat incomplete work list. A fuller list of works, shown here, can be compiled from information on Ferdinand Gajewski's website (listed here), which also provides links to scores of most of Filtsch's works, edited by Gajewski. Judging by the opus numbers, however, some works may still be lost.

In his piano works Filtsch shows a particular predilection for keys with many flats: The choral, andante, and nocturne are all in D flat major; the barcarolle and first impromptu are in G flat major; the mazurka is in E flat minor; and the second impromptu in B flat minor. The etude is in F major, but with a central section in A flat. The style owes much to Chopin (though it is less chromatic), and some pieces were evidently written as homage to him. Filtsch's largest work is a one-movement piano concerto in B minor. Formerly thought to be lost, it was discovered by Gajewski in private hands in England, along with a few other compositions by Filtsch (notably an overture in D for full orchestra). The concerto, though once again indebted to Chopin (especially in its opening theme, which is strongly reminiscent of Chopin's concerto in E minor), is an impressive work. In form it follows the traditional classical concerto first-movement form very regularly, suggesting that Filtsch may have intended a second and third movement—they could even have been written and subsequently lost. Though largely diatonic, it includes some striking modulations, notably to the flattened supertonic just before the end of the exposition and recapitulation. Its second subject is beautifully lyrical

Example 8.5.   Filtsch, Piano Concerto in B minor.

(ex. 8.5) and is skilfully developed during the movement, while the cadenza ranges from flamboyant virtuosity to a serious Bachian fugato based on the main theme of the work. Works:

Choral, 1839
Andante et Nocturne (Op. 1, Vienna: Mechetti):
  1. Andante, 1841 (?)
  2. Nocturne 1841 (?)
Introduction und Variationen über . . . Bellini, A (Op. 2, Vienna: Mechetti), 1842 (?)
Premières pensées musicales . . . pour le piano (Op. 3, Vienna: Mechetti, 1843):
  1. Romance sans paroles, 1840 (?)
  2. Barcarolle, 1842 (?)
  3. Mazurka, 1842
Etude (Op. 8, Pest: Joseph Wagner), 1843
Oeuvres posthumes (Vienna: Spina, c. 1845):
  1. Impromptu, 1843
  2. Impromptu, 1843 (?)
  3. Adieu (Das Lebewohl von Venedig), 11 Sep. 1844
Concerto for piano and orchestra, B minor (1 movement), 1843–44
Cadenza for Beethoven's Third Piano Concerto, 1840s
Overture for orchestra, D, 1840s

http://www.freewebs.com/fjgajewski

Camille Saint-Saëns (9 Oct. 1835–16 Dec. 1921)

Although neither of Saint-Saëns's parents showed any great musical inclinations, and his father died when Camille was just three months old, he began playing the piano before he was three, aided by his mother's aunt, with whom he and his mother were living. He immediately showed extraordinary ability, and was reportedly improvising descriptive pieces while still only two years old. His earliest known composition soon followed, dated 22 March 1839, when he was aged just 3 years and 164 days—only slightly older than Ouseley (*q.v.*) was at the time of his first composition. It is a short, unpretentious, galop-like piano piece in C major in 2/4 time, and only twelve bars long, but perfectly satisfactory as far as it goes. It was followed by two similar pieces of sixteen bars and eight bars, in G and A respectively, the latter dated 3 April 1839. All three pieces are written in pencil in a single manuscript preserved in the Bibliothèque Nationale, Paris (Ms 855),[5] and they are thoroughly competent compositions, like all his early works.

Much of what Saint-Saëns composed in the next few years is reported to have been destroyed by him almost as soon as it was written, including overtures, cantatas, piano pieces, and songs (see Studd 1999, 6). Nevertheless, many works from his childhood still survive in the Bibliothèque Nationale. A complete catalogue of the instrumental works has been produced by Sabina Teller Ratner (2002), and it lists twenty-four items for piano from before 1850, most of which were composed in the early 1840s. The first of these is a composite item containing several short pieces, including the three mentioned previously, but other items are incomplete pieces that were perhaps never finished, such as No. 23, an eighty-seven-bar fragment of a sonata in G from 1847. Several little pieces date from 1841, including galops, waltzes, and a berceuse. Among the longer of these is a sixty-four-bar galop in G, dated 6 June 1841, while a seventy-six-bar piece in E flat probably dates from the same year or earlier. About this time Saint-Saëns also began composing songs. Three of them ("Ariel," "Le soir," and "La maman") are thought to have been written that year, and altogether about fifteen are known that date from 1851 or earlier (in some cases the dates are uncertain).

Saint-Saëns was soon attempting more ambitious pieces, notably a three-movement sonata for piano and violin dated 8 January 1842, and he began studying composition in earnest at the age of seven. By the end of the decade he was composing still larger works, including part of an oratorio *Les Israelites sur la montagne d'Oreb* (Ms 862, written at the age of thirteen, according to a note added to the manuscript, perhaps at a later date); a cantata for soloists and chorus on words by Amable Tastu (Ms 863, aged fourteen according to the manuscript); another cantata entitled *Antigone* (Ms 864, aged fifteen), for solo voices, chorus, and orchestra; and several attempts at his first symphony. In the first attempt (Ms 858, aged thirteen; Ratner 2002, no. 154) Saint-Saëns completed the first movement in B flat major, with full orchestra, and began the second before abandoning the manuscript, leaving six empty pages. The second attempt, in D major (Ms 866; Ratner 2002, no. 155), resulted once again in just a first movement for full orchestra. This was succeeded by a scherzo in A (with trio section in D), a serenata for small orchestra, and the first movement of a symphony in A for woodwind and strings (Ratner 2002, nos. 156–58), all of which were composed around the age of fourteen or fifteen. Finally Saint-Saëns produced a complete four-movement symphony in

A, incorporating a version of the earlier scherzo in the same key, when he was still only fifteen (Ms 493; Ratner 2002, no. 159). It is said to have been much influenced by the little-known Henri Reber (Studd 1999, 21), though Reber's own symphonies may not have been familiar to Saint-Saëns at the time, as they were not actually published until 1858. Largely classical in style, with echoes of Haydn and perhaps early Schubert, it shows "an engaging degree of individuality in the boisterous finale" (Studd 1999, 21).

Altogether Saint-Saëns not only began composing exceptionally early, even compared with other child composers, but he also produced a very substantial output while still a child. More than fifty works still survive from before the age of sixteen, several being written on quite a large scale. If it is true that he actually destroyed the majority of his early works, then his overall output is even more impressive. Unfortunately, hardly any of it was published at the time, and he made far less impact than he would have done if, like Mozart, he had been taken on concert tours to perform new works. A few of the songs appeared in print not many years after they were composed, and the symphony in A was eventually published in Paris in 1913 (and again in 1974), but the vast majority of these works have remained in manuscript. Hence, a proper assessment of Saint-Saëns's ability as a child composer must remain some way in the future. What is clear, however, is that he mastered the techniques of composition when very young and was thereafter thoroughly fluent throughout his life. His fluency, indeed, tended to militate against any striking originality in later years: Berlioz once famously criticized him for knowing everything about music but lacking "inexperience" (Harding 1965, 90), implying that his approach was too facile. Although Saint-Saëns actually outlived Debussy, he continued composing in a rather conservative, pre-Debussy style right to the end, always showing excellent compositional technique, but relatively little stylistic development. Works:

Various short piano pieces (about twenty-five), 1839–47
About fifteen songs, 1841–51
Sonata in B flat, violin, and piano, 1842
Melodie in C, violin, pre-1845
Les Israelites (oratorio, incomplete), 1848
Three cantatas, c. 1848–50
Symphony in B flat (one movement only), c. 1849
Le martyre de Vivia (incidental music), 1850
Symphony in D (one movement only), c. 1850
Serenata in D, orchestra, c. 1850
Symphony in A (four movements), c. 1850
La rose, c. 1850

Moise sauvé des eaux, c. 1851
Many other unfinished works and fragments

Harding, James, *Saint-Saëns and His Circle* (London: Chapman & Hall, 1965).
Ratner, Sabina Teller, *Camille Saint-Saëns 1835–1921: A Thematic Catalogue of His Complete Works, vol. 1: The Instrumental Works* (Oxford: Oxford University Press, 2002).
Studd, Stephen, *Saint-Saëns: A Critical Biography* (London: Cygnus Arts, 1999).

Sound Recording

Symphony in A, cond. Jean Martinon. EMI 569683-2 (1974).

Mily Balakirev (2 Jan. 1837–29 May 1910)

Balakirev's musical inclinations were encouraged initially by his mother, who taught him piano for a time (his father seems to have shown little interest in music). Later he came under the influence of Alexander Ulïbïchev (Oulibicheff), a noted writer on music, but in compositional technique Balakirev was largely self-taught, mainly through studying scores in Ulïbïchev's library. His earliest known compositions are a lost septet for flute, clarinet, piano, and string quartet, and a *Grande Fantaisie* for piano and orchestra on Russian folksongs, which survives in manuscript in the State Public Library in St. Petersburg. Both works were written in 1852 at the age of fifteen. The ambitious scale and scoring of the *Fantaisie* suggests that many more works may have preceded it, but none have survived.

After the age of thirty-five, Balakirev composed very little, and much of what he did write was revisions of earlier works, with his style evolving hardly at all. Instead his role became mainly that of folksong collector, teacher, and leader of the group of Russian nationalist composers known as "The Five" or "The Mighty Handful."

Abraham, Gerald, "Balakirev's Symphonies," *Music & Letters* 14 (1933): 355–63.

Max Bruch (6 Jan. 1838–2 Oct. 1920)

Although his father showed no musical inclinations, Bruch's mother was a singing teacher and his two uncles owned a music shop in Cologne; he was taught to play the piano initially by his mother. His first composition was a song written at the age of nine for his mother's birthday. Soon he was composing prolifically, producing "motets, psalms, piano pieces, violin sonatas, a string quartet, and even orchestral works" while still a child (Fifield 2005, 19).

Almost all of these early works, which also include two piano trios and some lieder, appear to be lost. One notable work that does survive, however, is a septet in E flat, dated 28 August 1849. Scored for clarinet, horn, bassoon, two violins, cello, and double bass, it bears clear features of Bruch's later style, and much skill in form and harmonic planning (Fifield 2005, 20).

In 1850 Bruch became acquainted with the composer Ferdinand Hiller (1811–85), and learned much from him in the next few years. It is from Hiller's diaries that we learn of some of Bruch's early works, including a sonata for piano duet, a violin sonata and string quintet both performed in November 1852, and an eight-part mass composed the following year. The most ambitious work Bruch completed during this period was probably a symphony in F, which was publicly performed in Cologne in March 1852 but is now lost. Whether this work is the same as the symphony that Bruch showed to Hiller in August 1853, and again the next month after revision (Fifield 2005, 21), is unclear, but it seems unlikely that he would show a work already eighteen months old to his composition teacher for inspection, and so this may well be a second symphony. Meanwhile, in 1852 Bruch won a major prize for his compositions, enabling him to study composition formally with Hiller for four years. Thus it is clear that Bruch was a highly prolific and proficient composer as a child, and the loss of such a large number of his early works is particularly regrettable.

Fifield, Christopher, *Max Bruch: His Life and Works,* 2nd ed. (Woodbridge, U.K.: Boydell, 2005).

Sound Recording

Max Bruch, *Septet, Consortium Classicum.* Orfeo C167881A (n.d.).

Georges Bizet (25 Oct. 1838–3 Jun. 1875)

Bizet's father was a singing teacher and his mother also had exceptional musical ability, thus giving Bizet an ideal environment in which to develop as a musician. He made such good progress that he was able to enroll at the Paris Conservatoire at the age of nine, and he quickly gained a reputation as a fine pianist. His emergence as a composer was somewhat slower, but his first known works date from the early 1850s. These include more than a dozen piano pieces from the period 1850–54, a lost cantata, and three songs that were actually published as early as 1854: "La foi, l'espérance et la charité," "La rose et l'abeille," and "Petite Marguerite." From this time onward he progressed extremely rapidly, and it was probably when he was still only sixteen in 1855 that he completed his first opera, *La maison du docteur,* and an overture in A. His famous symphony in

C was written in November that year, and after remaining unknown until 1935, it quickly became one of the most celebrated works written by any seventeen-year-old. Works (based on communication from Hugh Macdonald):

> Barcarolle and vocalize, 1850
> Two *caprices originals,* May and Nov. 1851
> Nine short piano pieces, c. 1852–53
> Cantata (lost), 1854
> Fugues, 1854
> Nocturne in F, 1854
> *Grande valse de concert,* 1854
> Three songs ("La foi, l'espérance et la charité," "La rose et l'abeille," and "Petite Marguerite"), 1854

Bizet, Georges, *Oeuvres pour le piano,* ed. Michel Poupet (Paris: Mario Bois, 1984).

Sound Recording

Piano works in Georges Bizet, *Complete Piano Music,* Setrak. Harmonia Mundi HMA 190 5233/4 (1996).

Josef Rheinberger (17 Mar. 1839–25 Nov. 1901)

Although Rheinberger's parents were not professional musicians, he began learning the piano at the age of five, and by the age of seven he had become organist in Vaduz, Liechtenstein, and was starting to compose. The most notable of his very early works is a three-part mass with organ accompaniment, but, although he quickly became quite a prolific composer, he published nothing until 1859. Many of his early works appear to be lost, while others survive in unpublished manuscripts in the Bayerische Staatsbibliothek, Munich, still in need of exploration. On 1 August 1853 he began compiling an index of all new compositions, but none of the early ones on the list have appeared in the Rheinberger complete edition and most of them have never been published (for a catalogue of his works, see Irmen [1974]).

Today he is remembered mainly as a composer of organ music, having written much for the instrument during his lifetime, and this was already true while he was still a child. His earliest known organ compositions are three fugues, dated 1, 2, and 3 December 1851, which have been published as Nos. 15, 6, and 25 respectively in a recent volume edited by Martin Weyer. The fact that they were composed on consecutive days shows that Rheinberger was already at the age of twelve capable of composing a fugue a day; he may even have been doing so regularly, with these three being just the tip of a large iceberg. In style they are real textbook fugues, much influenced by Bach and his disciples, and showing great contrapuntal assurance throughout. Although music by child composers often shows limited variety of texture and little evidence of contrapuntal skill, Rheinberger's fugues clearly do not fit this pattern, for they show considerable resourcefulness in varying the basically four-part textures, and the part-writing is both harmonically and melodically secure. The fugues also display something of the rich but controlled chromaticism that is often evident in his later works. Indeed these fugues provide a clear foretaste of his later works, which continued to exhibit his great fluency, contrapuntal skill, and generally academic approach, as well as a conservatism that is typical of the later works of many notable child composers, displaying no great invention or originality. There is in these later works little evidence of influence by the more progressive composers of his day.

Irmen, Hans-Josef, *Thematisches Verzeichnis der musikalischen Werke Gabriel Josef Rheinbergers* (Regensburg, Germany: Gustav Bosse, 1974).

Weyer, Martin, ed., *Easy Organ Pieces from the 19th Century* (Kassel, Germany: Bärenreiter, 2000).

Sound Recording

Early organ works in Josef Rheinberger, *Complete Organ Works,* vol. 1, Rudolf Innig. Dabringhaus und Grimm MDG 317 0891-2 (1999).

Arthur Sullivan (13 May 1842–22 Nov. 1900)

Sullivan's earliest significant musical experiences were at Sandhurst, where his father was a bandmaster for a time, enabling Sullivan to gain familiarity with wind and brass instruments. Sullivan was soon also learning the piano, and began composing about the age of eight. His anthem "By the Waters of Babylon" is thought to date from about 1850, but most of his childhood compositions belong to 1854 or later, the year he joined the choir of the Chapel Royal. From that time he seems to have begun composing quite prolifically, although most of these early works are lost, including several songs and also an anthem, believed to be "Sing unto the Lord," that was performed at the Chapel Royal in early May 1855.

Sullivan's first extant composition is the sacred song "O Israel Return," which was published by Novello in 1855. The autograph is dated 1 September 1855 (its first page is reproduced in facsimile in Sullivan and Flower [1927, opposite page 14]). It has been described rather disparagingly by Percy Young as a "thinly disguised waltz . . . hardly more than a creditable exercise by a schoolboy," (Young 1971, 70), but this seems a far from fair assessment (ex. 8.6). Apart from the 3/4 time signature, the music has little in common with

Example 8.6. Sullivan, "O Israel Return."

any waltz, with its slow pace (crotchet = 69) and throbbing quaver accompaniment; meanwhile, its eloquent melodic line and well-controlled harmonies, its effective articulation marks and hand-crossing in the piano part, and its deeply expressive pleading for Israel's return to the Lord, give little if any indication that it was composed by a "schoolboy." Even though Sullivan was in fact only thirteen years old, this is no mere "exercise." Indeed, Young goes on to compliment the composer for his "not quite expected" transition from G major back to the tonic of B minor, and notes how his "timing of effect," so successful in his later music, is already in evidence (Young 1971, 70).

The autograph of "O Israel" appears in a manuscript book that was sold at Sotheby's, London, on 13 June 1956 and is currently unavailable. According to Young, this book was begun on 3 May 1855, and contains both works by other composers and original compositions. The latter include a setting of Psalm 103, "Bless the Lord, O My Soul," for four voices, unaccompanied, dated 1856; the madrigal "O Lady Dear," dated 26 March 1857; and two capriccios for piano from later that year. Three partsongs were also composed that year, including "Fair Daffodils," which was published posthumously in 1903 and displays quite sophisticated harmony and chord progressions, with some unusually executed modulations. Sullivan's most ambitious works of this period, however, can no longer be traced. They include an overture in C minor for Shakespeare's *Timon of Athens,* dated 1857; a fugue for chorus and orchestra to the words "Cum Sancto Spiritu," from the same year; and an overture in D minor from the following year. All three works are mentioned by Alexander C. MacKenzie

(1901–02, 543), who had access to their full scores. The second overture, which was dedicated to Sullivan's then composition teacher, John Goss, received a public performance in London at the Royal Academy of Music on 13 July 1858. MacKenzie describes these works as showing much influence of Mendelssohn, but also as being "full of experimental work" that gave little sign of Sullivan's later style. It is possible that these manuscripts are still in private hands and could resurface, but until they do, the summit of Sullivan's early achievement will remain shrouded in uncertainty. Works:

> "By the Waters of Babylon" (anthem), c. 1850
> Songs, c. 1854–55
> "Sing unto the Lord" (anthem), 1855
> "O Israel Return" (song), 1855
> "Bless the Lord, O My Soul" (anthem), 1856
> "O Lady Dear" (madrigal), 1857
> Two capriccios, 1857
> Three partsongs, 1857
> Overture, *Timon of Athens,* 1857
> "Cum Sancto Spiritu" (chorus and orchestra), 1857
> Overture in D minor, 1858

MacKenzie, Alexander C., "The Life-Work of Arthur Sullivan," *Sammelbände der Internationalen Musikgesellschaft* 3 (1901–02): 539–64.
Sullivan, Herbert, and Newman Flower, *Sir Arthur Sullivan: His Life, Letters and Diaries* (London: Cassell, 1927).
Young, Percy, *Sir Arthur Sullivan* (London: Dent, 1971).

Edvard Grieg (15 June 1843–4 Sep. 1907)

Grieg's early musical interest appears to have derived mainly from his mother, who was a very able pianist. He began composing at the age of nine, but all the works of his middle childhood are lost, and the earliest now known is his *Larvikspolka* (EG 101), a short piano piece in rondo form thought to have been composed soon after Grieg visited Larvik in summer 1858. A group of three piano pieces from slightly later (EG 102) survives in the handwriting of his brother Benedicte, while a further group of nine (EG 103) is dated 5 September 1859 and is dedicated to Fräulein Ludovisca Riis. Interestingly, it is described as "Op. 17," which gives some indication of the extent of earlier losses. Later in 1859 Grieg rearranged these two groups of pieces into a new order, interspersing them with eleven other similar short piano pieces to make a set of twenty-three *småstykker* (Little Pieces; EG 104). All twenty-four (including EG 101) survive in manuscripts in Bergen and have been published in volume twenty of the Grieg collected edition.

Many years after Grieg had assembled his set of twenty-three *småstykker,* he wrote in pencil in Norwegian at the head of the manuscript, "To be destroyed after my death; must never be printed" (Grieg 1995, 65). It is not to be supposed, however, that this was his wish at the time the works were composed. He clearly wanted them preserved at that stage, or he would not have written them down (twice in many cases), and he might well have been glad to have them printed at that stage. It was only in later years that he presumably grew anxious that they might harm his reputation if they became known; yet even then he had sufficient fondness for them to preserve them during his lifetime. They are, in fact, attractive little pieces, and well worth hearing in amateur and domestic contexts. What is most remarkable about them, however, is how many features of his later works are already present. Anyone familiar with these later works would surely have little difficulty in recognizing the composer of the twenty-three *småstykker.* Most striking, perhaps, is Grieg's fondness for constructing groups of small-scale piano pieces, each with a distinctive character, in fairly regular forms. None of the twenty-four early pieces is much more than sixty bars in length, and the shortest has only fourteen. Equally striking is his famous predilection for (some would say, limitation to) two-bar units, out of which virtually every piece is built, with only slight deviations. There is little sense of longer-range development over ten or twenty bars. The pieces also exhibit some typical Griegian chromatic harmony, occasional enharmonic modulation, a texture usually of melody plus accompaniment (often chordal), and much use of the middle registers of the piano. More than with most composers, Grieg's style, though continuing to evolve in later years, preserved many notable features present in his earliest extant compositions. Put another way, these pieces exerted a major influence on his later output, and we are most fortunate that they have survived. Works:

> *Larvikspolka,* 1858
> Twenty-three *småstykker,* 1858–59

Grieg, Edvard, *Samlede verker/Complete Works,* vol. 20, ed. Rune J. Andersen and others (Frankfurt: Peters, 1995).

Sound Recording

Larvikspolka and twenty-three *småstykker* in Edvard Grieg, *Piano Works,* vol. 10, Geir Henning Braaten. Victoria VCD19034 (1993).

Karel Šebor (13 Aug. 1843–17 May 1903)

Šebor wrote his first symphony, in E flat major, in 1858 and an orchestral overture in E the following year. He must have written other works before this, and had begun studying composition some years earlier, but no details have yet emerged. In the 1860s he played an important role in the development of Czech opera, but was less successful thereafter, and since his death his music has been largely neglected.

Emile Paladilhe (3 June 1844–8 Jan. 1926)

Paladilhe's father was a doctor and music lover who encouraged him to learn music with the local organist in Montpellier from the age of six. From the age of nine, Paladilhe was studying composition with Halévy at the Paris Conservatoire, and was soon studying piano and organ there too. Information about his early works (and indeed his later works) is sparse, but his first published composition appears to be a short work for two equal voices and piano, published in Montpellier in May 1855 when he was only ten. Another early publication was a verset for organ, published by Louise Niedermeyer and Joseph d'Ortigue in their journal *La Maîtrise: journal de musique religieuse* (1860). By this time, however, Paladilhe had composed much more ambitious works that were left unpublished and seem to have disappeared. These include a one-act *opéra comique* entitled *Le chevalier Bernard,* parts of which were performed on 16 February 1859; a three-act work *La reine Mathilde,* which was likewise performed incomplete on 28 February 1860; and a grand cantata *Ivan IV,* with which he won the Prix de Rome that year. Although this prize was awarded annually to a young composer, Paladilhe was the youngest ever to win it (Berlioz, by contrast, was already twenty-six when he succeeded in 1830). Like so many child composers, Paladilhe's later music is fluent and sophisticated but conservative, and he steered well clear of the modernist tendencies that surrounded him in the latter part of his life. Works:

> *Premier hommage d'une jeune pianiste à Marie,* 1855
> *Le chevalier Bernard* (opera), 1859
> *La reine Mathilde* (opera), 1860
> *Verset* (organ), 1860
> *Ivan IV* (cantata), 1860

La Maîtrise: journal de musique religieuse 4 (Paris: Heugel, 1860).

Hubert Parry (27 Feb. 1848–7 Oct. 1918)

Parry's father was a wealthy landowner and amateur musician, but his mother died of tuberculosis shortly after he was born. After showing early aptitude for music, he studied with the local organist at Highnam Church, near Gloucester, from 1860, and was soon composing hymn tunes and Anglican psalm chants that were performed at the church. *A Little Piano Piece,* a set of variations, followed in 1862, and then came some larger church compositions. These consisted mainly of a series of about seven anthems, beginning in 1863 with "In My Distress" and culminating in two that were actually published in 1865: "Blessed is He" and "Prevent Us, O Lord." Parry also composed a Te Deum in B flat and an evening service in A around 1864. Many of his earliest works still survive unpublished in manuscripts in the Bodleian Library, Oxford, and at Shulbrede Priory, Sussex. Works:

> Hymn tunes and Anglican chants, c. 1861–63
> *A Little Piano Piece,* 1862
> "In My Distress" (anthem), 1863

Dibble, Jeremy, *C. Hubert H. Parry: His Life and Music* (Oxford: Oxford University Press, 1992).

Zdeněk Fibich (21 Dec. 1850–15 Oct. 1900)

Fibich's father was a forestry official, while his mother was a cultured woman who began teaching him the piano when he was about six years old. His first composition, a setting of the sacred text *Pange lingua,* dates from 1862 and is now lost, but during the next four years he became very prolific, writing about fifty works by the middle of 1865 when he left Prague for Leipzig, and several more shortly thereafter. Most of these works were songs or piano pieces, including several that were actually published during 1865 and 1866: *Le printemps* for piano (Op. 1), Five Album Leaves for piano (Op. 2), two songs (Op. 3), and a scherzo for piano (Op. 4). Around this time he also composed two symphonies, which he wrote out in quartet score, but both are lost, apart from a piano-duet arrangement of one scherzo. By now he had also begun showing an interest in theater music, the genre in which he was to become most successful in later years. A fragment of an opera, *Medea,* dates from 1862 and/or 1863; this was followed by an overture and closing music for *Romeo and Juliet* (1865), and a comic opera *Kapellmeister in Venedig* (1866), which was actually performed in January 1868. Unfortunately all three works are lost. Thus the greater part of Fibich's early output, including all his large-scale works, has not survived. All these losses, coupled with general neglect in recent years of the smaller works that do survive, mean that his outstanding abilities as a child composer have never been fully appreciated. Works:

Pange lingua, 1862
Medea (opera fragment), 1862–63
Three songs ("Wunsch," "König Wiswamitra," "Ende"), 1865
Piano sonata, 1865
Music for *Romeo and Juliet,* 1865
Le printemps (Op. 1, piano), 1865–66
Five Album Leaves (Op. 2, piano), 1865–66
Two songs (Op. 3), 1865–66
Two symphonies (quartet score), 1865 and 1866
Scherzo (Op. 4, piano), 1866
Kapellmeister in Venedig (opera), 1866
Five songs ("Eisblumen," "Dein Bild," "Ihr Lied," "Am Meer," and "'Wand' ich in dem Wald"), 1866
Other lost piano music

· 9 ·

Composers Born between 1851 and 1900

Frederic Cowen (29 Jan. 1852–6 Oct. 1935)

Though born in Jamaica, Cowen moved to England in 1856 and quickly showed musical ability. There seems to have been no strong musical tradition in his family, although his father was treasurer to the Italian Opera at Her Majesty's Theatre, London. Nevertheless, Cowen began composing before he was six, and his first published composition appeared shortly afterward in 1858, issued in London by Leader and Cock. This was *The Minna Waltz* in E flat major, a lively and substantial piece occupying three pages (see the anonymous article "Frederick Hymen Cowen," [1898] from which much of the following information derives). Three more works were issued by Cocks and Company in 1859 and were reviewed by the noted critic J. W. Davison in *The Musical World* (28 May 1859), though no copies of them seem to be known today: *The Pet Polka, The Daisy Waltz,* and a song entitled "A Mother's Love." Davison described the song as being "really pretty, and gives much more evidence of promise than the Waltz and Polka."

Cowen was now ready to work on a much larger scale, and around the time of his eighth birthday he composed a "drawing room operetta" entitled *Garibaldi.* This is in two acts of five scenes each, with a libretto written by his seventeen-year-old cousin Rosalind, and consists of spoken dialogue that alternates with numerous airs, duets, and so on, with piano accompaniment. It was performed on 4 February 1860, with Cowen at the piano, and a cast of children all younger than seventeen. It was sufficiently successful to be published later that year, and consists of an impressive forty-three pages of score, supplemented at the end by the full libretto, including the spoken dialogue. The written-out cadenzas found in the songs are among the most striking features, notable for their floridity and the demands they place on the young voices (see

155

"Frederick Hymen Cowen," [1898, 714] for two examples). Equally interesting is some of Cowen's surprisingly advanced harmonic practice, in which he exploits conventional chords in an unconventional way, combining them with unusual melodic lines. In the first air, sung by Garibaldi's aide-de-camp Pietro, after an eight-bar introduction, the imaginative and agile vocal line produces some remarkable cross-relations with the accompaniment—an A natural against A flat in its second bar followed by C sharp against C natural in the third—while the chord accompanying the second bar resolves in an unexpected but convincing way (ex. 9.1). The whole phrase exudes a rather rough harmonic style that admirably suits the portrayal of the life of a soldier.

Toward the end of 1860 Cowen began studying harmony with John Goss, with whom he remained until 1865, when he went to study briefly in Leipzig and later Berlin. During this period, composition continued alongside harmony exercises and instrumental instruction (piano and organ), though little was published. Among several songs from this period, the only one printed appears to have been "My Beautiful, My Own," which was sold to the publisher for the excellent sum of five guineas and appeared in 1864. Other works are known to have been performed, including a piano trio in A (22 June 1865), a string quartet in C minor (14 January 1866), and, after his return from Leipzig, an orchestral overture in D minor (8 September 1866).

The highpoint of Cowen's early career came on 9 December 1869, when, at the age of seventeen, his First Symphony in C minor and his Piano Concerto in A minor were performed at a highly successful and enthusiastically reviewed concert. Everything seemed set for a great career as a composer.

Example 9.1.   Cowen, "Oh! Who Shall Say" from *Garibaldi*.

Instead, however, he turned increasingly to conducting, for which he was much in demand. Although he composed much in the next few decades, his style did not develop with the times, and by the time he died in 1935 very few of his works were being performed. The situation has changed little since then, except that he is even more neglected today. Works:

> *The Minna Waltz,* 1858
> *The Pet Polka,* 1859
> *The Daisy Waltz,* 1859
> "A Mother's Love" (song), 1859
> *Garibaldi* (operetta), 1860
> "My Beautiful, My Own" (song), 1864
> Other songs, c. 1861–65
> Piano trio in A, 1865
> String quartet in C minor, 1866
> Overture in D minor, 1866
> "The Stars Are with the Voyagers" (song), 1867

Anonymous, "Frederic Hymen Cowen," *The Musical Times* 39 (1898): 713–19.

Davison, J. W., review in *The Musical World* (28 May 1859).

Charles Villiers Stanford (30 Sep. 1852–29 Mar. 1924)

Stanford's father was a lawyer by profession but also a capable musician, and much music-making took place at his home when Stanford was a boy. His earliest known work is a march in D flat, supposedly written in 1860. At least three songs by him were performed in public during 1863 and 1864: "Once More My Love" (C minor, 3/8, performed 16 November 1863), "A Venetian Dirge" (6 June 1864), and "When Green Leaves" (September 1864). He is reported to have written several other songs during this period, and another one ("Heroes and Chieftains") was performed in February 1867. "A Venetian Dirge" was actually published at the time, and it shows excellent harmonic control and imagination. The remaining early works are lost, apart from the march, but those performed made some impact in his native Dublin and a bright future was predicted—a prediction he duly fulfilled. Works:

> March in D flat (piano), 1860 (?)
> Three songs ("Once More My Love," "A Venetian Dirge," "When
>   Green Leaves"), 1863–64
> "Heroes and Chieftains" (song), 1867

Rodmell, Paul, *Charles Villiers Stanford* (Aldershot, U.K.: Ashgate, 2002).

158   *Chapter 9*

Engelbert Humperdinck (1 Sep. 1854–27 Sep. 1921)

Humperdinck began composing at the age of seven, with a piece for piano duet entitled *Zu Mantua in Banden* and a song for two voices and piano entitled "Bahnwärters Abendlied." During 1867 and 1868 he wrote two singspiels, *Perla* and *Claudine von Villa Bella,* which betray a developing interest in music for the theater; both are lost except for the overture of the latter. None of his childhood compositions were published at the time, and much of his early output was destroyed in a house fire in 1874.

Edward Elgar (2 June 1857–23 Feb. 1934)

Elgar's musical gifts were perhaps inherited from his father, a versatile musician who was competent on both piano and violin, and tuned pianos for a time before opening a music shop in 1863. There Elgar was able to try numerous instruments, giving him early insight into the capabilities and character of each. He began composing around the age of ten, and one of his earliest efforts was some music for a children's play or opera (see Kent [1993] for a chronological catalogue). This work as a whole does not survive, but some of the themes from it were reworked many years later into his *Wand of Youth* suites, along with other very early material including a piece called "Humoreske[:] A Tune from Broadheath 1867," which is believed to be his earliest surviving composition (*Lbl,* Add. MS 63154, f. 57v). This was used for the opening motif of the movement entitled "Fairies and Giants," and although it is much modified in the *Wand of Youth,* Elgar claimed that the music in these suites was "as imagined by the author," rather than as it had actually been written down originally (Anderson 1993, 365–66). Other identifiable early works include an unfinished organ fugue in G minor (perhaps written as early as 1869, and published in the Elgar Complete Edition [1987, vol. 36, 91]) and a few from 1872: the piano piece *Chantant* in C minor, some litanies for unaccompanied chorus, and the song "The Language of Flowers." The sketchbooks that he began using in the 1870s include some copies of music written earlier (including the 1867 "Humoreske"), and could contain further childhood compositions not yet identified. None of his early works was published at the time, however, and his impact as a child composer did not extend much beyond his immediate circle. Works:

> Music for children's play or opera, c. 1867
> *Humoreske,* 1867
> Fugue in G minor (organ), 1869 (?)
> *Chantant* (piano), 1872
> Litanies (unaccompanied chorus), 1872
> "The Language of Flowers" (song), 1872

Anderson, Robert, *Elgar* (London: Dent, 1993).
Elgar, Edward, *Elgar Complete Edition,* vol. 36 (London: Novello, 1987).
Kent, Christopher, *Edward Elgar: A Guide to Research* (New York: Garland, 1993).

Hugo Wolf (13 Mar. 1860–22 Feb. 1903)

At about the age of five Wolf began learning the piano and violin with his father, a self-taught amateur musician, but he did not begin composing in earnest until 1875. Once he had started, however, he quickly indulged in a tremendous burst of creativity, with a large number of works written in quick succession. During this period he carefully allocated an opus number to almost all his completed works, even though they were not published at the time—a few are still unpublished—and within a year he was already working on Op. 14. In addition, he had composed or begun several other unnumbered works, notably several lieder now lost, the piano score of an unfinished violin concerto in D minor, and the first thirty-two bars of a string quartet in D major. Most of the early works have now appeared in the Wolf collected edition (Jancik and others 1960); manuscripts of most of the remainder survive in the Vienna Stadtbibliothek. A list of those with opus numbers is given here, with an indication of the relevant volume of the collected edition (further details of these, and of early unnumbered works, can be found in Ossenkop [1988]).

As can be seen, there were several occasions when Wolf was working on more than one composition at a time, making a strict chronological list impossible; in January 1876 he appears to have actually written two works, "Liebesfrühling" and "Erste Verlust," on consecutive days. But they are dated Thursday 29 and Sunday 30 January respectively (Jancik 1960, vol. vii/3), and the former date is incorrect for that year. Thus "Liebesfrühling" was presumably written on Thursday 27 January, since mistakes about days are far less common than incorrect dates. Nevertheless, Wolf was composing very fast, for the thirty-five-bar "Erste Verlust" is recorded as having been begun at 8:30 A.M. and finished at 10:30 the same morning.

What is most remarkable about the list, however, is the extent to which it is dominated by the genre for which Wolf was later to become mainly renowned—the lied or song for voice and piano: roughly half the works listed are lieder, and this is a fair reflection of his later output too. As in his later lieder, each of these early ones is strikingly differentiated and individual, with the words strongly characterized by vivid word-painting and evocative moods. These range from the swell of the rushing waters in "Der Fischer," in which the accompaniment features surging demisemiquaver runs and tremolando figures in a low register in C minor, to the playful and light texture of the accompaniment of "Liebesfrühling," with hints of cuckoo calls. There is also a great variety of word-setting styles, from the syllabic and chordal "Auf dem See" to the florid, cadenza-like Rossinian melismas in "Frühlingsgrüsse." A wide range of keys is exploited, and the harmony is certainly far from "elementary" as claimed by Jancik (1960, vol. vii/3, x), for there is much skilful use of seventh chords and other discords, with some abrupt but effective modulations. Although the music is not as chromatic as in some of Wolf's later songs, with no obvious Wagnerian influence, it is by no means reactionary. Works:

Sonata in E flat/D (Op. 1, piano), c. Apr. 1875
Variations in C (Op. 2, piano), 1875: vol. xviii
"Nacht und Grab" (Op. 3/1, song), 1875: vol. vii/3
"Sehnsucht" (Op. 3/2, song), 1875: vol. vii/3
"Der Fischer" (Op. 3/3, song), 1875: vol. vii/3
"Wanderlied" (Op. 3/4, incomplete song), 1875
"Auf dem See" (Op. 3/5, song), 1875: vol. vii/3
Op. 4/1–2, partsongs = Op. 3/4–5 arr. chorus, 1875
"Der Raubschütz" (Op. 5, incomplete song), 1875–24 June 1876
"Frühlingsgrüsse" (Op. 6, song), 3 Jan. 1876: vol. vii/3
Piano sonata in D (Op. 7, incomplete), 1875
Piano sonata in G (Op. 8, incomplete), Jan.–Feb. 1876: vol. xviii
"Meeresstille" (Op. 9/1, song), Jan. 1876: vol. vii/3
"Liebesfrühling" (Op. 9/2, song), 29 (27?) Jan. 1876: vol. vii/3
"Erste Verlust" (Op. 9/3, song), 30 Jan. 1876: vol. vii/3
"Abendglöcklein" (Op. 9/4, song), 18 Mar.–24 Apr. 1876: vol. vii/3
"Mai" (Op. 9/5, incomplete song, two versions), 25 Apr.–1 May 1876
"Der goldene Morgen" (Op. 9/6, song), 1 May 1876: vol. vii/3, xix/1
"Die Stimme des Kindes" (Op. 10, chorus and piano), 1876: vol. x
Piano fantasia in B flat (Op. 11, incomplete), 1876
March in E flat, lacking trio (Op. 12, piano duet), Feb. 1876
"Im Sommer" (Op. 13/1, partsong), Feb. 1876: vol. x, xix/2
"Geistesgruss" (Op. 13/2, partsong), Mar. 1876: vol. x
"Mailied" (Op. 13/3, partsong), 11 Mar.–13 Apr. 1876: vol. x
Piano sonata in G minor (Op. 14, incomplete), Mar.–Apr. 1876

Ossenkop, David, *Hugo Wolf: A Guide to Research* (New York: Garland, 1988).
Wolf, Hugo, *Sämtliche Werke: kritische Gesamtausgabe,* ed. Hans Jancik and others (Vienna: Musikwissenschaftliche Verlag, 1960–).

Sound Recording

Three partsongs Op. 13 in Cornelius and Hugo Wolf, *Choral Works,* cond. Uwe Gronostay. Globe GLO 5105 (1993).

Richard Strauss (11 June 1864–8 Sep. 1949)

Strauss is one of the most outstanding of child composers, having begun composing at the age of only six and producing around one hundred works by the time he reached the age of sixteen. His works have been listed in several catalogues—most recently the *Werkverzeichnis* edited by Franz Trenner, which for this period indicates around thirty lieder for voice and piano, a similar number of piano works, and a variety of other compositions. Strauss's father was an outstanding horn player, and also a conductor, professor, and occasional composer. He took a close interest in the young Strauss's compositions, giving the boy ample scope to develop his talents rapidly and successfully.

Strauss's very first composition may have been the song "Weihnachtslied" (Christmas Song), if it was not preceded by the piano piece *Schneiderpolka,* which was written about the same time. The song appears to date from Christmas 1870 (some have conjectured Christmas 1871), and it has been published, like all Strauss's extant early lieder, in the appendix to volume three of the Strauss *Lieder Gesamtausgabe.* Although the text of the song was inserted into the original manuscript by Strauss's mother, Josephine, the music was actually written out at the time by Strauss himself—unlike the first works of other very young composers such as Mozart and Ouseley, whose first compositions were invented at the piano and written down by a relative. "Weihnachtslied" is a very simple setting, as befits the words (a shepherds' lullaby for the infant Jesus), but its three-part harmony in E major is perfectly crafted, and it includes a neat modulation to G sharp minor at the central cadence.

In 1871 Strauss composed or at least sketched several more songs, of which the most notable is "Winterreise," with its expressive use of tremolando figures to suggest cold and shivering. (Both the poem by Uhland and Strauss's setting are slightly reminiscent of Schubert's song cycle of the same name.) Before long Strauss was composing more ambitious works, including his first orchestral composition, an overture to the singspiel *Hochlands Treue* (1872–73). In 1876 he composed his first major orchestral work, a *Festmarsch* in E flat that was eventually published in 1881 as his Op. 1 (modern edition in Werbeck [1999]). What is most striking about this work is the richness of the orchestration, clearly anticipating the later Strauss style: the scoring includes double woodwind plus piccolo, four horns, two trumpets, three trombones and tuba, timpani, and strings. Moreover, whereas Strauss acknowledged help with the orchestration in some of his earlier works, there is no clear indication that he received any assistance with Op. 1. The most unfortunate feature in the work is a little six-note decorative semiquaver figure developed extensively, which happens to be identical to a figure much used in the finale of Beethoven's Seventh Symphony, as several commentators have observed (in some cases they say little else about the *Festmarsch*). But the figure was clearly not copied from Beethoven, since it is introduced differently, handled differently, and thoroughly integrated into the motivic argument rather than grafted on; there is also no other resemblance to the Beethoven movement. It seems certain that, if Strauss had known this movement, he would not have adopted a motif that is so prominent in it. Each of the instruments is appropriately and skilfully handled, and the structure is carefully worked out, with a trio section in A flat and a coda that grows out of the reprise of the main section.

The year after the *Festmarsch,* Strauss composed an even larger work: a four-movement orchestral serenade. Again, the literature has not always been kind. Walter Werbeck's edition (1999) includes the following disparaging passage: "Schoolbook themes of almost universally four-square structure crop up with depressing regularity, making way for equally spatchcock transitions only to reappear later more or less unchanged" (xiii). Thus pejorative terms are used to describe features that can actually also be found in major masterpieces, such as regular four-bar phrase structure, themes giving way to transitional material, followed by reprise without variation. Part of the problem is that the serenade looks like a failed symphony, for it has the four-movement structure of a symphony, complete with slow introduction, without scaling the intellectual heights of contemporaneous symphonies. But it clearly was not Strauss's aim to scale such heights, as is apparent from his choice of title, which aptly suggests connections with the dance and with lighter styles. This is an unpretentious work, closer to Rossini than Brahms in its lightness of texture, directness of melodic style, and strong, simple rhythmic gestures. The development section in the opening movement is suitably short, again recalling a Rossini overture, and if it had had the structure of a typical serenade rather than a typical symphony it would be less often misjudged. The skillful development of rising scale figures in the first movement is particularly worthy of mention, as is the very varied orchestration, with well-crafted part-writing and imaginative use of the woodwind. There is a remarkably virtuosic flute solo in the first movement, and a lovely melody for horn (his father's instrument) in the trio section. A revival of the serenade on 9 June 1964 (to commemorate Strauss's centenary) showed the work to be "a graceful piece with a pleasing texture" (Schuh 1976, 44).

Many more works followed during the period 1877–80, culminating in a large-scale symphony in D minor, most of which was completed shortly before Strauss's sixteenth birthday. The work was premiered on 30 March 1881, to considerable success. Though not exhibiting a great deal of originality, it does show a few Straussian features, such as the rich orchestration and the numerous remote modulations in the slow introduction.

Unlike so many composers, Strauss seems to have retained some affection for his childhood compositions in later life. Although he recognized that they were by no means perfect masterpieces, he allowed a few to be published long after he had reached maturity, while the autograph of the song "Alphorn," composed in 1876, was presented to friends fifty years later for their golden wedding anniversary on 19 March 1926 (Strauss 1964, Notes). A useful discussion of the principal early works can be found in Schuh (1976, 42–52). Certain other seemingly relevant titles, however, are less revealing, such as Todd's (1992) study of "Strauss before Liszt and Wagner," which deals only with Strauss's music from the 1880s, rather than the works composed as a child. Works (T refers to Trenner's [1999] numbering):

> Overture, *Hochlands Treue* (T 17), 1872–73
> Four scenes for a singspiel with piano, 1876
> Concert overture in B minor (T 41), 1876
> *Festmarsch* (Op. 1, T 43), 1876 (Werbeck 1999)
> Piano sonata in E (T 47), 1877
> Serenade in G (T 52), 1877 (Werbeck 1999)
> Piano trio in A (T 53), 1877
> *Lila* (incomplete singspiel, T 61), 1878
> Piano variations in D (T 68), 1878
> Overture in E (T 69), 1878
> Variations for horn and piano (T 70), 1878
> Piano trio in D (T 71), 1878
> Variations for flute and piano (T 76), 1879
> Piano sonata in C minor (T 79), 1879
> *Romanza* (clarinet and orchestra, T 80), 1879
> Overture in A minor (T 83), 1879
> Symphony No. 1 in D minor (T 94), 1880
> String quartet in A (Op. 2, T 95), 1880
> About thirty lieder, beginning with "Weihnachtslied" (T 2–90, passim, published in Strauss 1964), 1870–80
> About twenty-four lesser piano works, beginning with *Schneiderpolka* (TrV 1–99, passim), 1870–80
> Other vocal works, minor chamber works, incomplete orchestral works

Schuh, Willi, *Richard Strauss: A Chronicle of the Early Years 1864–1898,* trans. Mary Whittall (Cambridge: Cambridge University Press, 1976).

Strauss, Richard, *Lieder Gesamtausgabe,* vol. 3, ed. Franz Trenner (London: Fürstner; Boosey & Hawkes, 1964).

Todd, R. Larry, "Strauss before Liszt and Wagner," in *Richard Strauss: New Perspectives on the Composer and His Work,* ed. Brian Gilliam (Durham N.C.: Duke University, 1992).

Trenner, Franz, ed., *Richard Strauss Werkverzeichnis,* 2nd ed., revised (Vienna: Dr. Richard Strauss GmbH, 1999).

Werbeck, Walter ed., *Richard Strauss Edition: Orchesterwerke,* vol. 24 (Vienna: Dr. Richard Strauss GmbH, 1999).

Sound Recordings

Festmarsch and symphony in D minor, cond. Klauspeter Seibel. Colosseum COL 34 9006 (n.d.).

Two piano trios, Odeon Trio. Capriccio 10 820 (1996).

Early songs in Richard Strauss, *Lieder,* Charlotte Margiono and others. Nightingale Classics NCO 71260-2 (1995).

Alexander Glazunov (10 Aug. [29 July] 1865–21 Mar. 1936)

Glazunov's musical gifts seem to have been inherited mainly from his mother, a pianist, for his father was not a musician. Glazunov began composing about the age of eleven, but his childhood works have attracted very little attention, although most have been published posthumously. There are two songs from 1881, five pieces for string quartet, and a *Romans* in B minor for cello and orchestra from about the same time, as well as some piano pieces, but his first major work was his Symphony in E. This was begun in 1880, but was not completed until two years later at the age of sixteen, and it was further revised in 1885 before appearing as his Op. 5. Meanwhile his Opp. 1 through 4 had appeared, though these were not composed until 1882 or later.

Ferruccio Busoni (1 Apr. 1866–27 July 1924)

Both of Busoni's parents were musical, his father being a leading clarinettist and his mother a pianist, and he was one of the most productive of all child composers. Of the 303 original works listed in the thematic catalogue by Jürgen Kindermann, the first 188 (i.e., well over half) were composed before Busoni reached the age of sixteen. Most of them survive complete, although a few are lost, unfinished, or fragmentary. There are also a few works referred to in programs and elsewhere that cannot be positively identified and may constitute additional material. By contrast, much of Busoni's later life was devoted to the concert platform and to making numerous arrangements of works by other composers. These activities, for which he has become best known, left him relatively little time for composition (and his later works tend to be much longer than his early ones; therefore there are fewer).

Busoni began composing at the age of seven, and his first extant composition, a twenty-four-bar *canzone* in C major for piano, dates from as early as June 1873. The autograph score, like many of Busoni's, is in the Staatsbibliothek zu Berlin, Preussische Kulturbesitz, and the piece opens unexpectedly on a dominant-seventh chord. More piano works quickly followed—six more (and a vocal duet) were written in 1873, another seven in the following year, and more than a dozen in 1875. These are mostly short, unpretentious pieces, nearly all in C major (or occasionally C minor), and generally ranging from about twenty to about eighty bars in length. A more ambitious work is a three-movement piano sonata completed on 20 August 1875 (nearly all of his early works are meticulously dated at the end). This was the first of a series of multi-movement instrumental works that he composed in the next few years. Table 9.1 is a full list of such works up to 1882.

Aside from instrumental works, more than half of which are for piano, Busoni also composed a number of vocal works during this period. Some are songs, such as *Lied der Klage* (K. 94, 14 October 1878). Most, however, are church compositions, including three settings of *Ave Maria* (K. 67, 91, and 95) and two complete masses for unaccompanied chorus (K. 103 and 169), and culminating in a large-scale requiem for soloists, chorus, and orchestra (K. 183). Six movements of this were completed during the period from 3 May to 10 July 1881, and sketches survive for the remaining movements. Busoni had already used the orchestra in a few earlier vocal works (K. 98a, 114a, and 174a), all being arrangements of works with piano accompaniment, but he wrote surprisingly few purely orchestral compositions during the period, and no complete ones: an overture in E major for large orchestra (K. 51) that included trombones, bells, and harp was left as a fragment, as were a piano concerto (K. 110), an andante maestoso (K. 141), and an introduction and fugue on a Bach chorale (K. 186).

Thus piano compositions formed the major part of Busoni's early output, and nearly all exhibit an already well-developed style and thoroughly secure

Table 9.1.   Busoni's Multimovement Instrumental Works before 1882

No.	Work	Date
K. 22	Piano Sonata in D major (three movements, 241 bars)	20 Aug. 1875
K. 38	String Quartet in C minor (four movements, 433 bars)	23 Feb. 1876
K. 41	Violin Sonata in C major (four movements, 535 bars)	19 Mar. 1876
K. 42	String Quartet in F minor (four movements, 484 bars)	28 Apr. 1876
K. 58	Piano Sonata in C major (four movements, 448 bars)	20 May 1877
K. 61	Piano Sonata in D major (three movements, 397 bars)	5 July 1877
K. 65	Piano Sonata in E major (two movements, 257 bars)	14 Sep. 1877
K. 80	Concerto in D minor, piano and string quartet (four movements, 486 bars)	21 Mar. 1878
K. 135	String Quartet in F minor (four movements, 502 bars)	by 1879
K. 164	Piano Sonata in F minor (four movements, 963 bars)	1 Sep. 1880
K. 168	Piano Sonata (lost or identical with K. 164)	Nov. 1880
K. 177	String Quartet in C major (four movements, 1,038 bars)	19 Feb. 1881

Example 9.2.   Busoni, Prelude in B minor.

compositional technique. They are generally serious in character, and without the highly florid, decorative writing beloved of so many Romantic piano composers. Busoni's tonality at this stage is often unsettled but rarely ambiguous, and there is relatively little use of Wagnerian chromaticism. The strongest influence is often that of Bach, with a rich vein of polyphonic thought often in evidence even where there is no actual imitative writing. Chopin is also a prominent influence, and signs of both composers can be found in Busoni's twenty-four preludes (one in each key), completed in May 1881, whose structure recalls both Chopin's Preludes Op. 28 and Bach's *Wohltemperirtes Clavier*. Chopin's influence is particularly evident in the prelude in B minor (ex. 9.2), whose solemn chords and unusual chromaticism recall those of Chopin's C minor prelude—especially in the chromatically moving bass octaves. Busoni's chromaticism, however, is more pervasive and intense than Chopin's, and at times quite extraordinary for a work of this date. The following prelude in A major, by contrast, is strongly Bachian, often resembling a two-part invention, though toward the end it greatly transcends its models by an extension of the compass and enrichment of the harmony and texture. Thus Busoni, at the age of barely fifteen, was no slavish imitator of Bach and Chopin even where he was clearly influenced by them, but was able to develop elements of their style in an imaginative and original way.

Busoni played many of his piano compositions in public shortly after they were written, making a name for himself in public as a pianist soon after he began composing, and it was not many years before some of his compositions themselves were published. The first to appear was probably Five Pieces for piano (K. 71), which appeared as Op. 3 in 1877, but it was quickly followed by Opp. 1 and 2, two settings of *Ave Maria* (K. 67 and 91). Altogether twenty of his childhood compositions were published within five years of being written, as listed here. The opus numbers allocated to each, however, bear little relation to the order in which they were composed (which normally matches their K. number), nor to the order in which they were published.

Many of these works, notably the twenty-four preludes, are very fine, and several have been reprinted in more recent editions. Very few of Busoni's unpublished works, however, have appeared since his death, and there is much scope here for exploration of a very interesting collection. The two masses and the requiem, as well as the larger instrumental works listed previously, may be particularly worth investigating with a view to publication and recording. For more information about these early works, see especially books by Beaumont (1985) and Roberge (1991). Works (published at the time):

Scherzo in F sharp minor, (Op. 8, K. 62), 1877, publ. 1882 (?)

Ave Maria, voice and piano (Op. 1, K. 67), 1877, publ. 1878

Five Pieces (Op. 3, K. 71), 1877, publ. 1877

Minuetto in F major (Op. 14, K. 77), 1878, publ. 1882 (?)

Preludio e Fuga in C minor (Op. 21, K. 85), 1878, publ. 1880

Gavotta in F major (Op. 25, K. 89), 1878, publ. 1880

Ave Maria No. 2, voice and piano (Op. 2, K. 91), 1878, publ. 1879

Lied der Klage, voice and piano (Op. 38, K. 94), 1878, publ. 1878

Des Sängers Fluch, voice and piano (Op. 39, K. 98), 1878, publ. 1879

Racconti fantastici, three character pieces (Op. 12, K. 100), 1881, publ. 1882

Album vocale, voice and piano (Op. 30, K. 114), 1879–84, publ. 1884

Menuetto capriccioso in C (Op. 61, K. 124), 1879, publ. 1880

Four *Danze antiche* (Op. 11, K. 126), 1878–79, publ. 1880

Gavotte in F minor (Op. 70, K. 152), 1880, publ. 1880

Praeludium und Fuge for organ (Op. 76, K. 157), 1880, publ. 1882

Three *pezzi nello stilo antico* (Op. 10, K. 159), 1880, publ. 1882

Two songs, voice and piano (Op. 31, K. 167), 1880, publ. 1884

Preludio e Fuga in C (Op. 36, K. 180), 1881, publ. 1882

Twenty-four preludes (Op. 37, K. 181), 1881, publ. 1882

Una festa di villagio, six pieces (Op. 9, K. 185), 1881, publ. 1882

Beaumont, Antony, *Busoni the Composer* (London: Faber, 1985).

Kindermann, Jürgen, *Thematisch-Chronologisches Verzeichnis der musikalischen Werke von Ferruccio B. Busoni* (Regensburg, Germany: Bosse, 1980).

Roberge, Marc-André, *Ferruccio Busoni: A Bio-Bibliography* (New York: Greenwood, 1991).

Sound Recordings

Ferruccio Busoni, *Clarinet Chamber Music* (includes K. 88, 101, 107–08, 138, 156, 176), Dieter Klöcker, clarinet. CPO 999 252-2 (1994).

Ferruccio Busoni, *Early Piano Works* (includes K. 9, 71, 100, 185), Ira Maria Witoschynskyj. Capriccio 10 546 (1994).

Aleksandr Scriabin (Skryabin) (6 Jan. 1872 [25 Dec. 1871]–27 [14] Apr. 1915)

Scriabin's mother was a virtuoso pianist and composer, but she died before he was one year old, and he was brought up mainly by an aunt, an amateur pianist who did much to foster his early interest. He was playing and improvising at the piano from the age of five, but did not learn to read music until somewhat later. His first known compositions, both for piano, are a nocturne in A flat, which may have been composed as early as 1882 but probably dates from 1884, and a canon in D minor from 1883, which has the unusual texture of a canon at the octave between treble and bass with a soft accompaniment in the middle, and interesting three-against-two rhythms. Scriabin's lifelong preference for triple rhythmic units is already evident here in its combination of both triplets and triple time.

Several more works, all also for piano, were composed before he was sixteen. All are listed in either *GMO* or *MGG,* but the two lists differ considerably in content, with several omissions in both. Further research is clearly needed before an accurate catalogue of these works is compiled, but a provisional list is given here. Among these works, two probably dating from 1885 were published as Op. 1 and Op. 5, No. 1—respectively a valse in F minor and a nocturne in F sharp minor (the nocturne may have been revised before publication in 1890). The etude in C sharp minor of 1886 was also published fairly promptly, as the first of Three Pieces, Op. 2, but an interesting sonata fantasie in G sharp minor from the same year remained unpublished during Scriabin's lifetime. This seven-minute piece is in two sections, slow then fast; both sections use characteristic triple metric units. It shows a thorough command of sonata form and pianistic figuration, and its second section, in sonata form, contains a lyrical second subject in B major that returns in A flat major in the recapitulation, before the coda reverts to the tonic minor. Although it is in places very reminiscent of Chopin, its complex and technically challenging textures clearly foreshadow Scriabin's later style. His penchant for unusual keys is also very much in evidence during this early period, for key signatures with four or five sharps or flats often appear. This tendency culminated in six flats in his sonata in E flat minor of 1887–89, the first movement of which was published in revised form as an *Allegro appassionato,* Op. 4, in 1892. Many of the unpublished works have been issued posthumously, while manuscripts of the remainder can be found in the National Scriabin Memorial Museum in Moscow. Works:

Canon in D minor, 1883
Nocturne in A flat, 1884 (?)
Valse in F minor, 1885

Nocturne in F sharp minor, 1885
Fuga, 1885–86
Etude in C sharp minor, 1886
Mazurka in C, 1886
Scherzo in E flat, 1886
Scherzo in A flat, 1886
Sonata fantasie in G sharp minor, 1886
Valse in C sharp minor, 1886
Valse in D flat, 1886
Valse in G sharp minor, 1886
Ballade in B minor, 1887
Etude in D flat, incomplete, 1887
Sonata in C sharp minor, incomplete, 1887
Valse impromptu in E flat, 1887
Yegorova variations, 1887
Sonata in E flat minor, 1887–89

Bowers, Faubion, *Scriabin*, 2 vols. (Tokyo and Palo Alto, Calif.: Kodansha, 1969).
Macdonald, Hugh, *Skryabin* (Oxford: Oxford University Press, 1987).

Sound Recording

Piano works in *The Early Scriabin,* Stephen Coombs. Hyperion CDA 67149 (2000).

Ralph Vaughan Williams (12 Oct. 1872–26 Aug. 1958)

There was no strong musical tradition in Vaughan Williams's family, but after moving from Gloucestershire to Surrey around the age of three after the death of his father, he began learning piano and music theory from an aunt. His first attempt at composition was a four-bar piano piece in C major dating from 1878 entitled *The Robin's Nest,* and headed "by mr R Williams" (see facsimile in Kennedy [1964, plate 1]). Curiously, it begins with the same theme as Ouseley's first composition (written at the age of three), though the key is different. An exercise book dated 5 June 1882 contains several more short pieces by Vaughan Williams, which were probably composed over an extended period rather than just in 1882. They include a few to which he gave opus numbers, such as a sonata in three movements, Op. 4, and a *Grand Marche des Bramas,* Op. 10 (Kennedy 1996, 1–2). Some numbers are not used, however, suggesting that other works from this period are lost.

Vaughan Williams continued composing at secondary school, where his most significant work was a piano trio in G major, performed on 5 August

1888. This met with no great success, however, and the score does not appear to survive. None of his childhood works was published at the time, and they have since been almost completely neglected: his earliest compositions listed in *NGD* date from 1891 or later.

Kennedy, Michael, *A Catalogue of the Works of Ralph Vaughan Williams*, 2nd ed. (Oxford: Oxford University Press, 1996).
———, *The Works of Ralph Vaughan Williams* (London: Oxford University Press, 1964).

Max Reger (19 Mar. 1873–11 May 1916)

Reger learned music initially from his father, a schoolteacher who could play several instruments and had published a book on harmony. Reger seems not to have begun composing until around the age of fifteen, but after a visit to Bayreuth in August 1888 he embarked rapidly on a series of ambitious compositions. The most notable of his childhood works is a three-movement string quartet in D minor, composed from winter 1888 to early 1889, which was published posthumously in volume twenty-five of the Reger complete edition. It is remarkable for adding a double bass in the finale, though Reger specifies that the instrument should if possible be one of half size, so as not to swamp the others, and it does relatively little beyond simply reinforcing the bass line. The quartet has generally thick textures and frequent use of "layered" counterpoint, in which two, three, or even four different types of figuration are being played simultaneously by the four instruments. Both these features are prominent in Reger's later music (Grim 1988, 5). The first movement is essentially in sonata form, but it tends to fall into distinct sections, each with its own character, resulting in many sharp contrasts and considerable variety of style overall. The adagio in B flat starts extremely slow and relaxed, but builds to an agitated middle section and back to a gentle conclusion. The finale is again full of contrast, from a very dynamic opening to a slow, chorale-like second subject in F major in plain four-part block chords. Other works by Reger from his late childhood include an overture in B minor (now possibly lost), and a scherzo in G minor for flute and string quintet.

Grim, William E., *Max Reger: A Bio-Bibliography* (Westport, Conn.: Greenwood, 1988).
Reger, Max, *Sämtliche Werke*, vol. 25, ed. Hermann Grabner (Wiesbaden, Germany: Breitkopf & Härtel, c. 1960).

Serge Rachmaninoff (1 Apr. [20 Mar.] 1873–28 Mar. 1943)

Both of Rachmaninoff's parents were capable pianists, and he was initially taught piano and theory by his mother. He began composing about 1886. A piano piece in D minor sometimes dated 1884 probably dates from 1886 or later (Threlfall and Norris 1982, no. II/14). A lost etude (II/10) may also date from that year, and a short song without words (II/11) was one of ten composed around that time and the only one that survives, Rachmaninoff having written it out from memory in 1931. Much more impressive than anything he had previously written, however, was an orchestral scherzo in D minor (II/40) of February 1887, though this owes much to Mendelssohn's Scherzo in *A Midsummer Night's Dream.*

Later the same year Rachmaninoff composed his first significant piano pieces, a group of four (II/12) entitled *Romance, Prélude, Mélodie,* and *Gavotte,* and described on the manuscript as Op. 1. The manuscript is dated 1887 in an unidentified hand, but there is no reason to doubt the date. In November of that year he began a set of three nocturnes, which were completed in January 1888. These early piano pieces are clearly influenced by Tchaikovsky, but they also display a firm grasp of pianistic figuration and fine melodic invention—features that continued to be prominent in Rachmaninoff's later music. After these piano pieces he embarked on a much more ambitious work, a three-act opera entitled *Esmeralda* (II/72), but only small sections of this were ever written, and only in piano score. No other large-scale works were composed at this time, and his first full opera, the one-act *Aleko,* was not completed until 1892. Works:

> Piano piece in D minor, 1886 (?)
> Etude in F sharp, c. 1886
> Ten Songs without Words, c. 1886
> Scherzo in D minor for orchestra, 1887
> Four pieces, Op. 1, 1887
> Three nocturnes, 1887–88
> *Esmeralda* (unfinished opera), 1888

Norris, Geoffrey, "Rakhmaninov's Apprenticeship," *The Musical Times* 124 (1983): 602–05.
Threlfall, Robert, and Geoffrey Norris, *A Catalogue of the Compositions of S. Rachmaninoff* (London: Scolar, 1982).

Sound Recordings

Four pieces Op. 1, Three Nocturnes, in Serge Rachmaninov, *Piano Works,* vol. 7, Idil Biret. Naxos 8 553004 (1996). Several recordings of Scherzo in D minor.

Arnold Schoenberg (13 Sep. 1874–13 July 1951)

Neither of Schoenberg's parents was very musical, but he began learning the violin at the age of eight, and shortly after that began composing elementary violin duets (see Schoenberg 1952), though most of these are now lost. The few other compositions that survive from his childhood might well have been destroyed by Schoenberg himself, had they not been saved by his cousin Hans Nachod, who passed them to Ena Steiner, who in turn described them in an article in 1974. Steiner notes an eighty-one-bar romance for two violins and viola, labelled "Opus 1," which Schoenberg apparently composed around the age of thirteen or fourteen, and from the same period an eighty-eight-bar *Nocturne für kleines Orchester,* of which the second-violin part and a piano arrangement survive. The opening of this, quoted by Steiner, is quite striking in that it seems to suggest G major before settling into B minor. Less helpful are Steiner's comments about how Schoenberg must have struggled at first to learn how to write four-bar phrases, and how he betrayed his inexperience by placing his downward stems on the "wrong" side of the notes. Such comments seem unduly patronizing, like those in so many other accounts of children's compositions; placing downward stems on the right-hand side of notes was actually a common feature in handwritten music of that time.

Virtually no other compositions from Schoenberg's childhood are known to survive, except a few ländler for piano (whose opening bars are quoted by Steiner) and a violin polka. Thus the total is quite small and insignificant for a composer who was to play a leading role in the development of music in the early twentieth century. What does survive exhibits a certain awkwardness of style that contrasts with the fluency of some child composers, though this feature is not necessarily a weakness and may be a pointer toward Schoenberg's later music.

Schoenberg, Arnold, "My Evolution," *The Musical Quarterly* 38 (1952): 517–27.
Steiner, Ena, "Schoenberg's Quest: Newly Discovered Works from His Early Years," *The Musical Quarterly* 60 (1974): 401–20.

Charles Ives (20 Oct. 1874–19 May 1954)

Ives began learning music from his father, an able and versatile musician, at the age of five, and the father's predilection for using mind-stretching and ear-stretching exercises (using two keys simultaneously, for example) in order to develop the son's musical abilities are legendary. Ives quickly absorbed the influences of at least three musical traditions: church music (he became a paid church organist when only thirteen), American light music (his father was a bandmaster among other things), and European Classical music. He began composing about the age of twelve, and all three traditions quickly became apparent in his music, with more than one sometimes appearing within a single work. He had written more than a dozen works in several different genres by 1890, but the dates of most are very uncertain: Ives's own retrospective datings made around the 1920s are not always reliable or even consistent, and his works also frequently underwent revision, so that the surviving manuscripts do not always represent the original date of composition. Fifteen works are dated to 1890 or earlier by Geoffrey Block, who catalogued them as W17, 66–67, 85, 102–107, 125, and 245–248. They have since been renumbered in a more recent catalogue by James B. Sinclair, as 28, 120, 109, 52, 149, 170, 159, 178, 164, 144, 202, 349, 212, 205, and 246 respectively. Sinclair, however, dates some of these works to slightly later years, while adding a few extra ones not in Block, such as a hymn and chant, Op. 2, and a minuetto, Op. 4. More detailed comments on some of these early works are provided in a dissertation by Laurence Wallach (1973).

Ives's first work to attract attention was a march for small orchestra entitled *Holiday Quickstep,* which was composed in December 1887 and performed publicly in Danbury, Connecticut, on 16 January 1888. Written within the light-music tradition, it was given a very favorable review in the local newspaper, which described Ives as a "musical genius." Two other similar pieces of popular music, a New Year's dance and a march (S 120 and S 109), are scored for piano. Another early work is a fantasia on "Jerusalem the Golden" (the well-known hymn tune by Alexander Ewing). This is described by Block as being for organ, but Sinclair points out that it is not really organ music but a short score of a work for unspecified medium, which would work on an organ only with some difficulty. Nevertheless, the use of a hymn tune as the basis for the composition clearly places it within the church-music tradition, and foreshadows many later Ives works that make use of similar tunes. Several other church pieces for choir and organ were also composed around this time. Works with a more Classical orientation include the aforementioned minuetto, which may date from as early as 1886; the song "This Year's at the Spring," a four-part setting of words by Browning, which Sinclair dates as circa 1892 (S 202); and the song "Slow March," which paraphrases the Dead March from Handel's *Saul* in its introduction and postlude, and which was eventually published by Ives as the last of his collection of *114 Songs* in 1922. Some of the harmony in the early works could be described as either experimental or incompetent (the chant, Op. 2, No. 2, seems particularly poor), but much of it is in a conventional and rather Romantic vein, with little sign of the chromaticism of some of Ives's later music. As with many composers, therefore, Ives's childhood compositions exhibit several features that remained distinctive aspects of his style, but these features were developed alongside new ones in later works. Works (S refers to Sinclair's numbering):

Minuetto Op. 4, piano (S 119), 1886
New Year's Dance, piano (S 120), 1886–87

Holiday Quickstep, six instruments (S 28), 1887
Hymn and chant, Op. 2/1–2, four voices (S 168, 163), July 1887
"Slow March" (song, S 349), c. 1887–88
Psalm 42 (S 149), c. 1885–88 (or later)
Fantasia on "Jerusalem the Golden," band (S 52), 1888
"At Parting" (song, S 212), 1888 or later
"Hear My Prayer" (song, S 355c), c. 1889–90
Other works (S 109, 144, 159, 164, 170, 178, 202, 205, 212, 246) may
date from 1890 or before, at least in early, lost versions.

Block, Geoffrey, *Charles Ives: A Bio-Bibliography* (New York and London: Greenwood, 1989).
Sinclair, James B., *A Descriptive Catalogue of the Music of Charles Ives* (New Haven, Conn.: Yale University Press, 1999).
Wallach, Laurence, *The New England Education of Charles Ives* (Ph.D. diss., Columbia University, 1973).

Samuel Coleridge-Taylor (15 Aug. 1875–1 Sep. 1912)

The illegitimate son of a doctor from Sierra Leone, Coleridge-Taylor was raised in Croydon by his English mother. There was no strong musical tradition, but his mother was evidently gifted musically, for all four of her children showed musical aptitude, and her father, Benjamin Holmans, was a violinist who gave Coleridge-Taylor his first music lessons on the violin. The boy was beginning to compose violin melodies by the age of eleven, and after joining the local church choir he composed a Te Deum, his first substantial work, in 1890. All these early efforts are now lost, but the following year he wrote an anthem, "In Thee O Lord," which was promptly published by Novello when Coleridge-Taylor was only sixteen. The anthem was described as a "melodious and very vocal setting" in *The Musical Times* (1898, 600), and possesses a "sweet harmonious chromaticism" typical of the composer (Self 1995, 18). Novello published four more of his anthems in 1892, but all his other known works are later.

Self, Geoffrey, *The Hiawatha Man: The Life and Work of Samuel Coleridge-Taylor* (Aldershot, U.K.: Scolar, 1995).

William Hurlstone (7 Jan. 1876–30 May 1906)

Hurlstone was initially taught the piano by his mother, but had had no instruction in composition when he published a set of *Five Easy Waltzes* for piano at the age of nine. No copy of this can be found in the British Library, however, and its circulation must have been very small. He presumably continued composing intermittently in the following few years, but nothing more is heard of his output until around the time when he entered the Royal College of Music in 1894. His manuscripts are now preserved there, but it is doubtful whether any date back to his childhood.

Louis Aubert (19 Feb. 1877–9 Jan. 1968)

The treble soloist in the first performance of Fauré's Requiem, Aubert published two songs at the age of fifteen but the rest of his output dates from somewhat later. Works:

> "Sous bois," 1892
> "Vieille chanson espagnole," 1892

Nicolas (Nikolay) Medtner (Metner) (5 Jan. 1880 [24 Dec. 1879]– 13 Nov. 1951)

Medtner's father was a successful businessman, but Medtner began learning the piano from his mother at the age of six. It appears that he was starting to compose by the age of nine, though nothing survives from that time. In 1892 he insisted on training to become a musician, and his parents reluctantly agreed. That same year he produced a list of seventeen compositions, numbered as Opp. 1–17, though virtually nothing survives of them and they may merely have been projected or planned. The precision of the titles, however, such as Second Song without Words (*Gondelied*), Op. 4, suggests that these works were already more or less composed in his head, even if he had not actually yet written them down. A second list of six further works, numbered Opp. 1–6, was compiled shortly afterward, followed by a third list from the period 1892–95, which includes some thematic material but no complete works (Martyn 1995, 4–5). These works, too, have some detailed titles and keys, and may have been partly or fully written out, but the only complete work surviving from his childhood appears to be an *Adagio funebre (cacofoniale)* for piano, of 1894 and 1895. Several more piano pieces date from around 1896, and some of these are dated 1895–96 in *NGD*, but Martyn places none of them before March 1896. The most striking feature about Medtner's early output is its emphasis on piano compositions, while the title "cacofoniale" can be seen as "a hint of the penchant for unusual Italian terms that came to be an intriguing feature of Medtner's titles" (Martyn 1995, 9).

Martyn, Barrie, *Nicolas Medtner: His Life and Music* (Aldershot, U.K.: Scolar, 1995).

Ernest Bloch (24 July 1880–15 July 1959)

Neither of Bloch's parents showed strong musical inclinations, his father being a businessman, and Bloch's first significant musical experiences were at the synagogue in his native Geneva. He then studied the violin and composition before leaving home at the age of sixteen. He did not begin composing particularly early, and his first known works date from 1895; once he had started, however, he composed several substantial and ambitious works in quick succession. The earliest works are still unpublished, but the manuscripts survive in the Library of Congress in Washington, D.C., and have been listed by David L. Sills (1986). Nearly all are meticulously dated, enabling Bloch's progress to be monitored.

The earliest work is the first movement of a string quartet, written at the age of fourteen and dated May 1895. The rest of the quartet was completed by 1 February the following year. Meanwhile, Bloch had completed the short score of a *Symphonie funèbre,* written from 11 September to 17 September 1895 and consisting of a single-movement maestoso that appears never to have been fully orchestrated. An eleven-page *Pastorale* for piano followed (March 1896), but by far his most important early work was a *Symphonie orientale.* This large-scale work of eighty-seven pages in full score is sometimes said to have been composed during the period 1894–96, but the manuscript makes clear that the first movement was begun on 19 April 1896 and finished on 5 May. The remaining two movements were completed by 20 July, a few days before Bloch's sixteenth birthday, but the three movements form only the first part of a projected six-movement work. No trace remains of the other movements, apart from their titles. Oriental elements in the three existing movements are reflected in titles such as "Caravane en Marche" and "l'Oasis," as well as some use of traditional Jewish tunes within a generally Romantic idiom.

From this time onward Bloch became quite prolific, with about eight works dated 1897. In his later period the vaguely Oriental leanings already present in his *Symphonie orientale* (and in a slightly later orchestral piece, *Orientale,* of 1898) became crystallized into explicitly Jewish and Hebraic elements, and the Jewish aspects of his style have been the subject of much investigation. Some of these elements clearly originated in the music he composed before he was sixteen. Works:

> String quartet (first movement), May 1895
> *Symphonie funèbre* (one movement, short score), Sep. 1895
> String quartet (completed), Feb. 1896
> *Pastorale* for piano, Mar. 1896
> *Symphonie orientale* (first three of projected six movements), completed
>   July 1896

Chapman, Ernest, "Ernest Bloch," *The Musical Times* 75 (1934): 121–23.
Sills, David L., "Bloch Manuscripts at the Library of Congress," *Notes* 42 (1986): 726–53.

Béla Bartók (25 Mar. 1881–26 Sep. 1945)

Bartók's parents were teachers and amateur musicians, and his mother taught him piano from the age of five. His first compositions date from four years later, in 1890, and his extensive early output has been documented in detail by Denis Dille (1976). By 1894 Bartók had composed thirty-two works, all for piano. He listed them all in two separate lists that show only minor discrepancies, and allocated opus numbers from 1 to 32. Op. 32 was a substantial sonata in G minor in three or four movements (it is unclear whether a scherzo in the same key is part of the sonata, though it probably is), and Bartók renumbered it as Op. 1 in a new series, the implication being that all the previous works could now be discounted (a similar approach can be found with a few other child composers). The second series eventually extended to Op. 21 by 1898, as noted in a third list, after which he composed several unnumbered pieces before a third and final Op. 1 appeared in 1904. The second series is again dominated by piano works, but it includes two violin sonatas (Opp. 5 and 17), three further works for violin (Opp. 7–9), two string quartets (Opp. 10 and 11), a piano quintet (Op. 14), and a late piano quartet from 1898 (Op. 20). Unfortunately, all of these chamber works are lost except for the two violin sonatas and the piano quartet.

Bartók's early preference for short piano pieces recalls a similar tendency in Grieg's early works, but Bartók's pieces are on average much longer than Grieg's. Although many of them are dances (waltz, mazurka, polka, and ländler are all represented), they are usually developed at some length. Even Op. 1, a waltz in D major, extends to ninety-six bars, whereas Grieg had never gone much beyond sixty bars. Much the longest is *A Duna folyása* (The Course of the Danube), Op. 20, a large-scale programmatic work of 573 bars and lasting more than seventeen minutes in performance. It divides into about twelve sections, each depicting a different stage of the river from its source to its mouth, although the connection between the musical style of the themes and the underlying poetic idea is not always obvious. The piece was composed at the age of eleven and was first performed in public by Bartók in May 1892, to much applause. It may have been revised later, and was also arranged for violin and piano around 1894.

All of Bartók's childhood compositions remained unpublished at the time, and hardly any have been published since. A rare exception is a *Klavierstück* in B minor from a set of three composed in early 1897 (Op. 13 in Bartók's second series), which has appeared in *The Young Bartók* (Dille

Example 9.3.   Bartók, *Változó darab*.

1965, 1–3). (All the remaining items in this collection are of later date.) A charming if unpretentious piece, it shows a clear grasp of pianistic style and harmonic control, but nothing particularly exceptional. Most significant in these early works, including this *Klavierstück,* is the characteristic texture that so often prevails, with a right-hand melody supported by firm left-hand chords, often of only two notes. This type of texture, combined with small-scale, dance-related forms, reappears in several later Bartók pieces such as some in his famous *Mikrokosmos* collection. The sound of the very early *Változó darab op. 2* of 1890 (ex. 9.3, from Dille 1965, 53) is notably forward-looking and probably quite new, even though one can find precursors of it in much piano music of the nineteenth century; and its textural similarity to his "Peasant Dance," No. 128 from *Mikrokosmos* (ex. 9.4, showing bars 5–8), is conspicuous. The main difference between these two extracts is the harmonic idiom, but it is surprising how Bartókian the first extract sounds if, for instance, one adds a two-flat key signature to the right-hand part; indeed, its resemblance to the second extract then becomes quite uncanny in many ways. Thus what Bartók discovered as a child composer was to remain with him for many years. Works:

> Nineteen short piano pieces, Opp. 1–19 (first series), 1890–91
> *A Duna folyása* (The Course of the Danube), Op. 20 (first series), 1890–94
> Eleven short piano pieces, Opp. 21–31 (first series), 1891–94
> Piano sonata in G minor, Op. 32 (first series), Op. 1 (second series), 1894
> Two short piano pieces, Opp. 2 and 4 (second series), 1895
> Piano sonata in F, Op. 3 (second series), 1895
> Violin sonata in C minor, Op. 5 (second series), 1895
> Piano sonata in C, Op. 6 (second series), 1895

Example 9.4.   Bartók, "Peasant Dance" from *Mikrokosmos*.

Three short pieces for violin, Opp. 7–9 (second series), 1895–96
String quartets in B flat and C minor, Opp. 10 and 11 (second series), 1896
Andante, scherzo, and finale, Op. 12 (second series), 1897
Three piano pieces, Op. 13 (second series), 1897
Note: Opp. 14–21 (second series) date from after March 1897

Dille, Denis, *Thematisches Verzeichnis der Jugendwerke Béla Bartóks 1890–1904,* 2nd ed. (Kassel, Germany: Bärenreiter, 1976)
Dille, Denis, ed., *The Young Bartók: Piano Pieces* (Budapest: Editio Musica, 1965).

George (Gheorghe) Enescu (19 Aug. 1881–3 or 4 May 1955)

Enescu is undoubtedly one of the most naturally talented of all twentieth-century composers, and was described by Sir Yehudi Menuhin in 1990 as "the greatest musician . . . I have ever experienced" (Malcolm 1990, 9; most of the following information is derived from this book). Not surprisingly, this talent exhibited itself at an unusually early age. Although Enescu's father could play the violin and sing, and his mother could play the guitar and piano, neither was a professional musician and Enescu's early upbringing in the Romanian countryside might not seem a likely environment for a prospective composer. But he began playing the violin at the age of four, and as soon as he had begun learning the piano and musical notation at the age of five he started composing. His first known piece, a twenty-four-bar "opera" for violin and piano, was written in 1886, and was followed in 1887 by a waltz for piano.

Enescu's exceptional ability enabled him to enroll at the Vienna Conservatoire in 1888, and he graduated in 1893, though he remained there for another year. During his time at the conservatoire he composed more than a dozen works, including three orchestral overtures, some piano works, and a quartet for four violins, plus other chamber music. In 1895 he moved to the Paris Conservatoire, where he remained until 1899, mostly using the French form of his name, Georges Enesco. During his first two years there the extent of his output increased sharply. Three symphonies were written in 1895 and 1896 (plus a fourth in 1898), and the first two movements of his only violin concerto were composed during the same period; the first movement was performed in March 1896, though he never wrote a final third movement. Two more orchestral overtures, one "tragic" and the other "triumphal," date from the same period, while vocal music was represented by two cantatas (*La Vision de Saül* and *Ahasvérus,* both dating from 1895); chamber music was represented by a violin sonata and a piano quintet plus other works. Altogether, by the time he reached the age of sixteen he had composed at least fifty works, several of them of considerable size, as well as of undoubted quality. Massenet described the first symphony, in D minor, as "very remarkable, extraordinary for his instinct for development," and he praised *La Vision de Saül* for display-ing "an instinct for symphonic writing, development, unity, and a very true conception from the dramatic point of view" (Malcolm 1990, 50). It seems clear that by the end of 1895, if not before, Enescu was already a thorough master of the art of composition.

None of the works produced before 1897 seems to have been written with publication in mind, and indeed nearly all of them are still unpublished, though thankfully Enescu preserved the manuscripts of most of them and they are now in the Enescu Museum in Bucharest. Two short piano pieces (a prelude and a scherzo from 1896) were eventually published in 1898, and a four-part fugue from about the same time appeared in 1900, but the big break-through in terms of publication came with works composed in 1897. Enescu was by now ready to launch himself officially as a composer, and his Op. 1 was a symphonic suite for orchestra entitled *Poème Roumain* written that year. A somewhat programmatic piece incorporating some Romanian folk tunes, it was first performed with great success in Paris in January 1898, and it met with even greater success when he conducted it in Bucharest two months later. Roughly contemporary with the *Poème Roumain* were a violin sonata (Op. 2) and a *Suite dans le style ancien* for piano (Op. 3), completed respectively on 2 June and 6 May 1897. These two works came out in 1898, although Op. 1 was delayed until the following year.

Like many child composers, his late works are more retrospective than progressive, and this may be one reason for the relative neglect of his work today. This neglect has meant that his childhood works are even less likely to be published and to receive the attention that they apparently deserve. Works (from Malcolm 1990):

> *Opera,* violin and piano, 1886
> Waltz, piano, 1887
> *Pièce d'église,* piano, 1889
> Three orchestral overtures, 1891–94
> Quartet for four violins, 1894
> Suite for two violins, 1894
> Symphony No. 1 in D minor, 1895
> Two cantatas (*Vision de Saül, Ahasvérus*), 1895
> *Tragic Overture,* 1895
> Symphony No. 2 in F, 1895
> Violin concerto (two movements only), 1896

Symphony No. 3 in F, 1896
Triumphal Overture, 1896
Piano quintet, 1896
Fantaisie for piano and orchestra, 1896
Poème Roumain, orchestra, 1897 (publ. 1899 as Op. 1)
First Piano Suite, May 1897 (publ. 1898 as Op. 3)
Violin sonata in D, June 1897 (publ. 1898 as Op. 2)
Various short piano pieces, violin pieces, further cantatas, and unfinished
  works

Malcolm, Noel, *George Enescu: His Life and Music* (London: Toccata Press, 1990).

Sound Recordings

Poème roumain Op. 1, cond. Cristian Mandeal. Arte Nova 74321 65425-2 (2000).
Violin Sonata Op. 2 in George Enescu, *Violin Sonatas,* Vilmos Szabadi. Hungaroton
  HCD 31778 (1997).
Suite for Piano Op. 3 in George Enescu, *Piano Suites,* Aurora Ienei. Olympia OCD
  414 (1981).

Zoltán Kodály (16 Dec. 1882–6 Mar. 1967)

Both of Kodály's parents were amateur musicians—his father could play the
violin and his mother the piano—and he grew up in an environment of much
music-making. He was apparently starting to improvise songs at the age of
four, and he quickly learned to play several instruments. By the age of fourteen, if not earlier, he was writing down some compositions for performance.
His earliest works include several settings of the "Ave Maria," one dated 20
October 1897, and other sacred compositions presumably written for his local
church choir, of which he was a member. His earliest dated work appears to
be a minuet in B flat major for string quartet, with a trio section in G major,
the manuscript of which is dated 10 July 1897 (see Laki 1992). Although its
style scarcely advances beyond Haydn, and may have been modeled partly
on the minuets in two of Haydn's quartets—Op. 55, No. 3, and Op. 74,
No. 1—it has been described as a "forceful and coherent composition full
of invention and almost flawless from a technical point of view" (Laki 1992,
30). It exhibits thoroughly idiomatic quartet writing, and contains interesting
tonal excursions to D flat major and E flat minor during the minuet section,
and from G major to E flat major during the trio. His overture in D minor
for full orchestra was a more substantial work, written in 1897 and performed

the following February, and his personal style began to emerge clearly during the next few years as he composed many more works. Works:

> Lost sacred works (including incomplete Mass), c. 1895–97
> Minuet in B flat, string quartet, July 1897
> *Ave Maria* (several settings), 1897–98
> Overture in D minor, 1897
> *Stabat mater,* unaccompanied voices, 1898
> *Romance lyrique,* cello and piano, 1898

Laki, Peter G., "*Minuet for String Quartet* (1897): Kodály's First Surviving Composition Rediscovered," *Notes* 49 (1992): 28–38.

Arnold Bax (8 Nov. 1883–3 Oct. 1953)

Although Bax's parents were not musicians, his father, a man of property, was highly cultured, and Bax grew up learning to play the piano without ever being taught music formally. He began composing at the age of twelve, his first efforts being a song ("Butterflies All White") and a piano sonata, both of which are now lost. Some notable early works do survive, however, in a manuscript now in the British Library (Add. 54768), entitled "Clavierstücke by A. E. T. Bax 1897–8" and containing twenty-eight pages of compositions from that period. These include a minuet in E minor; two Hungarian dances ("Ra's Dance" and "On the Mountains"); three mazurkas; two scherzi; a prelude; a nocturne in B somewhat in the style of Chopin; an arrangement of the minuet in E minor for flute, oboe, clarinet, bassoon, and string quartet; and an incomplete piano sonata in D. The sonata is described as "No. 5," and so there must be earlier ones now missing. The nocturne has been published in *Selected Works for the Piano,* edited by Connie Mayfield (1986), and its opening is quoted in Foreman (1983, 7). Also from this period are a few pieces, mostly unfinished, preserved in the Bax Memorial Room of the University Library in Cork, Ireland, including some variations in G minor for piano, dated 31 October 1897, and the piano score of an ambitious orchestral *Symphonische Dichtung nach "Rubaiyat" von Omar Khayyam* from the following year. The fifty-six-bar score, however, may represent just the introduction to a much longer work that was never completed. A piano sonata dated 27 February 1898 is described as Op. 1, suggesting that Bax, like several child composers, hoped to make a fresh start with a numerical series of more advanced compositions; but again it was left unfinished, with little written down beyond the first movement.

These early works seem to have been composed more for private amusement than public consumption, and only the nocturne has so far been printed. They should not be completely dismissed, however. The desire to compose was clearly present long before Bax had any particular training or encouragement to do so. Works:

Clavierstücke (miscellaneous piano pieces), 1897–98
Piano variations in G minor, Oct. 1897
Piano sonata, Op. 1, Feb. 1898
Symphonische Dichtung nach "Rubaiyat" von Omar Khayyam (piano score), 1898
Other short piano pieces and unfinished works

Bax, Arnold, *Selected Works for Piano*, ed. Connie Mayfield (London: Thames, 1986).
Foreman, Lewis, *Bax: A Composer and His Times* (London: Scolar, 1983), 7, 449.
Parlett, Graham, *A Catalogue of the Works of Sir Arnold Bax* (Oxford: Clarendon, 1999).

Wilhelm Furtwängler (25 Jan. 1886–30 Nov. 1954)

Born into a highly cultured family (his father was an archaeologist, his mother a painter), Furtwängler quickly showed exceptional musical gifts, and began composing at the age of seven. His earliest works are short piano pieces, followed by eight piano sonatas written between 1896 and 1898. Further piano works followed during the next few years, as well as choral music, fifteen songs from the period between 1895 and 1900, and several chamber works. In this last group were three for string quartet written between 1896 and about 1901, a string trio written during 1896 and 1897, a piano quartet written in 1899, three piano trios written between 1896 and 1900, one sonata for piano with cello written in 1896, and one sonata for piano with violin written in 1898 and 1899. An orchestral overture in E flat composed in 1899 was designated as Op. 3, suggesting that Furtwängler regarded two of his earlier compositions as being quite significant. All of this very substantial collection of early works, however, has remained unpublished, and has attracted very little attention at the time or since, although all are duly included in a detailed list of works compiled by Chris Walton (1996).

Once he reached adulthood, Furtwängler quickly established himself as one of the greatest conductors of the day. As a consequence, he found little time for composition, and composed very little after 1903 except for three symphonies and a concerto. Thus he is one of the few composers whose childhood works form a major part of their total output. Publication of these works seems a necessary first step toward their appraisal, and there is likely to be much of interest in such a substantial collection of compositions by a child of such remarkable talent. Works:

>   Various piano pieces, 1894–1900
>   Fifteen songs, 1895–1900
>   Cello sonata, 1896
>   Piano trio, 1896
>   String quartet, 1896
>   String trio, 1897
>   Eight piano sonatas, 1896–98
>   Variations for string quartet, 1897
>   *Die erste Walpurgisnacht,* voices and instruments, 1897–98
>   "Ich wandelte," voices and piano, 1898
>   Violin sonata, 1898–99
>   Overture (Op. 3), 1899
>   Piano quartet, 1899
>   Piano trio, 1900
>   Phantasie for piano trio, 1900
>   String quartet in F sharp minor, c. 1901

Walton, Chris, ed., *Wilhelm Furtwängler in Diskussion* (Winterthur, Del.: Amadeus Press, 1996), especially 85–114 (list of works).

Sound Recordings

Wilhelm Furtwängler, *Early Orchestral Works,* cond. Alfred Walter. Marco Polo 8 223645 (1995).
Eleven early songs (1895–1900) in Wilhelm Furtwängler, *Lieder and Choral Works,* Guido Pikal. Marco Polo 223546 (1995).

Nadia Boulanger (16 Sep. 1887–22 Oct. 1979)

Boulanger's father, Ernest (1815–1900), was a singer and composer, and former winner of the Prix de Rome. He was older than seventy when Nadia and her sister Lili (1893–1918; see "Lili Boulanger") were born, having married one of his singing pupils in 1878. Three songs written by Nadia Boulanger at the age of fourteen, which appear to be her first compositions, are preserved in the Bibliothèque Nationale: "Extase" (16 September 1901), "Aubade" (1 April 1902), and "Désespérance" (14 April 1902). She did not begin composing in earnest until 1905, however, and in later years made her name mainly as a teacher. A chronological list of her compositions is in Potter (2006, 165–73).

Potter, Caroline, *Nadia and Lili Boulanger* (Aldershot, U.K.: Ashgate, 2006).

Bohuslav Martinů (8 Dec. 1890–28 Aug. 1959)

Martinů lived initially at the top of the tower of his village church, where his father, a cobbler by trade, was a bell-ringer. It would be hard to imagine a more unpromising environment for a child composer, for there was no significant musical tradition within the family and for several years he hardly ever ventured from the tower. Nevertheless, he began learning the violin at the age of seven, not long after starting school, and he was soon improvising compositions. His earliest efforts are said to date from 1900, but only one work survives from before 1907 (Halbreich 1968, 17, 155), and it is uncertain how much has been lost. Since manuscript paper was not generally available to him, other compositions may never have been written down.

The surviving work is a three-movement string quartet in D major entitled *Tři Jezdci* (The Three Riders, H. 1), after a programmatic ballad by Jaroslav Vrchlický. It is thought to have been composed about 1902 or even 1901; but this was the work that he took to Prague in August 1906 to gain admission to the Conservatoire, and it seems doubtful that he would take a work already four years old rather than something more recent. He was duly admitted to the Conservatoire, and his mother reports that the director there "was so impressed by Bohuš's composition that at first he doubted whether the score was my son's own work, and asked who had helped him" (Large 1975, 10). Such an attitude is common in those confronted by a well-written composition by a child. In Martinů's case, however, not only had he received no assistance, but nobody in his village would have had sufficient skill to give him any (he had not even learned the alto clef, and used the treble clef instead for the viola part).

Halbreich, Harry, *Bohuslav Martinů: Werkverzeichnis, Dokumentation und Bibliographie* (Zurich: Atlantis, 1968).
Large, Brian, *Martinů* (London: Duckworth, 1975).

Sound Recording

Tři Jezdci in Bohuslav Martinů, *String Quartets,* vol. 1, Martinů Quartet. Naxos 8 553782 (1997).

Sergei Prokofiev (23 [11] Apr. 1891–5 Mar. 1953)

Prokofiev began composing when he was barely five years old, shortly after his mother, who was an accomplished pianist though not a professional musician, began teaching him the piano. His earliest composition was a nine-bar "Indian Galop" in F for piano, dating from summer 1896 and written down by his mother before he had fully learned notation; it is published in Prokofiev's autobiography (1979, 10). He continued composing piano pieces throughout his childhood, producing around eighty altogether by the time he was sixteen, including a few works that are more substantial, notably a sonata in B flat in 1904. For a recent chronological list of all Prokofiev's early works, see Nice (2003, 63–65). He also composed six pieces for piano duet, three for violin and piano (including a three-movement sonata in C minor in 1903), and five songs for voice and piano during this period. Many of the shorter piano pieces from the period 1902–6 were written in five groups of twelve *Pesenki* ("Little Songs"), at the suggestion of his teacher, Reinhold Glière. Prokofiev's most ambitious instrumental work from this period was a symphony in G (1902), dedicated to Glière, who had provided some assistance in the work. Altogether, sixty-one pages of this symphony survive in score, including a fully orchestrated first movement and the rest in short score.

More significant than his instrumental compositions, however, were Prokofiev's early attempts at writing operas. He had first seen an opera in Moscow at the age of eight, and quickly set about composing one of his own: *Velikan* (The Giant), which dates from February to about June 1900. Written in vocal score, it is divided into three acts (seven scenes) and was performed privately in 1901. About half of the twenty-seven-page score is now lost (Nice 2003, 12, 363). *Velikan* is notable for some extreme dynamics and some powerful music for the Giant, whose footsteps are portrayed by loud, ponderous chords that uncannily foreshadow the heavy chords accompanying the main theme in "The Montagues and the Capulets" in Prokofiev's *Romeo and Juliet.* There are also some bird calls that could be seen as anticipating those in *Peter and the Wolf. Velikan* was soon followed by *Na pustïnnïkh ostrovakh* (On Desert Islands), but this was left incomplete; only the overture and three scenes of Act I were written, and only fragments of these survive. His third operatic effort was the one-act *Pir vo vremya chumï* (A Feast in Time of Plague), written between July and October 1903; and his fourth and final childhood opera was the four-act *Undina,* begun in 1904 and completed in vocal score in 1907. None of his four early operas exists in a performable version in full score, however.

All of Prokofiev's one hundred or more childhood compositions remained unpublished during his lifetime, and even today little beyond a few excerpts of this music has been printed. Much of it still survives, however, either complete or at least partially, and all the manuscripts can be found in the *Rossiyskiy gossudarstvennïy arkhiv literaturï i iskustva* in Moscow. Unlike so many composers, Prokofiev continued to treat his early works with respect after reaching maturity, and he even discussed them in some detail in his autobiography (abridged version in Prokofiev 1979), pointing out certain stylistic features that remained with him in later life, such as his use of ostinato structures. Other writers have also noted characteristic features of the later style in his early works, such as "a bent for sharp, strong, terrifying effects . . . and for a graphic reproduction of the sounds of nature" (Nestyev 1961, 7). Works:

> Four short piano pieces, 1896
> *Velikan* (The Giant), opera (vocal score), Feb.–Jun. 1900
> *Na pustïnnïkh ostrovakh* (On Desert Islands), opera (unfinished), 1900–02
> Symphony in G, 1902
> Five sets of twelve "Little Songs" for piano, 1902–06
> Violin sonata in C minor, 1903
> *Pir vo vremya chumï* (A Feast in Time of Plague), opera (unfinished?), July–Oct. 1903, later rewritten
> Five songs, 1903–07
> Piano sonata in B flat, 1904
> *Undina,* opera, partly scored, 1904–07
> Four piano sonatas, 1907–08
> Further chamber music and piano pieces

Nestyev, Israel, *Prokofiev* (London: Oxford University Press, 1961).

Nice, David, *Prokofiev: From Russia to the West 1891–1935* (New Haven, Conn., and London: Yale University Press, 2003).

Prokofiev, Serge, *Prokofiev by Prokofiev: A Composer's Memoir*, ed. Francis King (London: Macdonald & Jane's, 1979).

Sound Recording

Many piano works in Serge Prokofiev, *Piano Works,* vols. 7–8, Frederic Chiu. Harmonia Mundi HMU 7190/1 (1998).

Rued Langgaard (28 July 1893–10 July 1952)

Langgaard was brought up surrounded by music, for his father was a piano teacher and occasional composer at the Copenhagen Conservatoire, while his mother was also a pianist. His talents were therefore quickly noticed by his parents and he was able to develop fast, starting to compose as early as 1901 (for a complete catalogue of his works, see Nielsen 1991; a summary catalogue of his works and short biography are also available on the Langgaard website). His earliest dated composition is an andante and scherzo of April 1901, one of a number of short piano pieces (BVN 1) that he composed in the first five years of the twentieth century. Another, a prelude in D major (BVN 2) of 18 May 1902, was actually published in Copenhagen later that year.

Langgaard's later childhood works include two substantial compositions for full orchestra, *Drapa* and *Heltedød* (BVN 20 and 24), dating 1907–9 and 1907–8, lasting seven and ten minutes respectively. Also notable are two cantatas for choir and orchestra, *Musae triumphantes* and *En Sommeraften* (BVN 14 and 27), dating 1906–7. Other early works include several songs, chamber music, short piano pieces, and an organ fantasia. Altogether Langgaard had composed some forty works (BVN 1 through 40) by his sixteenth birthday, though some of these were later revised. The most outstanding is undoubtedly his First Symphony (BVN 32), the five movements of which were composed between March 1908 and March 1909, before being substantially revised. The work reached its final form in 1911 and was publicly performed with considerable success at an all-Langgaard concert in Berlin in 1913. Lasting about an hour, it exhibits a rich and expressive late-Romantic style reminiscent of Bruckner or Richard Strauss, with much powerful use of brass instruments, but also many tender passages.

In the ensuing years, Langgaard engaged with modernism for a time, but around 1925 he made a dramatic about-face back to a late-Romantic style, adopting an explicitly antimodernist stance and reverting uncompromisingly to the sound-world of his childhood. Thus, like many child composers, he became notably conservative in later life, but in a much more extreme way than usual. Consequently, his compositions were almost entirely neglected in the middle decades of the twentieth century, and he came to be regarded very much as an outsider. In more recent years his music has undergone something of a revival in his native Denmark, where much of his music, including his childhood works, has been published by Samfundet or Edition Wilhelm Hansen, but he is still largely ignored in most other countries. Works:

> *Musae triumphantes,* voices and orchestra (BVN 14), 1906–07
> *Fantasia patetica,* organ (BVN 19), 1907–10
> *Drapa* (On the Death of Edvard Grieg), orchestra (BVN 20), 1907–09
> *Heltedød,* orchestra (BVN 24), 1907–08
> *For Danmark (Festmarsch),* wind orchestra (BVN 25), 1907
> *En Sommeraften,* voices and orchestra (BVN 27), 1907
> Symphony No. 1 (BVN 32), 1908–09 (later revised)
> *Kong Volmer,* voices and orchestra (BVN 33), 1908–10
> Short piano pieces (BVN 1–3, 6, 7, 21, 22, 28, 29, 38, 40), 1901–09
> Short chamber pieces (BVN 10, 23, 34), 1906–08
> Single songs (BVN 5, 8, 10, 15–17, 26, 30, 31, 35, 36, 44), 1906–09

Nielsen, Bendt Viinholdt, *Rued Langgaards kompositioner: annoteret vaerkfortegnelse* (Odense, Denmark: Odense Universitetsvorlag, 1991).
http://www.langgaard.dk

Sound Recording

Symphony No. 1, *Drapa, Heltedød,* in Rued Langgaard, *Complete Symphonies,* vols. 1–3, cond. Ilya Stupel. Danacord DACOCD 404/6 (1994).

Lili Boulanger (21 Aug. 1893–15 Mar. 1918)

Both Boulanger's parents were musicians, but the greatest help and encouragement in her early development as a musician probably came from her elder sister, Nadia (1887–1979; see "Nadia Boulanger"). Her earliest compositions apparently date from 1906: these are two lost songs, "La lettre de mort" and "Les pauvres," and the opening four bars of a violin sonata. An incomplete valse in E for piano also dates from around this time. Some larger works—mainly psalm settings for voices and orchestra—followed during 1907 through 1909, but these too are lost and it is unclear whether they were ever completed or even progressed much beyond the planning stage. Her first extant work, a *Morceau* for melody instrument (possibly the flute) and piano, dates from 1910, though its harmony is strikingly advanced and suggests that several earlier works must have been composed.

Potter, Caroline, *Nadia and Lili Boulanger* (Aldershot, U.K.: Ashgate, 2006).

Max Darewski (1894 [?]–26 Sep. 1929)

Darewski's date of birth is given variously as 1892 and 1894, but even if the older date is accepted, his early progress is remarkable. He is reported in his obituary to have composed a waltz at the age of five and conducted an orchestral composition of his own three years later; no fewer than fourteen publications from before 1911 are listed in *Lbl* (see the following list of works). He later developed mainly in the field of light and popular music, as both pianist and composer. Works (all piano unless specified):

> *Le Reve,* valse, Op. 1, 1904
> *England's Crown,* march, Op. 2, 1904
> *"The Kilties,"* march, Op. 3, 1904
> *Barcarolle,* Op. 4, 1905
> *Nelson's Victory,* march, 1905
> *Royal Standard,* march, 1906

"A World of Roses," song, 1906
Fantasia Impromptu, 1907
"I Dreamed of a Beautiful Garden," song, 1907
Franco-British March, 1908
The Diamond Jubilee, march, 1909
The Trumpeter's March, 1909
"A Nightingale's Courtship," song, 1910
"Rose of Night," song, 1910

Anonymous, "Obituary," *The Musical Times* 70 (1929): 1039.

Erwin Schulhoff (8 June 1894–18 Aug. 1942)

Schulhoff composed a *Melodie* for violin and piano that appeared in Prague as early as 1903, but he did not begin composing prolifically until 1910. That year he wrote several works, including a set of three pieces for string orchestra, and many more followed in later years.

Mario Castelnuouvo-Tedesco (3 Apr. 1895–16 Mar. 1968)

Castelnuouvo-Tedesco was first taught the piano by his mother, and his earliest published compositions appeared when he was ten years old. Among his early works are a few songs, but most are for piano, including *Arie antiche* (1905) and an *English Suite* for piano or harpsichord—a very surprising choice of instrument for that time (1909). Another piano work, his *Cielo di settembre* (September Sky) of 1910 was designated as his Op. 1 and was orchestrated five years later. In later life he continued as a composer and pianist, and settled in the United States in 1939. Works (piano, except where stated):

Arie antiche, 1905
Nocturne and Berceuse, 1905
English Suite, piano or harpsichord, 1909
Calma a Giramonte, 1910
Cielo di settembre, Op. 1, 1910
Chansons grises (songs), 1910
Primavera fiorentina, 1911

Otero, Corazon, *Mario Castelnuovo-Tedesco* (Newcastle-upon-Tyne, U.K.: Ashley Mark, 1999).

Paul Hindemith (16 Nov. 1895–28 Dec. 1963)

Neither of Hindemith's parents was a musician by profession, but his father was very knowledgeable about music and sufficiently interested in it to ensure that Hindemith, along with his younger brother and sister, received intensive musical training from an early age. Hindemith appears to have begun composing around the age of nine; a fragment of one of his manuscripts, from circa 1904 or 1905, is reproduced in Heinrich Strobel's *Paul Hindemith: Zeugnis in Bildern* (1955, 4). Most of his later childhood compositions are lost (destroyed in World War II), but they included two piano trios, some violin sonatas, cello sonatas, piano fantasias, a string quartet, and about twenty lieder (Strobel 1955, 5), all written before he began studying composition at the Hoch Conservatory in Frankfurt in 1912.

Among the surviving works, the most prominent is a set of seven lieder that date from about 1908 and 1909, published in volume VI/1 in the Hindemith collected edition (1983, 149–61). In these songs Hindemith's word setting is almost entirely syllabic, with careful attention to verbal rhythm, but the accompaniments are quite varied, from the florid but evocative "Nachtlied" (No. 1) to the whimsical "Georgslied" (No. 7). "Mein Sterben" (No. 4) is noteworthy for Hindemith's experimental and forward-looking use of dissonance, with several unusual combinations that arise from the relatively independent lines of voice and piano. Another interesting feature of these songs is that not all end in the same key as they began. "Die Rosen" (No. 2) ends in the dominant, while "Heimatklänge" (No. 5) begins in F minor and ends on the dominant of F sharp minor; similarly "Frühlingstraum" (No. 6) opens in B major, but after several modulations concludes with a final section in F minor. These songs as a whole show plenty of imagination, while a certain lack of refinement should be seen simply as part of their style rather than a defect. Their relegation to an appendix in the complete edition is unfortunate and seems inappropriate.

Other early works that have escaped destruction are the two piano trios, although they are not yet published and one is incomplete. They are thought to date from 1909 and 1910, and the first is headed "Op. 2." Thus, at least at this stage, Hindemith acknowledged one earlier composition as worthy of an opus number. Later work lists that he compiled, however, make no mention of either the piano trios or any works that preceded them. As is the case with many composers, Hindemith seems in later life to have accorded little value to his early compositions, and more or less discounted them. Works:

Seven songs, 1908–09
Two piano trios, 1909–10
Lost chamber music, piano pieces, and songs, 1904–11

Hindemith, Paul, *Sämtliche Werke, Bd. 6, 1: Klavierlieder,* ed. Kurt von Fischer (Mainz, Germany: Schott, 1983).
Strobel, Heinrich, *Paul Hindemith: Zeugnis in Bildern* (Mainz, Germany: Schott, 1955).

Roger Sessions (28 Dec. 1896–16 Mar. 1985)

Although in his later life Sessions was a prolific composer and writer on music, his only early work listed is an unpublished opera, *Lancelot and Elaine,* dating from 1910.

Erich Wolfgang Korngold (28 May 1897–29 Nov. 1957)

One of the most outstanding of all child composers, Korngold began composing at the age of six, no doubt encouraged by his father, Julius, a well-known music critic. He continued to excel throughout his childhood, and later took his style to Hollywood, where it became the archetypal norm for film scores toward the middle of the century. Yet by the time he died his adherence to a late-Romantic style and his refusal to embrace modernism meant that, like Langgaard (see "Rued Langgaard" on page 187), he had become marginalized by the musical establishment and largely forgotten as a composer of concert music. In recent years he has attracted greater attention, including several recordings and two important biographies, one by Jessica Duchen and a more detailed one by Brendan G. Carroll. The latter includes a complete list of surviving works (Carroll 1997, 396–406).

Korngold showed musical talent from the age of three (unlike his elder brother Hanns, who seems never to have shown any real talent for anything), and was playing the piano with some fluency by the age of five. His earliest surviving works are two pieces from 1905, each entitled *Melodie* and labeled as "Opus 1" and "Opus 2." Soon he was filling notebooks with short compositions and sketches—mainly piano pieces but also a few songs and some chamber music. These were followed in 1906 by a cantata entitled *Gold,* which was completed by Easter of that year. Though now lost apart from a fragmentary sketch, it was such a well-written work that when Gustav Mahler heard it played he was extremely impressed and immediately recommended Korngold to Alexander Zemlinsky for instruction in composition. There Korngold continued to make rapid progress, and produced another cantata-like work in 1908, *Die Nixe,* which is also lost apart from a fragment. Soon he was writing scores that would astonish the world. Three of these written in 1908 and 1909, a piano sonata in D minor, a group of six pictorial piano pieces entitled *Don Quixote,* and a two-act ballet pantomime, *Der Schneemann* (The Snowman), were printed privately in 1909 and circulated to some eminent musicians, including Richard Strauss, who were all amazed at the quality of the music. The testimony of Strauss is particularly significant since he himself had been a notable child composer (see "Richard Strauss" on page 161), writing an impressive orchestral *Festmarsch* at the age of eleven. Of Korngold,

Strauss states, "The first feeling one has when one realizes that this was written by an 11-year-old boy is that of awe. . . . This assurance of style, this mastery of form, this characteristic expressiveness in the sonata, this bold harmony, are truly astonishing" (Carroll 1997, 43). Of the three works, the one that had the greatest impact was *Der Schneemann,* which was completed as early as Easter 1909 and received a prestigious and highly successful public premiere in Vienna on 4 October 1910. A second piano sonata was completed in December 1910, which was promptly championed by the great pianist Artur Schnabel and was soon published as Op. 2 (Op. 1 was a piano trio).

From the time that news of Korngold's ability began spreading around Vienna in 1909, many people suspected a hoax, claiming that it was impossible for a child of his age to compose such ravishing music. Their suspicions were increased by the fact that his middle name was Wolfgang, an obvious reference to Mozart; and the fact that he was Jewish meant that his music was also liable to face hostility because of widespread anti-Semitism. As Duchen explains, a "skeptical populace" concluded that this music "could not have been written by an eleven-year-old boy," (1996, 34) and suggested it must be by his father. Julius Korngold replied, "If I could write such music, I would not be a critic." To that there was no answer.

It is easy to see why Julius, along with Strauss, Mahler, and others, was such an admirer of Korngold's compositions from that period. Korngold's major works from around 1910, such as *Der Schneemann* and his *Schauspiel Ouvertüre,* Op. 4 (first performed in December 1911 and published the following year), are remarkable in so many ways: the wealth of melody and the skill with which it is developed; the rhythmic variety and control of pacing; the inventiveness and assuredness of the tonal direction; the structural organization of the material; and particularly the richness of the harmony, which extends to highly chromatic chords, sometimes suffused with sevenths, ninths, and other dissonances but always used in a thoroughly logical yet often highly original way. The textures are not particularly complex, and the orchestration of *Der Schneemann* was done by Zemlinsky (though later revised by Korngold); but in his *Schauspiel Ouvertüre* Korngold produced his own orchestral score, and demonstrated an extremely deft handling of the instruments.

Korngold composed many more works in the next few years, and by the time he was sixteen he had produced around fifty compositions (Carroll 1997, 396–401), several of which had been published. Manuscripts of the unpublished works and sketches are preserved in the Library of Congress in Washington, D.C. The whole sound of these early works, especially the harmony and orchestration, exhibits an unmistakable individuality, and at this stage his style was thoroughly up-to-date, even if not as advanced as the recent experiments of the Second Viennese School of Schoenberg, Webern, and Berg. Some early critics were struck by his "modernity"—even "dubious modernity"—and by his "virility" and "daring" (Duchen 1996, 30–31). Having achieved success with this style, however, Korngold seems to have felt no urge to move forward, and instead of developing alongside the intellectualism of the Second Viennese School, his style hardly advanced at all in later years. Fortunately, however, it proved to be particularly well suited to the demands of film music when he moved to Hollywood in 1934, although later attempts to reestablish himself as a concert composer met with limited success. Works:

> Two *Melodies,* piano (Opp. 1 and 2), 1905
> Intermezzo, piano, 1905
> *Gold* (cantata), 1906
> *Die Nixe* (cantata), 1908 (?)
> *Don Quixote,* six piano pieces, 1908
> *Caprice fantastique,* violin and piano, 1908
> Piano sonata in D minor, 1908–09
> *Der Schneemann,* ballet, 1908–09
> Piano trio in D (Op. 1), 1909
> Piano sonata in E (Op. 2), 1910
> *Märchenbilder* (Op. 3), 1910
> *Schauspiel* overture (Op. 4), 1911
> Sinfonietta in B flat (Op. 5), 1912
> Violin sonata in G (Op. 6), 1913
> Six songs (Op. 9), 1911–16
> Other piano pieces, songs, chamber music

Carroll, Brendan G., *The Last Prodigy: A Biography of Erich Wolfgang Korngold* (Portland, Ore.: Amadeus Press, 1997).
Duchen, Jessica, *Erich Wolfgang Korngold* (London: Phaidon, 1996).

Sound Recording

Erich Korngold, *Orchestral Works,* vol. 1, Nordwestdeutsche Philharmonie, cond. Werner Andreas Albert. CPO 999 037-2, 1991.

Sonia (Sophie-Carmen) Fridman (later Fridman-Gramatté, then Eckhardt-Gramatté) (6 Jan. 1899 [N.S.]–2 Dec. 1974)

Fridman began composing as early as 1905, writing a series of fourteen "Alphabet" pieces between 1905 and 1910 depicting particular letters of the alphabet. Her *Etude de concert* was published in Paris in 1910, and altogether she wrote around thirty compositions, nearly all for piano solo, by the time she was sixteen. In later life she was celebrated as a virtuoso on both piano and violin. Works (for full catalogue see her website):

> Fourteen "Alphabet" pieces, piano, 1905–10
> *Der Geiger,* violin and piano, 1907
> Twelve miscellaneous pieces, piano, 1907–11
> *Ein wenig Musik,* piano trio, 1910

http://www.egre.mb.ca/sc

Alexander Tcherepnin (20 [8] Jan. 1899–29 Sep. 1977)

Son of the composer Nikolai Tcherepnin (1873–1945), Alexander learned music initially from his mother rather than his father, who had surprisingly little influence on his childhood years. As early as 1913, perhaps earlier, he was apparently composing an opera, *The Death of Ivan the Terrible* (somewhat reminiscent of Musorgsky's *Boris Godunov*), and at one point threw a large metal sheet on the floor to imitate the sound of a huge bell. By the age of fourteen he had also written several piano pieces that were later incorporated into published collections, notably:

> *Bagatelles* Op. 5 (c. 1912–18, publ. 1922), of which No. 7 was the earliest, composed c. 1912, and derives from the third movement of his "Piano Concerto No. 3" of that date (not to be confused with his later Piano Concerto No. 3, Op. 48, of 1931–32)
> *Pièces sans titres,* Op. 7, No. 4, dates from 1913 (publ. c. 1923–4)
> *Dix études,* Op. 18, No. 10, dates from 1914
> *Episodes Priskaski* (Short Stories): No. 5 "Scherzando," 1912

The main Tcherepnin collection was catalogued by Paul Radzievsky (*Catalog of the Tcherepnin Archive,* 1983) and is now housed in the Paul Sacher Foundation in Basel, Switzerland. A more recent study by Enrique Arias uses Radziewsky's catalogue and lists the unpublished material in the Archive (1989, 116–26). Whereas most of these unpublished works are listed individually, however, the early ones are lumped together under a single number, TA 78, entitled "Childhood Works," with this laconic description: "including a Sonatina, Impromptu, Humoresque etc. Dated 1912–13" (Arias 1989, 117). Whether any material survives for either *The Death of Ivan the Terrible* or the early piano concerto No. 3 (not to mention Nos. 1 and 2) remains unclear. Meanwhile Arias's chronological list of compositions "by Tcherepnin" includes only published works and begins with works written in 1915. This seems a good example of unthinking prejudice against composers' early works. Arias does, however, recognize that Tcherepnin "wrote hundreds of pieces in his early years" (1989, 134), though the dating is usually uncertain and needs detailed investigation. Works:

Various short piano pieces, 1912–14
Three (?) piano concertos, c. 1910–12
The Death of Ivan the Terrible (opera), c. 1913

Arias, Enrique Alberto, *Alexander Tcherepnin: A Bio-Bibliography* (Westport, Conn.: Greenwood, 1989).

Bibliography

MAJOR REFERENCE WORKS

British Library Integrated Catalogue (Lbl). At http://catalogue.bl.uk (accessed 3 June 2008).

Die Musik in Geschichte und Gegenwart (MGG). Edited by Friedrich Blume. Kassel and Basel, Germany: Bärenreiter, 1949–68.

Die Musik in Geschichte und Gegenwart, Supplement. Kassel and Basel, Germany: 1970–86.

Die Musik in Geschichte und Gegenwart, 2nd ed. Edited by Ludwig Finscher, 1994–2008.

Grove Music Online (GMO). Edited by L. Macy. At http://www.grovemusic.com (accessed 25 June 2008).

The New Grove Dictionary of Music and Musicians (NGD). Edited by Stanley Sadie. London: Macmillan, 1980.

The New Grove Dictionary of Music and Musicians (NGD), 2nd ed. Edited by Stanley Sadie and John Tyrrell. London: Macmillan, 2001. See also *GMO*.

Oxford Dictionary of National Biography (ODNB). At http://www.oxforddnb.com (accessed 31 March 2008).

BOOKS AND ARTICLES

Abraham, Gerald. "Balakirev's Symphonies," *Music & Letters* 14 (1933): 355–63.

Anderson, Julian. "La Note Juste," *The Musical Times* 136 (1995): 22–27.

Anderson, Robert. *Elgar*. London: Dent, 1993.

Anonymous. "Frederic Hymen Cowen," *The Musical Times* 39 (1898): 713–19.

———. "Music in Manchester," *The Musical Times* 38 (1897): 835.

———. "Obituary [of Max Darewski]," *The Musical Times* 70 (1929): 1039.

Arias, Enrique Alberto. *Alexander Tcherepnin: A Bio-Bibliography*. Westport, Conn.: Greenwood, 1989.

Arnold, Denis. *The Master Musicians: Monteverdi*, 3rd ed. London: Dent, 1990.

Ashbee, Andrew, and David Lasocki. *A Biographical Dictionary of English Court Musicians 1485–1714*. Aldershot, U.K.: Ashgate, 1998.

Auda, Antoine. *Barthélemy Beaulaigue, poète et musicien prodige*. Brussels: Antoine Auda, 1957(?).

Barrington, Daines. *Miscellanies by the Honourable Daines Barrington*. London: J. Nichols, 1781.

Beaumont, Antony. *Busoni the Composer*. London: Faber, 1985.

Beechey, Gwilym. "Thomas Linley, Junior. 1756–1778," *The Musical Quarterly* 54 (1968): 74–82.

Bennett, Joseph. "Facts, Rumours, and Remarks," *The Musical Times* 38 (1897): 742–43.

Blacking, John. *Venda Children's Songs: A Study in Ethnomusicological Analysis*. Johannesburg, South Africa: Witwatersrand University Press, 1967.

Block, Geoffrey. *Charles Ives: A Bio-Bibliography*. New York and London: Greenwood, 1989.

Bowers, Faubion. *Scriabin*, 2 vols. Tokyo and Palo Alto: Kodansha, 1969.

Bowers, Jane, and Judith Tick, eds. *Women Making Music: The Western Art Tradition, 1150–1950*. Urbana: University of Illinois Press, 1986.

Boyd, Malcolm. *Domenico Scarlatti*. London: Weidenfeld & Nicolson, 1986.

Boynton, Susan, and Isabelle Cochelin. "The Sociomusical Role of Child Oblates at the Abbey of Cluny in the Eleventh Century." In *Musical Childhoods and the Cultures of Youth*. Edited by Susan Boynton and Roe-Min Kok, 3–24. Middletown, Conn.: Wesleyan University Press, 2006.

Boynton, Susan, and Roe-Min Kok, eds. *Musical Childhoods and the Cultures of Youth*. Middletown, Conn.: Wesleyan University Press, 2006.

Boynton, Susan, and Eric Rice, eds. *Young Choristers, 650–1700*. Woodbridge, U.K.: Boydell Press, 2008.

Brett, Philip, Elizabeth Wood, and Gary C. Thomas, eds. *Queering the Pitch: The New Gay and Lesbian Musicology*. New York: Routledge, 1994.

Briscoe, James R., ed. *Historical Anthology of Music by Women*. Bloomington: Indiana University Press, 1987.

Brown, Clive. *Louis Spohr: A Critical Biography*. Cambridge: Cambridge University Press, 1984.

Carroll, Brendan G. *The Last Prodigy: A Biography of Erich Wolfgang Korngold*. Portland, Ore.: Amadeus Press, 1997.

Cattell, James McKeen. "A Statistical Study of Eminent Men," *Popular Science Monthly* 62 (1903): 359–77.

Chapman, Ernest. "Ernest Bloch," *The Musical Times* 75 (1934): 121–23.

Chissell, Joan. *Clara Schumann: A Dedicated Spirit*. London: Hamilton, 1983.

Citron, Marcia J. *Gender and the Musical Canon*. Cambridge: Cambridge University Press, 1993.

Clapham, John. *Smetana*. London: Dent, 1972.

Clifford, James. *The Divine Services and Anthems Usually Sung in His Majesties Chappell and in All Cathedrals and Collegiate Choires in England and Ireland.* London: Nathaniel Brooke and Henry Brome, 1664.

Cole, Hugo. "Children's Opera." In *The New Grove Dictionary of Opera,* vol. 1. Edited by Stanley Sadie, 842–44. London: Macmillan, 1992.

Cooper, Barry. "The Amazing Early Works of Frederick Ouseley," *The Musical Times* 147 (summer 2006): 49–58.

———, ed. *The Beethoven Compendium,* 2nd ed. London: Thames & Hudson, 1996.

———. "Beethoven's Childhood Compositions: A Reappraisal," *The Beethoven Journal* 12 (1997): 2–6.

———. *English Solo Keyboard Music of the Middle and Late Baroque.* New York: Garland, 1989.

———. "Major Minors," *The Musical Times* 137 (August 1996): 5–10.

———. "'Miss Bonwick' Identified: An Eighteenth-Century Composer and Organist," *The Musical Times* (forthcoming).

Czerny, Carl. "Recollections from My Life," translated and edited by Ernest Sanders, *The Musical Quarterly* 42 (1956): 302–17.

Davies, Laurence. *Franck.* London: Dent, 1973.

Del Mar, Norman. *Richard Strauss: A Critical Commentary on His Life and Works,* vol. 1. London: Barrie & Rockliff, 1962.

Dennison, Peter. *Pelham Humfrey.* Oxford: Oxford University Press, 1986.

Deutsch, Otto Erich. *Franz Schubert: thematisches Verzeichnis seiner Werke in chronologischer Folge,* 2nd ed. Kassel, Germany: Bärenreiter, 1978.

———. *Handel: A Documentary Biography.* London: A. & C. Black, 1955.

Dibble, Jeremy. *C. Hubert H. Parry: His Life and Music.* Oxford: Oxford University Press, 1992.

Dille, Denis. *Thematisches Verzeichnis der Jugendwerke Béla Bartóks 1890–1904,* 2nd ed. Kassel, Germany: Bärenreiter, 1976.

Dobbins, Frank. *Music in Renaissance Lyons.* Oxford: Clarendon, 1992.

Duchen, Jessica. *Erich Wolfgang Korngold.* London: Phaidon, 1996.

Eddie, William A. *Charles Valentin Alkan: His Life and His Music.* Aldershot, U.K.: Ashgate, 2007.

Eisen, Cliff. "Problems of Authenticity among Mozart's Early Symphonies: The Examples of K. Anh. 220 (16a) and 76 (42a)," *Music & Letters* 70 (1989): 505–16.

Epstein, Dena J. Review of *Little Red Riding Hood,* by Seymour Barab. *Notes* 23, no. 2 (1966): 337.

Evans, John, Philip Reed, and Paul Wilson. *A Britten Source Book,* 2nd ed. Aldeburgh, U.K.: Britten Estate, 1987.

Fallows, David. "Henry VIII As a Composer." In *Sundry Sorts of Music Books: Essays on the British Library Collections, Presented to O. W. Neighbour on His 70th Birthday.* Edited by Chris Banks and others, 27–39. London: British Library, 1993.

Farnsworth, Paul R. "Elite Attitudes in Music as Measured by the Cattell Space Method," *Journal of Research in Music Education* 10 (1962): 65–68.

Fellowes, E. H. *The Catalogue of Manuscripts in the Library of St. Michael's College, Tenbury.* Paris: Oiseau-Lyre, 1934.

Fifield, Christopher. *Max Bruch: His Life and Works,* 2nd ed. Woodbridge, U.K.: Boydell Press, 2005.

Ford, Anthony. "Giovanni Bononcini," *The Musical Times* 111 (1970): 695–99.

Foreman, Lewis. *Bax: A Composer and His Times.* London: Scolar, 1983.

Gallo, Denise P. *Gioachino Rossini: A Guide to Research.* London and New York: Routledge, 2002.

Gatens, William. *Victorian Cathedral Music in Theory and Practice.* Cambridge: Cambridge University Press, 1996.

Gibbs, Christopher H. "'Komm, geh' mit mir': Schubert's Uncanny 'Erlkönig,'" *19th-Century Music* 19 (1995): 115–35.

Glover, Joanna. *Children Composing: 4–14.* London: Falmer, 2000.

Göthel, Folker. *Thematisch-bibliographisches Verzeichnis der Werke von Louis Spohr.* Tutzing, Germany: Schneider, 1981.

Griffiths, Paul. *Bartók,* 2nd ed. London: Dent, 1988.

Grim, William E. *Max Reger: A Bio-Bibliography.* Westport, Conn.: Greenwood, 1988.

Halbreich, Harry. *Bohuslav Martinů: Werkverzeichnis, Dokumentation und Bibliographie.* Zurich: Atlantis, 1968.

Hall, Michael. *Harrison Birtwistle.* London: Robson, 1984.

Harding, James. *Saint-Saëns and His Circle.* London: Chapman & Hall, 1965.

The Harmonicon: A Journal of Music, 11 vols. London: Pinnock, 1823–33. Reprint, Farnborough, U.K.: Gregg, 1971.

Hennessee, Don A. *Samuel Barber: A Bio-Bibliography.* Westport, Conn.: Greenwood, 1985.

Higgins, Paula. "Tracing the Careers of Late Medieval Composers: The Case of Philippe Basiron," *Acta Musicologica* 62 (1990): 1–28.

Hill, Cecil. *The Music of Ferdinand Ries: A Thematic Catalogue.* Armidale, Australia: University of New England, 1977.

Holman, Peter. *Henry Purcell.* Oxford: Oxford University Press, 1994.

Holoman, D. Kern. *Catalogue of the Works of Hector Berlioz.* Kassel, Germany: Bärenreiter, 1987.

Horvath, Emmerich. *Franz Liszts Kindheit (1811–27).* Eisenstadt, Austria: Nentwich, 1978.

Hummel, Walter. *W. A. Mozarts Söhne.* Kassel, Germany: Bärenreiter, 1956.

Huys, Bernard. *François-Joseph Fétis et la vie musicale de son temps, 1784–1871.* Brussels: Bibliothèque Royale Albert I, 1972.

Irmen, Hans-Josef. *Thematisches Verzeichnis der musikalischen Werke Gabriel Josef Rheinbergers.* Regensburg, Germany: Gustav Bosse, 1974.

Jackson, Barbara Garvey. *"Say Can You Deny Me": A Guide to Surviving Music by Women from the 16th through the 18th Centuries.* Fayetteville: University of Arkansas Press, 1994.

Jähns, Friedrich Wilhelm. *Carl Maria von Weber in seinen Werken: chronologisch-thematisches Verzeichniss seiner sämmtlichen Compositionen.* Berlin: Schlesinger, 1871.

Johannson, Cari. *J. J. & B. Hummel Music-Publishing and Thematic Catalogues.* Stockholm: Library of the Royal Swedish Academy of Music, 1972.

Johnson, Douglas. *Beethoven's Early Sketches in the "Fischhof Miscellany": Berlin, Autograph 28*, Ann Arbor, Mich.: UMI Research Press, 1980.

Joyce, F. W. *The Life of Rev. Sir F. A. G. Ouseley, Bart.* London: Methuen, 1896.

Kassler, Michael, and Philip Olleson. *Samuel Wesley (1766–1837): A Source Book.* Aldershot, U.K.: Ashgate, 2001.

Kennedy, Michael. *A Catalogue of the Works of Ralph Vaughan Williams*, 2nd ed. Oxford: Oxford University Press, 1996.

———. *The Works of Ralph Vaughan Williams.* London: Oxford University Press, 1964.

Kenneson, Claude. *Musical Prodigies: Perilous Journeys, Remarkable Lives.* Portland, Ore.: Amadeus Press, 1998.

Kent, Christopher. *Edward Elgar: A Guide to Research.* New York: Garland, 1993.

Kindermann, Jürgen. *Thematisch-Chronologisches Verzeichnis der musikalischen Werke von Ferruccio B. Busoni.* Regensburg, Germany: Bosse, 1980.

Kobylańska, Krystyna. *Frédéric Chopin: thematisch-bibliographisches Werkverzeichnis.* Munich: Henle, 1979.

Köchel, Ludwig Ritter von. *Chronologisch-thematisches Verzeichniss sämmtlicher Tonwerke Wolfgang Amade Mozart's.* Leipzig, Germany: Breitkopf & Härtel, 1862. 6th ed., edited by Franz Giegling. Wiesbaden: Breitkopf & Härtel, 1964.

Köhler, Karl-Heinz, and others, eds. *Ludwig van Beethovens Konversationshefte,* vols. 3 and 4. Leipzig, Germany: Deutscher Verlag für Musik, 1983, 1968.

Kramer, Lawrence. "*Carnaval,* Cross-Dressing, and the Woman in the Mirror." In *Musicology and Difference: Gender and Sexuality in Music Scholarship.* Edited by Ruth Solie, 305–25. Berkeley: University of California Press, 1993.

Kroll, Mark. *Johann Nepomuk Hummel.* Lanham, Md.: Scarecrow Press, 2007.

Laki, Peter G. "*Minuet for String Quartet* (1897): Kodály's First Surviving Composition Rediscovered," *Notes* 49 (1992): 28–38.

Landon, H. C. Robbins, ed. *The Mozart Compendium.* London: Thames & Hudson, 1990.

Large, Brian. *Martinů.* London: Duckworth, 1975.

Latham, Alison, ed. *The Oxford Companion to Music.* Oxford: Oxford University Press, 2002.

Lindeman, Stephan D. *Structural Novelty and Tradition in the Early Romantic Piano Concerto.* Stuyvesant, N.Y.: Pendragon, 1999.

Macdonald, Hugh. *Skryabin.* Oxford: Oxford University Press, 1987.

MacKenzie, Alexander C. "The Life-Work of Arthur Sullivan," *Sammelbände der Internationalen Musikgesellschaft* 3 (1901–02): 539–64.

Malcolm, Noel. *George Enescu: His Life and Music.* London: Toccata Press, 1990.

Marshall, Kimberly, ed. *Rediscovering the Muses: Women's Musical Traditions.* Boston: Northeastern University Press, 1993.

Martyn, Barrie. *Nicolas Medtner: His Life and Music.* Aldershot, U.K.: Scolar, 1995.

Maxwell Davies, Peter. "Music Composed by Children." In *Music in Education.* Edited by Willis Grant, 108–15. London: Butterworth, 1963.

McClary, Susan. "Of Patriarchs . . . and Matriarchs, Too," *The Musical Times* 135 (1994): 364–69.

Nestyev, Israel. *Prokofiev*. London: Oxford University Press, 1961.

Nice, David. *Prokofiev: From Russia to the West 1891–1935*. New Haven and London: Yale University Press, 2003.

Nielsen, Bendt Viinholdt. *Rued Langgaards kompositioner: annoteret vaerkfortegnelse*. Odense, Denmark: Odense Universitetsvorlag, 1991.

Norris, Geoffrey. "Rakhmaninov's Apprenticeship," *The Musical Times* 124 (1983): 602–05.

Ossenkop, David. *Hugo Wolf: A Guide to Research*. New York: Garland, 1988.

Otero, Corazon. *Mario Castelnuovo-Tedesco*. Newcastle-upon-Tyne, U.K.: Ashley Mark, 1999.

Pargeter, Shirley. *A Catalogue of the Library at Tatton Park, Knutsford, Cheshire*. Chester, U.K.: Cheshire Libraries and Museums, 1977.

Parlett, Graham. *A Catalogue of the Works of Sir Arnold Bax*. Oxford: Clarendon, 1999.

Pazdírek, Franz. *Universal-Handbuch der Musikliteratur*. Vienna: Franz Pazdírek, 1904–10. Reprint, Hilversum: F. Knuf, 1957.

Perényi, Eleanor. *Liszt*. London: Weidenfeld & Nicolson, 1975.

Phillips-Matz, Mary Jane. *Verdi: A Biography*. Oxford: Oxford University Press, 1993.

Pinker, Stephen. *The Language Instinct*. New York: W. Morrow, 1994.

Potter, Caroline. *Nadia and Lili Boulanger*. Aldershot, U.K.: Ashgate, 2006.

Prokofiev, Serge, *Prokofiev by Prokofiev: A Composer's Memoir*. Edited by Francis King. London: Macdonald & Jane's, 1979.

Radcliffe, Philip. "Piano Music." In *The Age of Beethoven, New Oxford History of Music*, vol. 8. Edited by Gerald Abraham, 325–75. London: Oxford University Press, 1982.

Ratner, Sabina Teller. *Camille Saint-Saëns 1835–1921: A Thematic Catalogue of His Complete Works, vol. 1: The Instrumental Works*. Oxford: Oxford University Press, 2002.

Reese, Gustave. *Music in the Middle Ages*. London: Dent, 1942.

Reich, Nancy B. *Clara Schumann: The Artist and the Woman*. London: Gollancz, 1985.

Rennert, Jonathan. *William Crotch 1775–1847*. Lavenham, U.K.: Dalton, 1975.

Révész, Géza. *The Psychology of a Musical Prodigy (Erwin Nyiregyházy)*. London: Kegan Paul, 1925. Originally published as *Erwin Nyiregyházy: psychologische Analyse eines musikalisch hervorragenden Kindes*. Leipzig, Germany: 1916.

Roberge, Marc-André. *Ferruccio Busoni: A Bio-Bibliography*. New York: Greenwood, 1991.

Rodmell, Paul. *Charles Villiers Stanford*. Aldershot, U.K.: Ashgate, 2002.

Rosselli, John. "Child Performers." In *The New Grove Dictionary of Opera*, vol. 1. Edited by Stanley Sadie, 842. London: Macmillan, 1992.

Rössl, Elisabeth. "Leopoldine Blahetka: Eine Pianistin und Komponistin der Biedermeierzeit." In *Biographische Beiträge zum Musikleben Wiens im 19. und 20. Jahrhundert: Leopoldine Blahetka, Eduard Hanslick, Robert Hirschfeld*. Edited by Friedrich C. Heller, 112–211. Vienna: Verband der Wissenschaftliche Gesellschaft Oesterreichs, 1992.

Rushton, Julian. *Mozart: An Extraordinary Life*. London: The Associated Board of the Royal Schools of Music, 2005.

Sachs, Joel. "A Checklist of the Works of Johann Nepomuk Hummel," *Notes* 30 (1973–74): 732–54.

Sadie, Julie Anne, and Rhian Samuel, eds. *The New Grove Dictionary of Women Composers*. London: Macmillan, 1994.

Sadie, Stanley. *Mozart: The Early Years*. New York: Oxford University Press, 2006.

———, ed. *The New Grove Dictionary of Opera*, 4 vols. London: Macmillan, 1992.

Schoenberg, Arnold. "My Evolution," *The Musical Quarterly* 38 (1952): 517–27.

Schuh, Willi. *Richard Strauss: A Chronicle of the Early Years 1864–1898*. Translated by Mary Whittall. Cambridge: Cambridge University Press, 1976.

Seaton, Douglas, ed. *The Mendelssohn Companion*. Westport, Conn.: Greenwood, 2001.

Self, Geoffrey. *The Hiawatha Man: The Life and Work of Samuel Coleridge-Taylor*. Aldershot, U.K.: Scolar, 1995.

Silberman, Israel. "Teaching Composition via Schenker's Theory," *Journal of Research in Music Education* 12 (1964): 295–303.

Silburn, Muriel. "The Most Extraordinary Creature in Europe," *Music & Letters* 3 (1922): 200–05.

Sills, David L. "Bloch Manuscripts at the Library of Congress," *Notes* 42 (1986): 726–53.

Sinclair, James B. *A Descriptive Catalogue of the Music of Charles Ives*. New Haven, Conn.: Yale University Press, 1999.

Sitwell, Sacheverell. *Liszt*. London: Faber & Faber, 1934.

Smith, Ronald. *Alkan Volume One: The Enigma*. London: Kahn and Averill, 1976.

Solie, Ruth, ed. *Musicology and Difference: Gender and Sexuality in Music Scholarship*. Berkeley: University of California Press, 1993.

Stainer, John. "The Character and Influence of the Late Sir Frederick Ouseley," *Proceedings of the Musical Association* 16 (1889): 25–39.

Steiner, Ena. "Schoenberg's Quest: Newly Discovered Works from His Early Years," *The Musical Quarterly* 60 (1974): 401–20.

Strobel, Heinrich. *Paul Hindemith: Zeugnis in Bildern*. Mainz, Germany: Schott, 1955.

Studd, Stephen. *Saint-Saëns: A Critical Biography*. London: Cygnus Arts, 1999.

Sullivan, Herbert, and Newman Flower. *Sir Arthur Sullivan: His Life, Letters and Diaries*. London: Cassell, 1927.

Taylor, Ronald. *Franz Liszt: The Man and the Musician*. London: Grafton, 1986.

Thompson, Kenneth. *A Dictionary of Twentieth-Century Composers 1911–1971*. London: Faber, 1973.

Threlfall, Robert, and Geoffrey Norris. *A Catalogue of the Compositions of S. Rachmaninoff*. London: Scolar, 1982.

Tillard, Françoise. *Fanny Mendelssohn*. Paris: Belfond, 1992. Translated by Camille Naish. Portland, Ore.: Amadeus Press, 1996.

Todd, R. Larry. *Mendelssohn: A Life in Music*. New York: Oxford University Press, 2005.

———. *Mendelssohn's Musical Education*. Cambridge: Cambridge University Press, 1983.

———. "Strauss before Liszt and Wagner." In *Richard Strauss: New Perspectives on the Composer and His Work*. Edited by Brian Gilliam. Durham, N.C.: Duke University, 1992.

Tolley, Thomas. "Haydn, the Engraver Thomas Park, and Maria Hester Park's 'little Sonat,'" *Music & Letters* 82 (2001): 421–31.

Treitler, Leo. "Gender and Other Dualities of Music History." In *Musicology and Difference: Gender and Sexuality in Music Scholarship.* Edited by Ruth Solie, 23–45. Berkeley: University of California Press, 1993.

Trenner, Franz, ed. *Richard Strauss Werkverzeichnis,* 2nd ed. Vienna: Dr. Richard Strauss GmbH, 1999.

Tyler, Linda. "Bastien und Bastienne: The Libretto, Its Derivation, and Mozart's Text Setting," *Journal of Musicology* 8 (1990): 520–52.

Tyson, Alan. *Thematic Catalogue of the Works of Muzio Clementi.* Tutzing, Germany: Schneider, 1967.

Van Boer, Bertil H. *Joseph Martin Kraus (1756–1792): A Systematic-Thematic Catalogue of His Music.* Stuyvesant, N.Y.: Pendragon, 1998.

Vitercik, Greg. *The Early Works of Felix Mendelssohn: A Study in the Romantic Sonata Style.* Philadelphia: Gordon & Breach, 1992.

Walker, Alan, ed. *Franz Liszt: The Man and His Music.* London: Barrie & Jenkins, 1970.

Wallach, Laurence. "The New England Education of Charles Ives." Ph.D. diss., Columbia University, 1973.

Walton, Chris, ed. *Wilhelm Furtwängler in Diskussion.* Winterthur, Del.: Amadeus Press, 1996.

Wangermée, Robert. *François-Joseph Fétis: musicologue et compositeur.* Brussels: Palais des Académies, 1951.

Warrack, John. *Carl Maria von Weber,* 2nd ed. Cambridge: Cambridge University Press, 1976.

Watson, Derek. *The Master Musicians: Liszt.* London: Dent, 1989.

Wilson, Sarah J., and Roger J. Wales. "An Exploration of Children's Musical Compositions," *Journal of Research in Music Education* 43 (1995): 94–111.

Wolff, Christoph. "Recovered in Kiev: Bach et al. A Preliminary Report of the Music Collection of the Berlin Sing-Akademie," *Notes* 58 (2001): 259–71.

Wolff, Konrad. "Johann Samuel Schroeter," *The Musical Quarterly* 44 (1958): 338–59.

Wotquenne, Alfred. *Catalogue de la Bibliothèque du Conservatoire Royal de Musique.* Brussels: Coosemans, 1898–1912.

Young, Percy. *Sir Arthur Sullivan.* London: Dent, 1971.

Zimmerman, Franklin B. *Henry Purcell 1659-1695: An Analytical Catalogue of His Music.* London: Macmillan, 1963.

SCORES

Arriaga, Juan Crisóstomo. *Obra completa 1.* Edited by Christophe Rousset. Madrid: Instituto Complutense de Ciencias Musicales, 2006.

Aspull, George. *The Posthumous Works of G. Aspull . . . Edited by His Father.* London: Thomas Aspull, 1837.

Bartók, Béla. *The Young Bartók: Piano Pieces.* Edited by Denis Dille. Budapest: Editio Musica, 1965.

Bax, Arnold. *Selected Works for Piano.* Edited by Connie Mayfield. London: Thames, 1986.

Beethoven, Ludwig van. *Ludwig van Beethovens Werke,* 25 vols. Leipzig, Germany: Breitkopf & Härtel, 1862–65, 1888.

Bizet, Georges. *Oeuvres pour le piano.* Edited by Michel Poupet. Paris: Mario Bois, 1984.

Blahetka, Leopoldine. *Music for Piano.* Edited by Lydia Hailparn Ledeen. Bryn Mawr, Pa.: Hildegard Publishing, 1992.

Brook, Barry S., ed. *The Symphony 1720–1840,* Series F, vol. III. New York: Garland, 1983.

———, ed. *The Symphony 1720–1840: Reference Volume.* New York: Garland, 1986.

Chopin, Frédéric. *Complete Works,* vol. 8. Edited by Ignacy Paderewski and others. Warsaw: Fryderyk Chopin Institute, 1949.

Clementi, Muzio. *Muzio Clementi: Opera Omnia,* vol. 51. Edited by Andrea Coen. Bologna: Ut Orpheus Edizioni, 2004.

Diabelli, Anton, ed. *Vaterlandischer Künstlerverein,* facsimile. In *Denkmäler der Tonkunst in Österreich,* vol. 136. Edited by Günter Brosche. Graz, Austria: Akademische Druck- und Verlagsanhalt, 1983. Originally published Vienna: Diabelli, 1824.

Elgar, Edward. *Elgar Complete Edition,* vol. 36. London: Novello, 1987.

Gipps, Ruth. *The Fairy Shoemaker.* London: Forsyth, 1929.

Grieg, Edvard. *Edvard Grieg: Samlede verker/Complete Works,* vol. 20. Edited by Rune J. Andersen and others. Frankfurt: Peters, 1995.

Handel, George Frideric. *The Works of George Frederic Handel,* vol. 27. Edited by Friedrich Chrysander. Leipzig, Germany: German Handel Society Edition, 1879.

Hindemith, Paul. *Sämtliche Werke, Bd. 6, 1: Klavierlieder.* Edited by Kurt von Fischer. Mainz, Germany: Schott, 1983.

Humfrey, Pelham. *Complete Church Music* [part 1]. In *Musica Britannica,* vol. 34. Edited by Peter Dennison. London: Stainer & Bell, 1972.

Hummel, Johann Nepomuk. *The Complete Works for Piano: A Six-Volume Collection of Reprints and Facsimiles.* Edited by Joel Sachs. New York: Garland, 1989–90.

Jackson, Barbara Garvey, ed. *Lieder by Women Composers of the Classic Era,* vol. 1. Fayetteville, Ark.: ClarNan Editions, 1987.

Loewe, Carl. *Carl Loewes Werke: Gesamtausgabe der Balladen, Legenden, Lieder und Gesänge für eine Singstimme. . . .* Edited by Max Runze. Leipzig, Germany: Breitkopf & Härtel, 1899–1904. Reprint, Farnborough, U.K.: Gregg, 1970.

Mendelssohn, Felix. *Felix Mendelssohn Bartholdy's Werke: kritisch durchgesehene Ausgabe.* Edited by Julius Rietz. Leipzig, Germany: Breitkopf & Härtel, 1874–77.

———. *Leipziger Ausgabe der Werke Felix Mendelssohn Bartholdys.* Leipzig, Germany: Internationale Felix-Mendelssohn-Gesellschaft, 1960–77. Continued by Sächsische Akademie der Wissenschaften, 1997– .

Monteverdi, Claudio. *Claudio Monteverdi: Tutte le opere,* vol. 14/1. Edited by G. F. Malipiero. Vienna: Universal Edition, 1926–42.

Mozart, Wolfgang Amadeus. *Neue Ausgabe sämtlicher Werke*. Edited by the Internationale Stiftung Mozarteum Salzburg. Kassel, Germany: Bärenreiter, 1955–2007.

Pinto, George Frederick. *Complete Works for Solo Piano*. In *The London Pianoforte School*, vol. 14. Edited by Nicholas Temperley. New York: Garland, 1985.

Purcell, Henry, *The Works of Henry Purcell*, vol. 25. Edited by Margaret Laurie. Borough Green, U.K.: Novello, 1985.

Reger, Max. *Sämtliche Werke*, vol. 25. Edited by Hermann Grabner. Wiesbaden, Germany: Breitkopf & Härtel, c. 1960.

Rossini, Gioachino. *Sei sonate a quattro*. In *Quaderno Rossiniani* 1. Edited by Alfredo Bonaccorsi. Pesaro, Italy: Fondazione Rossini, 1954.

Schleifer, Martha F., and Sylvia Glickman, eds. *Women Composers: Music through the Ages*. New York: G. K. Hall, 1998.

Schubert, Franz. *Neue Ausgabe sämtlicher Werke*. Edited by Walther Dürr and others. Kassel, Germany: Bärenreiter, 1964– .

Strauss, Richard. *Lieder Gesamtausgabe*, vol. 3. Edited by Franz Trenner. London: Fürstner; Boosey & Hawkes, 1964.

———. *Richard Strauss Edition: Orchesterwerke*, vol. 24. Edited by Walter Werbeck. Vienna: Dr. Richard Strauss GmbH, 1999.

Weyer, Martin, ed. *Easy Organ Pieces from the 19th Century*. Kassel, Germany: Bärenreiter, 2000.

Wolf, Hugo. *Sämtliche Werke: kritische Gesamtausgabe*. Edited by Hans Jancik and others. Vienna: Musikwissenschaftliche Verlag, 1960– .

SOUND RECORDINGS

Arriaga, Juan Crisóstomo. Overture Op. 1 and Overture *Los esclavos felices*. In *Orchestral Works*. Conductor Jordi Savall. Auvidis Astrée E8532 (1995).

Beethoven, Ludwig van. *The Complete Beethoven Edition*, vols. 2, 6, 14, 16. Various performers. Deutsche Grammophon 453 707-2GCB5; 453 733-2GCB8; 453 772-2GCB6; 453 782-2GCB3 (1997).

Bizet, Georges. *Complete Piano Music*. Setrak. Harmonia Mundi HMA 190 5233/4 (1996).

Bruch, Max. *Septet, Consortium Classicum*. Orfeo C167881A (n.d.).

Busoni, Ferruccio. *Clarinet Chamber Music* (includes K. 88, 101, 107–08, 138, 156, 176). Dieter Klöcker, clarinet. CPO 999 252-2 (1994).

———. *Early Piano Works* (includes K. 9, 71, 100, 185). Ira Maria Witoschynskyj. Capriccio 10 546 (1994).

Clementi, Muzio. Sonata in A flat. In *Piano Sonatas*. Pietro Spada. Arts Music 472232 (1983).

Enescu, George. *Poème roumain* Op. 1. Conductor Cristian Mandeal. Arte Nova 74321 65425-2 (2000).

———. Suite for Piano Op. 3. In *Piano Suites*. Aurora Ienei. Olympia OCD 414 (1981).

———. Violin Sonata Op. 2. In *Violin Sonatas.* Vilmos Szabadi. Hungaroton HCD 31778 (1997).

Franck, César. Piano Concerto No. 2, Op. 11. Martijn van den Hoek. Naxos 8 553472 (1997).

———. Variations brillantes Op. 5. In *Piano Music.* Marios Papadopoulos. Meridian CDE 84206 (n.d.).

Furtwängler, Wilhelm. *Early Orchestral Works.* Conductor Alfred Walter. Marco Polo 8 223645 (1995).

———. Eleven early songs (1895–1900). In *Lieder and Choral Works.* Guido Pikal. Marco Polo 223546 (1995).

Grieg, Edvard. *Larvikspolka* and twenty-three *småstykker.* In *Piano Works,* vol. 10. Geir Henning Braaten. Victoria VCD19034 (1993).

Hummel, Johann Nepomuk. Piano Sonata No. 1. In *Piano Sonatas.* Dana Proto-popescu. Koch DICD 920237 (1995).

Korngold, Erich. *Orchestral Works,* vol. 1. Conductor Werner Andreas Albert. CPO 999 037-2 (1991).

Langgaard, Rued. Symphony No. 1, *Drapa, Heltedød.* In *Complete Symphonies,* vols. 1–3. Conductor Ilya Stupel. Danacord DACOCD 404/6 (1994).

Liszt, Franz. *Don Sanche.* Notes by András Batta. Hungaroton HCD 12744/5 (1986).

———. *Piano Works,* vol. 26. Leslie Howard. Hyperion CDA 66771/2 (1994).

Martinů, Bohuslav. *Tři Jezdci.* In *String Quartets,* vol. 1. Martinů Quartet. Naxos 8 553782 (1997).

Mendelssohn, Felix. *Die beiden Pädagogen.* Conductor Heinz Wallberg. CPO 999 550-2 (1998). Many recordings of thirteen string symphonies, early concertos, and some early piano music.

Monteverdi, Claudio. *Sacrae cantiunculae.* Conductor Miklós Szabó. Hungaroton HCD 12921 (1977).

Mozart, Wolfgang Amadeus. *Mozart Edition.* Various performers. Philips 422 501-2PME6 *et seq.* (1990–91).

Prokofiev, Sergei. *Piano Works,* vols. 7–8. Frederic Chiu. Harmonia Mundi HMU 7190/1 (1998).

Rachmaninoff, Serge. *Piano Works,* vol. 7. Idil Biret. Naxos 8 553004 (1996).

Rheinberger, Josef. *Complete Organ Works,* vol. 1. Rudolf Innig. Dabringhaus und Grimm MDG 317 0891-2 (1999).

Rossini, Gioachino. Many recordings of six sonatas.

Saint-Saëns, Camille. *Symphony in A.* Conductor Jean Martinon. EMI 569683-2 (1974).

Schubert, Franz. Early quartets including fragments in *String Quartets,* vols. 1–3, 8–9. Leipzig Quartet. Dabringhaus und Grimm MDG 307 0601-2 (n.d.). Many record-ings of the Piano Trio D. 28.

———. Fantasies, D. 1 and 9. In *Piano Duets,* vol. 4. Yaara Tal and Andreas Groethuy-sen. Sony Classical SK68243 (1995).

Scriabin, Aleksandr. Piano works in *The Early Scriabin.* Stephen Coombs. Hyperion CDA 67149 (2000).

Strauss, Richard. Early songs in *Lieder.* Charlotte Margiono and others. Nightingale Classics NCO 71260-2 (1995).

———. *Festmarsch* and Symphony in D minor. Conductor Klauspeter Seibel. Colosseum COL 34 9006 (n.d.).

———. Two piano trios. Odeon Trio. Capriccio 10 820 (1996).

Weber, Carl Maria von. Six fughettas in *Salzburg Organ Landscape.* Florian Pagitsch. Dabringhaus und Grimm MDG 319 0990-2 (1999). Several recordings of overture (only) of *Peter Schmoll.*

Wesley, Samuel. Violin Concerto No. 2 in D. In *English Classical Violin Concertos.* Elizabeth Wallfisch. Hyperion CDA 66865 (1996).

Wieck (Schumann), Clara. *Complete Piano Works.* Jozef de Beenhouwer. CPO 999 758-2 (1991). Several recordings of Piano Concerto in A minor.

Wolf, Hugo. Partsongs Op. 13. In Cornelius and Wolf, *Choral Works.* Conductor Uwe Gronostay. Globe GLO 5105 (1993).

WEBSITES

Neue Mozart-Ausgabe: http://dme.mozarteum.at (accessed 27 June 2008).

Works by Alexander Prior: http://www.alexprior.co.uk (accessed 27 June 2008).

British Broadcasting Corporation: http://www.bbc.co.uk (accessed 25 April 2008).

Britten-Pears Foundation: http://www.brittenpears.org (accessed 25 April 2008).

Chopin's First Editions Online: http://www.cfeo.org.uk/apps (accessed 25 June 2008).

Works by Sonia Fridman (Eckhardt-Gramatté): http://www.egre.mb.ca/sc (accessed 11 August 2008).

Works by Carl Filtsch: http://www.freewebs.com/fjgajewski (accessed 11 April 2008).

The Juilliard Journal Online: http://www.juilliard.edu (accessed 25 April 2008).

Works by Rued Langgaard: http://www.langgaard.dk (accessed 25 June 2008).

Composer Index

Bold page numbers indicate a main entry in part 2. Italic numbers reference a table. To locate music examples, see the list on pages v–vi.

About the Author

Barry Cooper is professor of music at the University of Manchester. He began learning the piano at the age of four and began composing at seven. Later he studied music at University College, Oxford (M.A., 1973; D. Phil., 1974), where he also studied the organ (F.R.C.O., 1968). After a temporary lectureship at the University of St. Andrews he moved to the University of Aberdeen (1974) before transferring to Manchester in 1990.

He has a wide range of research interests from medieval to nineteenth-century music, notably on English Baroque music and the music of Beethoven and his contemporaries. His dissertation was revised and published as *English Solo Keyboard Music of the Middle and Late Baroque* (1989), and his other writings include a monograph on music theory in Britain in the seventeenth and eighteenth centuries, three catalogues of musical source material, and numerous journal articles and reviews.

Cooper's main research in recent years has been on Beethoven, and he is regarded as a world authority on this composer. His books on Beethoven include *Beethoven and the Creative Process* (1990; 2nd ed. 1992), *Beethoven's Folksong Settings* (1994), and *Beethoven* (2000; 2nd ed. 2008). He is also the general editor and coauthor of *The Beethoven Compendium* (1991; 2nd ed. 1996), which has been translated into five other languages.

In 1988 his completion of the first movement of Beethoven's unfinished Tenth Symphony attracted widespread international attention when it was premiered at the Royal Festival Hall, London. It has since been performed in more than a dozen countries and recorded several times. The score is published by Universal Edition, London.

In 2007 he completed a new and widely acclaimed scholarly performing edition of Beethoven's thirty-five piano sonatas, published by the Associated Board of the Royal Schools of Music, who described it as undoubtedly the highlight of their publishing program that year.